NELSON • MORA • CASSATA

HEXED

THE HARLOT & THE THIEF VOLUME TWO

BOOM!
STUDIOS

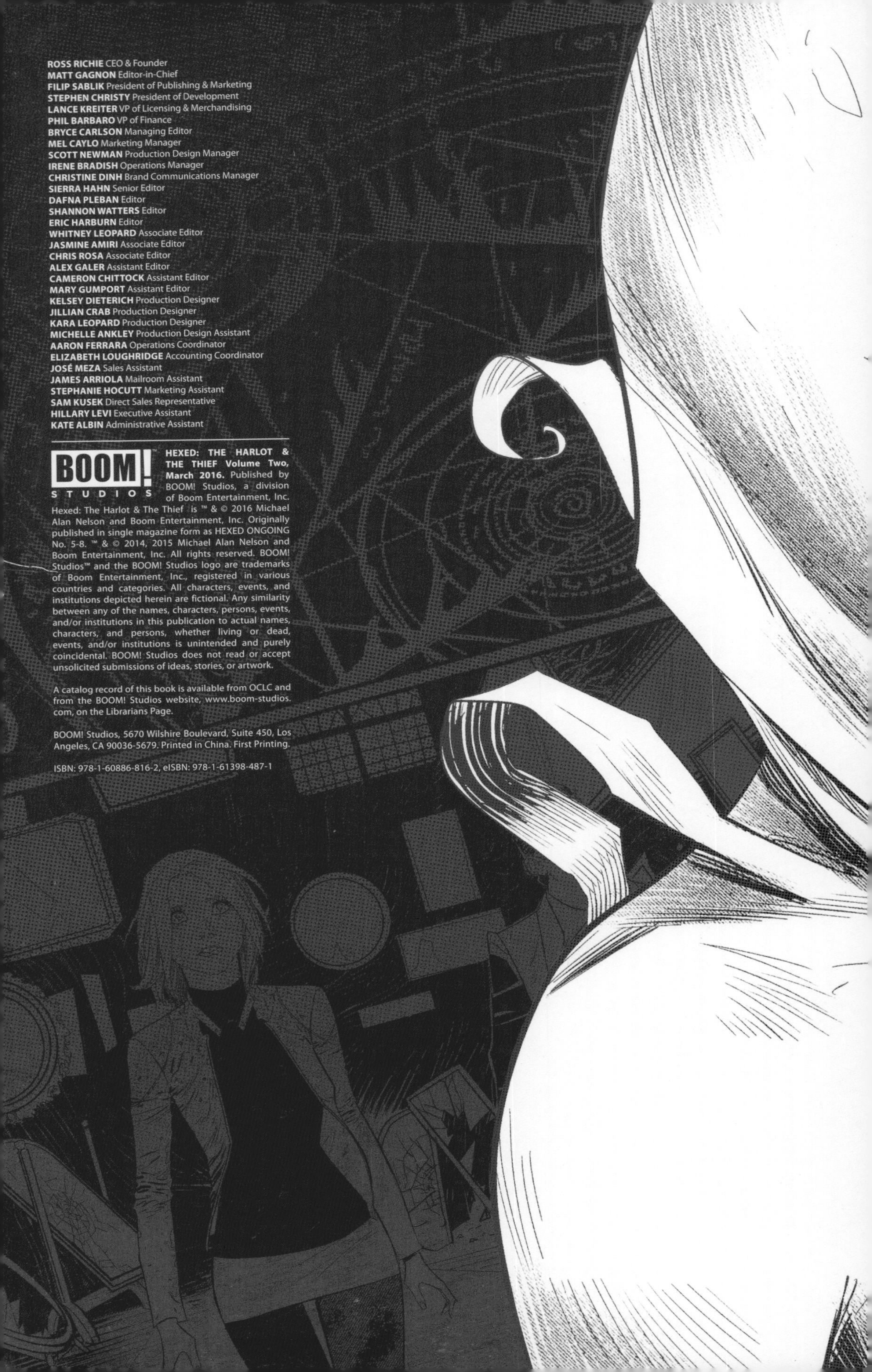

BOOM! STUDIOS

HEXED: THE HARLOT & THE THIEF Volume Two, March 2016. Published by BOOM! Studios, a division of Boom Entertainment, Inc. Hexed: The Harlot & The Thief is ™ & © 2016 Michael Alan Nelson and Boom Entertainment, Inc. Originally published in single magazine form as HEXED ONGOING No. 5-8. ™ & © 2014, 2015 Michael Alan Nelson and Boom Entertainment, Inc. All rights reserved. BOOM! Studios™ and the BOOM! Studios logo are trademarks of Boom Entertainment, Inc., registered in various countries and categories. All characters, events, and institutions depicted herein are fictional. Any similarity between any of the names, characters, persons, events, and/or institutions in this publication to actual names, characters, and persons, whether living or dead, events, and/or institutions is unintended and purely coincidental. BOOM! Studios does not read or accept unsolicited submissions of ideas, stories, or artwork.

A catalog record of this book is available from OCLC and from the BOOM! Studios website, www.boom-studios.com, on the Librarians Page.

BOOM! Studios, 5670 Wilshire Boulevard, Suite 450, Los Angeles, CA 90036-5679. Printed in China. First Printing.

ISBN: 978-1-60886-816-2, eISBN: 978-1-61398-487-1

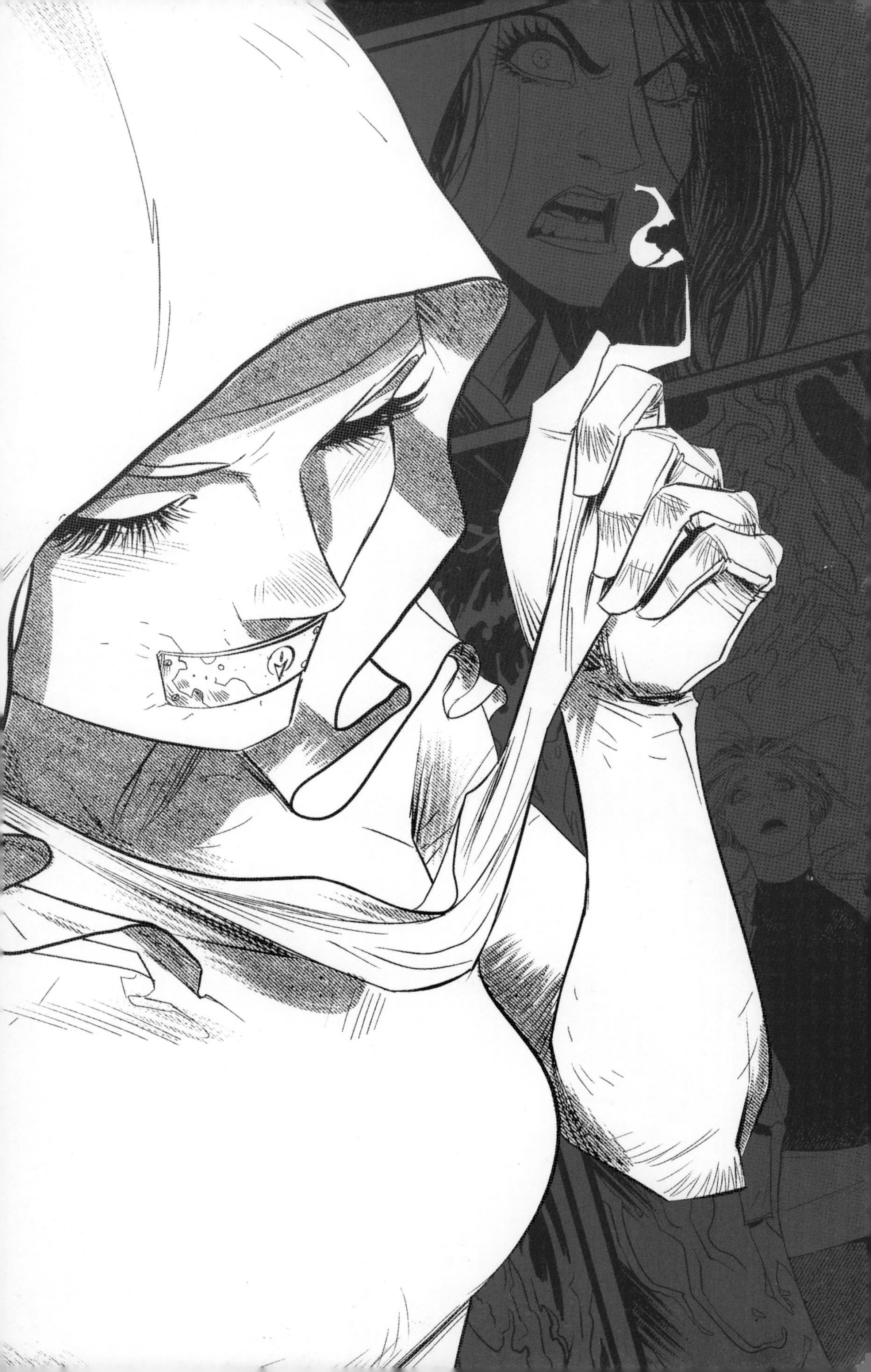

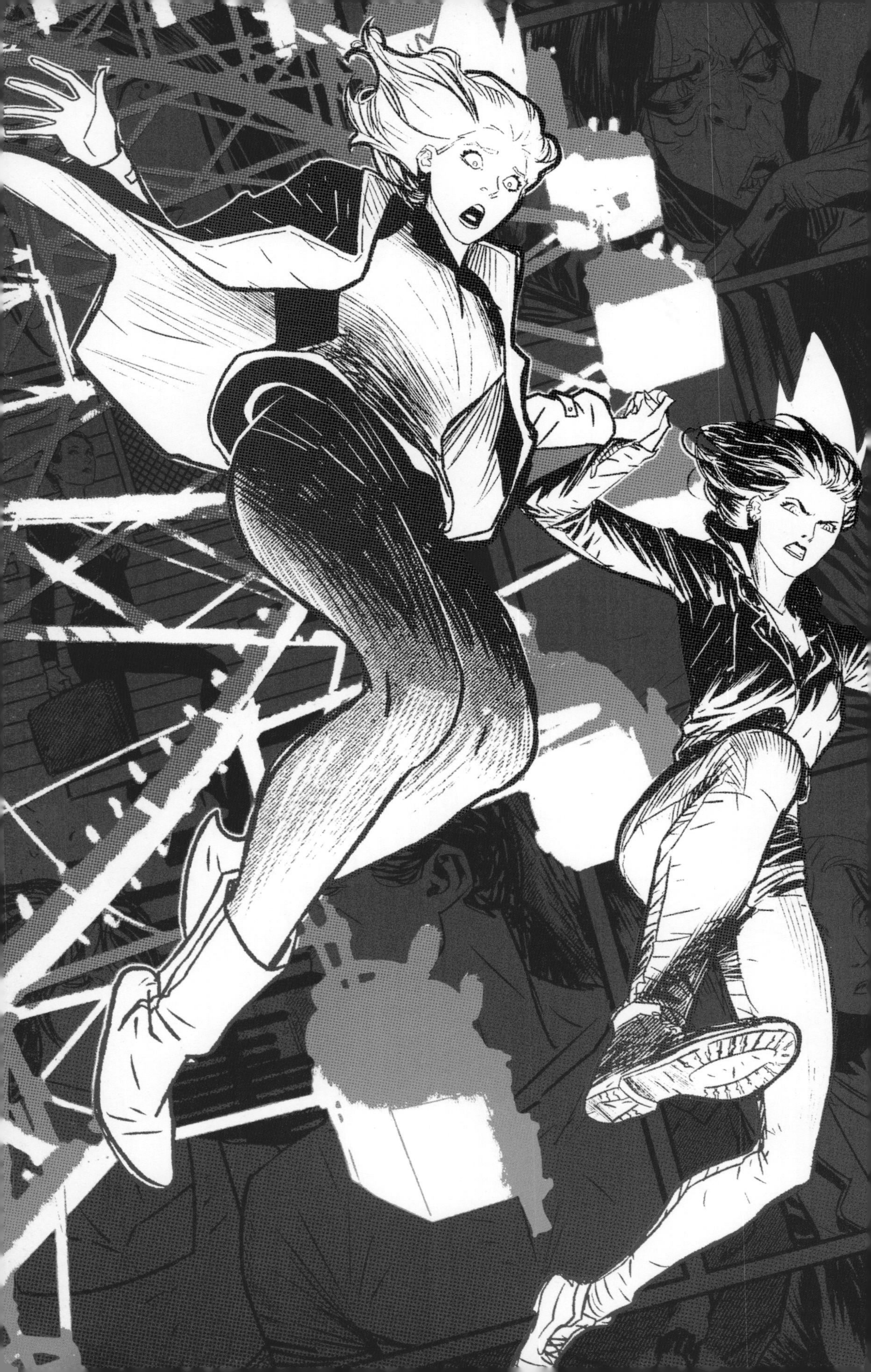

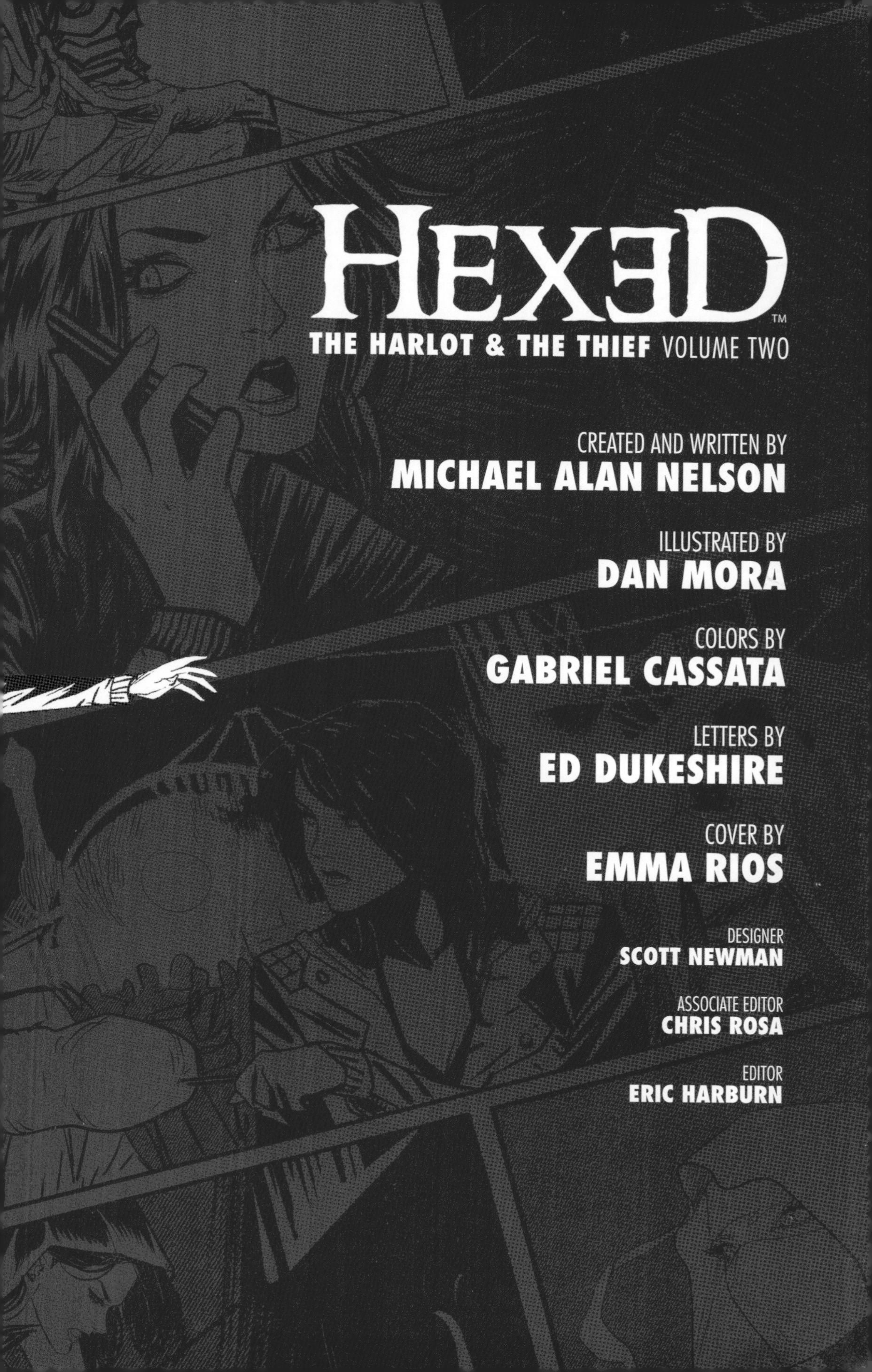

HEXED™

THE HARLOT & THE THIEF VOLUME TWO

CREATED AND WRITTEN BY
MICHAEL ALAN NELSON

ILLUSTRATED BY
DAN MORA

COLORS BY
GABRIEL CASSATA

LETTERS BY
ED DUKESHIRE

COVER BY
EMMA RIOS

DESIGNER
SCOTT NEWMAN

ASSOCIATE EDITOR
CHRIS ROSA

EDITOR
ERIC HARBURN

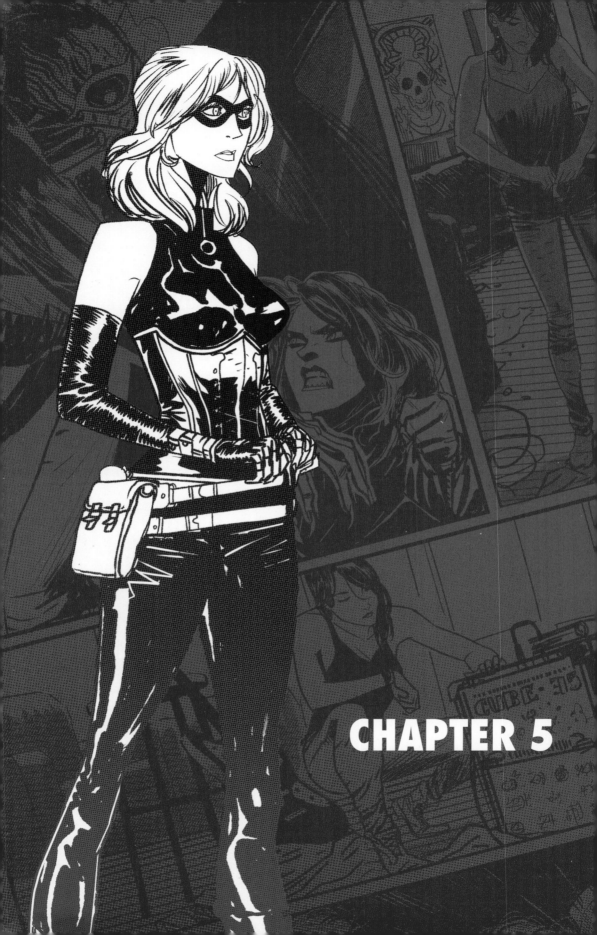

CHAPTER 5

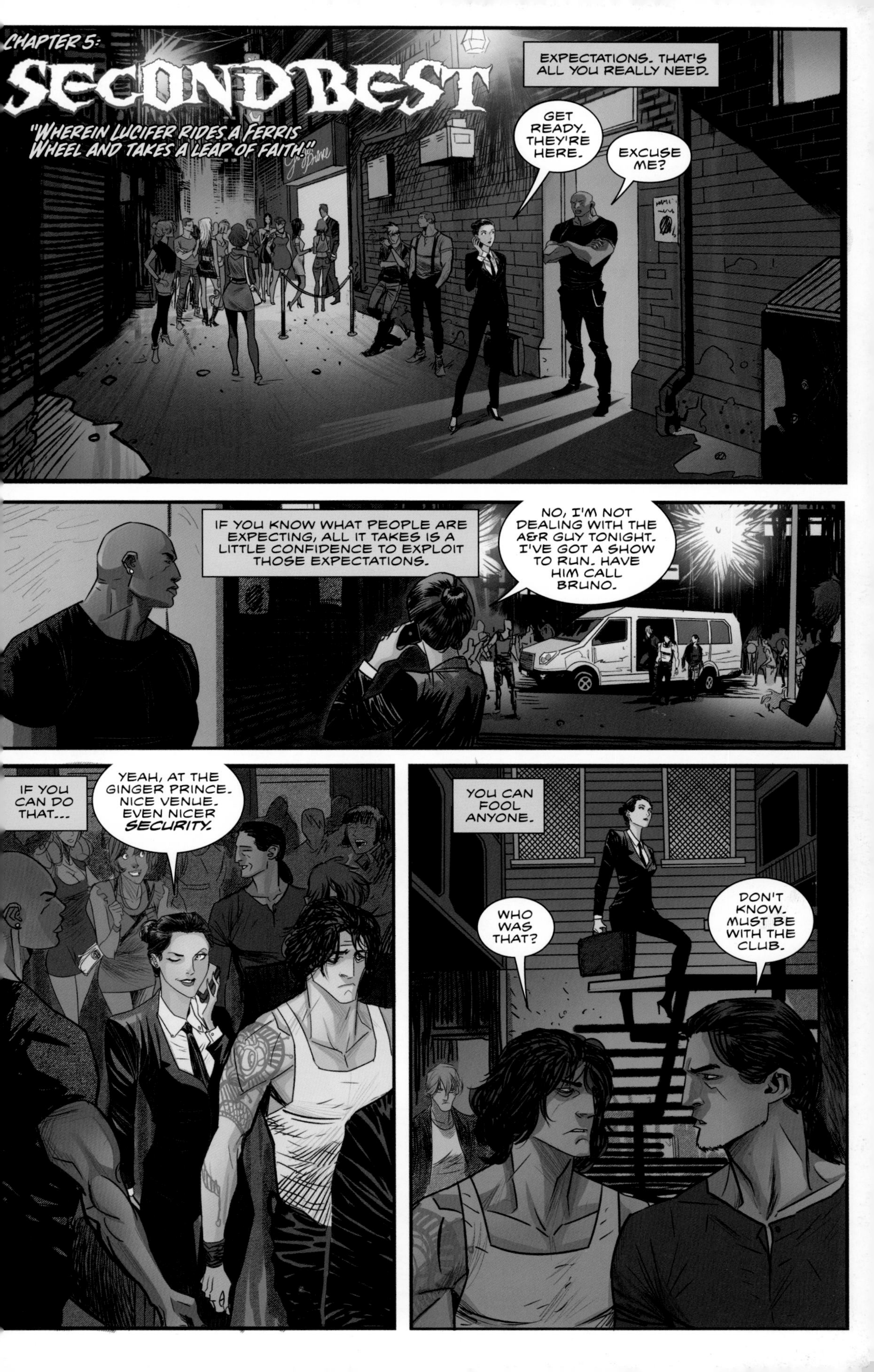
CHAPTER 5:
SECOND BEST
"WHEREIN LUCIFER RIDES A FERRIS WHEEL AND TAKES A LEAP OF FAITH."
EXPECTATIONS. THAT'S ALL YOU REALLY NEED.
GET READY. THEY'RE HERE.
EXCUSE ME?
IF YOU KNOW WHAT PEOPLE ARE EXPECTING, ALL IT TAKES IS A LITTLE CONFIDENCE TO EXPLOIT THOSE EXPECTATIONS.
NO, I'M NOT DEALING WITH THE A&R GUY TONIGHT. I'VE GOT A SHOW TO RUN. HAVE HIM CALL BRUNO.
IF YOU CAN DO THAT...
YEAH, AT THE GINGER PRINCE. NICE VENUE. EVEN NICER SECURITY.
YOU CAN FOOL ANYONE.
WHO WAS THAT?
DON'T KNOW. MUST BE WITH THE CLUB.

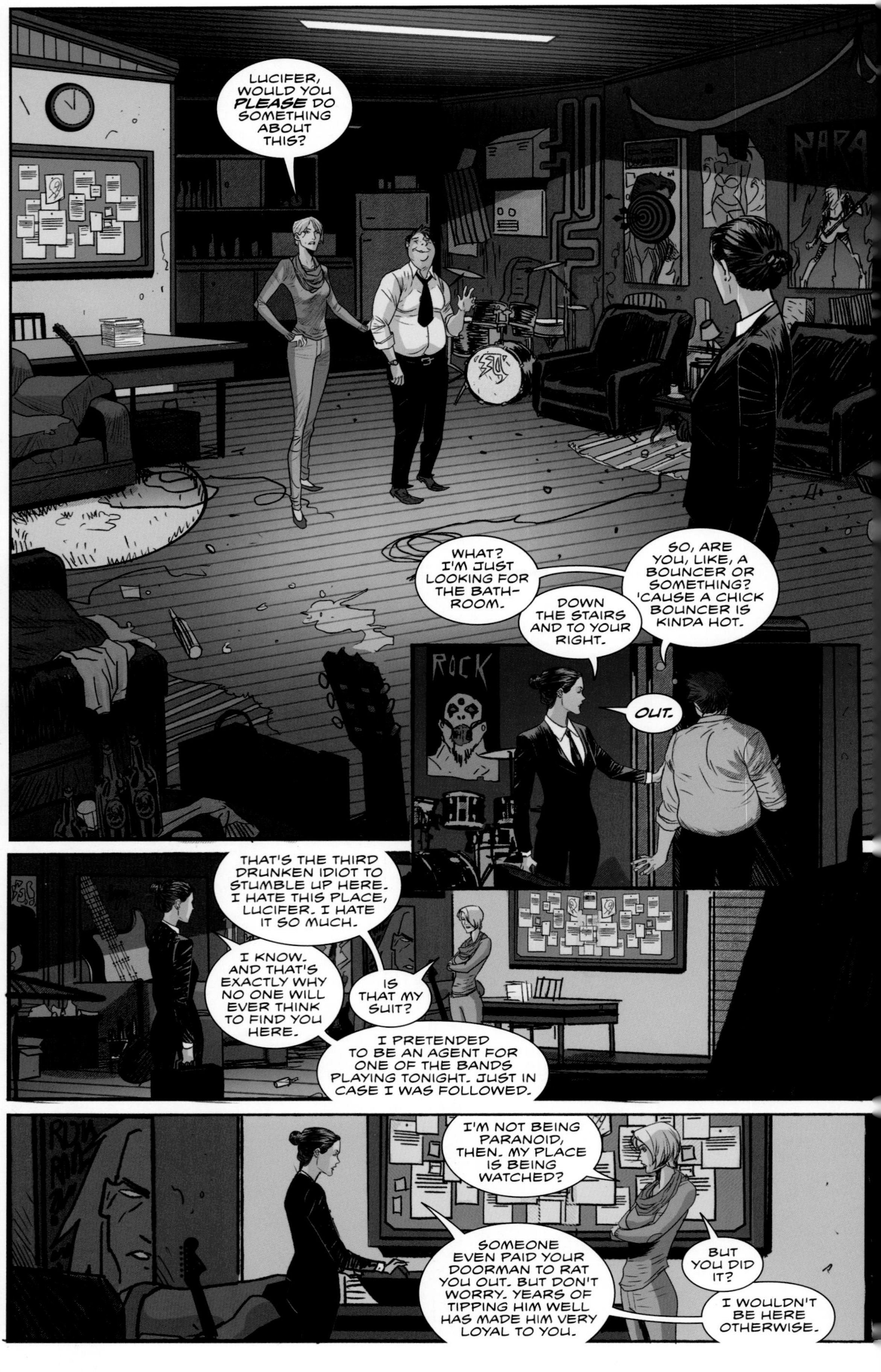

LUCIFER, WOULD YOU *PLEASE* DO SOMETHING ABOUT THIS?
WHAT? I'M JUST LOOKING FOR THE BATH-ROOM.
SO, ARE YOU, LIKE, A BOUNCER OR SOMETHING? 'CAUSE A CHICK BOUNCER IS KINDA HOT.
DOWN THE STAIRS AND TO YOUR RIGHT.
ROCK
OUT.
THAT'S THE THIRD DRUNKEN IDIOT TO STUMBLE UP HERE. I HATE THIS PLACE, LUCIFER. I HATE IT SO MUCH.
I KNOW. AND THAT'S EXACTLY WHY NO ONE WILL EVER THINK TO FIND YOU HERE.
IS THAT MY SUIT?
I PRETENDED TO BE AN AGENT FOR ONE OF THE BANDS PLAYING TONIGHT. JUST IN CASE I WAS FOLLOWED.
I'M NOT BEING PARANOID, THEN. MY PLACE IS BEING WATCHED?
SOMEONE EVEN PAID YOUR DOORMAN TO RAT YOU OUT. BUT DON'T WORRY. YEARS OF TIPPING HIM WELL HAS MADE HIM VERY LOYAL TO YOU.
BUT YOU DID IT?
I WOULDN'T BE HERE OTHERWISE.

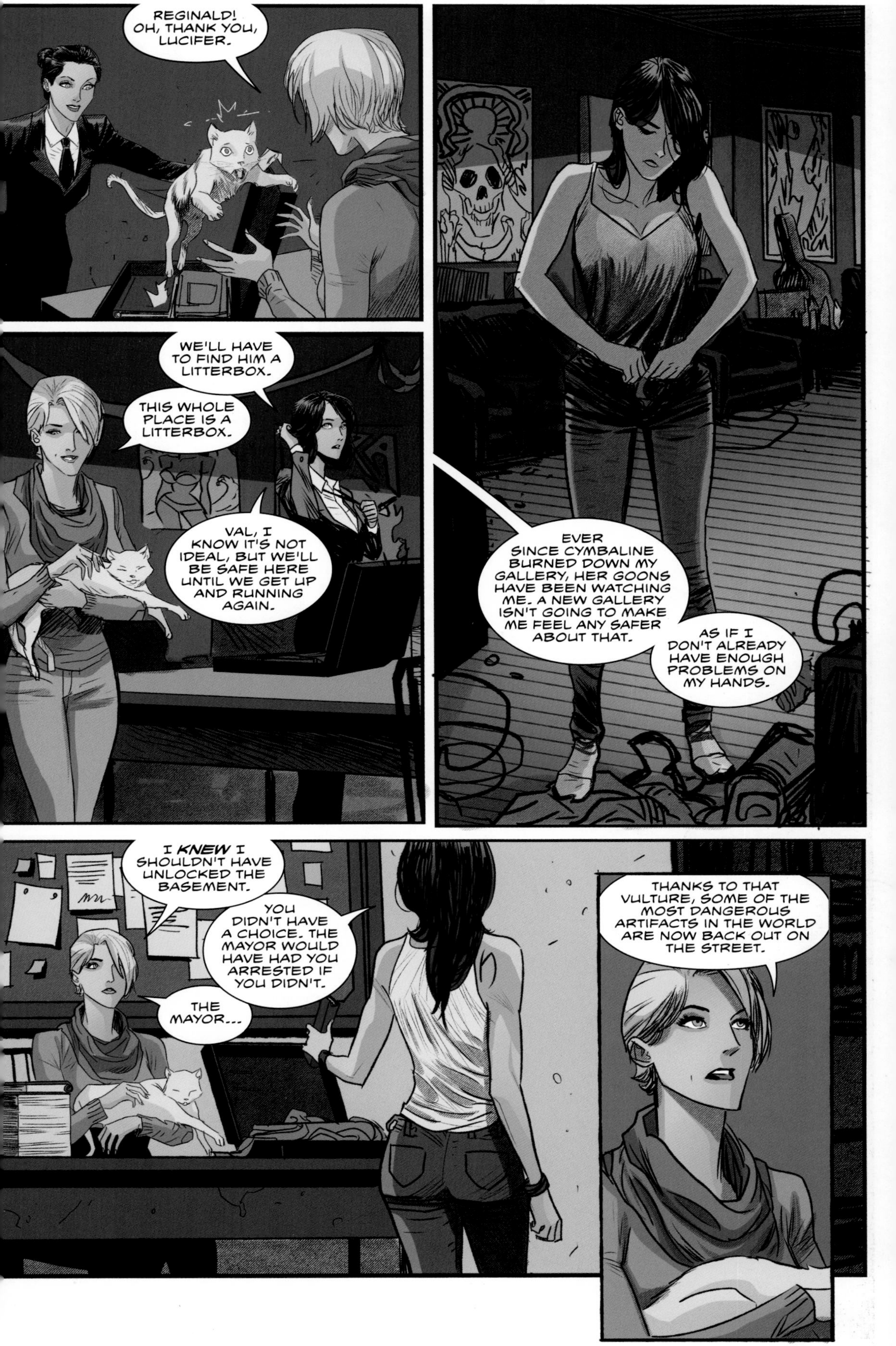
REGINALD! OH, THANK YOU, LUCIFER.
WE'LL HAVE TO FIND HIM A LITTERBOX.
THIS WHOLE PLACE IS A LITTERBOX.
VAL, I KNOW IT'S NOT IDEAL, BUT WE'LL BE SAFE HERE UNTIL WE GET UP AND RUNNING AGAIN.
EVER SINCE CYMBALINE BURNED DOWN MY GALLERY, HER GOONS HAVE BEEN WATCHING ME. A NEW GALLERY ISN'T GOING TO MAKE ME FEEL ANY SAFER ABOUT THAT.
AS IF I DON'T ALREADY HAVE ENOUGH PROBLEMS ON MY HANDS.
I *KNEW* I SHOULDN'T HAVE UNLOCKED THE BASEMENT.
YOU DIDN'T HAVE A CHOICE. THE MAYOR WOULD HAVE HAD YOU ARRESTED IF YOU DIDN'T.
THE MAYOR...
THANKS TO THAT VULTURE, SOME OF THE MOST DANGEROUS ARTIFACTS IN THE WORLD ARE NOW BACK OUT ON THE STREET.

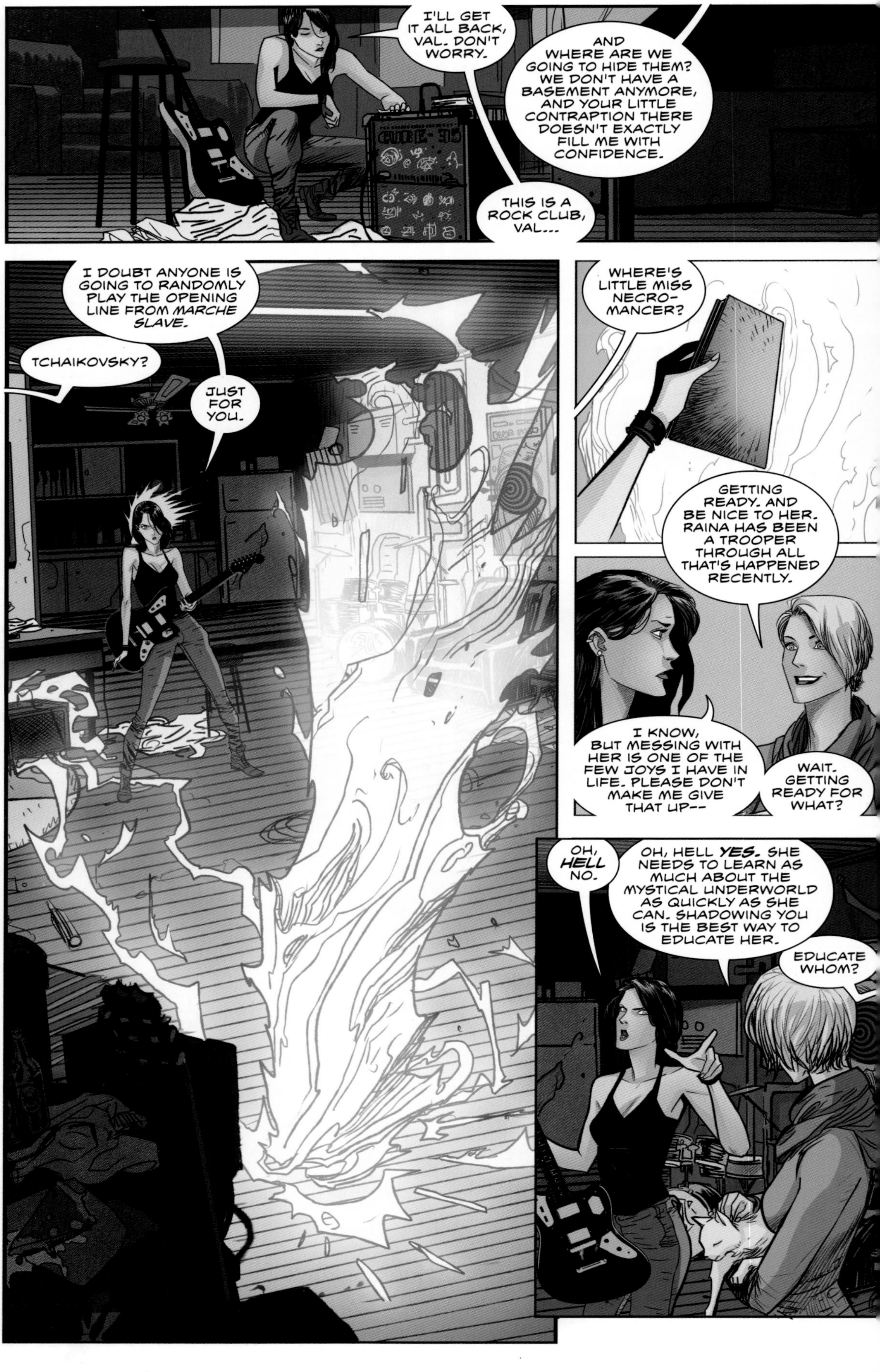
I'LL GET IT ALL BACK, VAL. DON'T WORRY.
AND WHERE ARE WE GOING TO HIDE THEM? WE DON'T HAVE A BASEMENT ANYMORE, AND YOUR LITTLE CONTRAPTION THERE DOESN'T EXACTLY FILL ME WITH CONFIDENCE.
THIS IS A ROCK CLUB, VAL...
I DOUBT ANYONE IS GOING TO RANDOMLY PLAY THE OPENING LINE FROM *MARCHE SLAVE*.
TCHAIKOVSKY?
JUST FOR YOU.
WHERE'S LITTLE MISS NECRO-MANCER?
GETTING READY. AND BE NICE TO HER. RAINA HAS BEEN A TROOPER THROUGH ALL THAT'S HAPPENED RECENTLY.
I KNOW, BUT MESSING WITH HER IS ONE OF THE FEW JOYS I HAVE IN LIFE. PLEASE DON'T MAKE ME GIVE THAT UP--
WAIT. GETTING READY FOR WHAT?
OH, ***HELL*** NO.
OH, HELL ***YES***. SHE NEEDS TO LEARN AS MUCH ABOUT THE MYSTICAL UNDERWORLD AS QUICKLY AS SHE CAN. SHADOWING YOU IS THE BEST WAY TO EDUCATE HER.
EDUCATE WHOM?

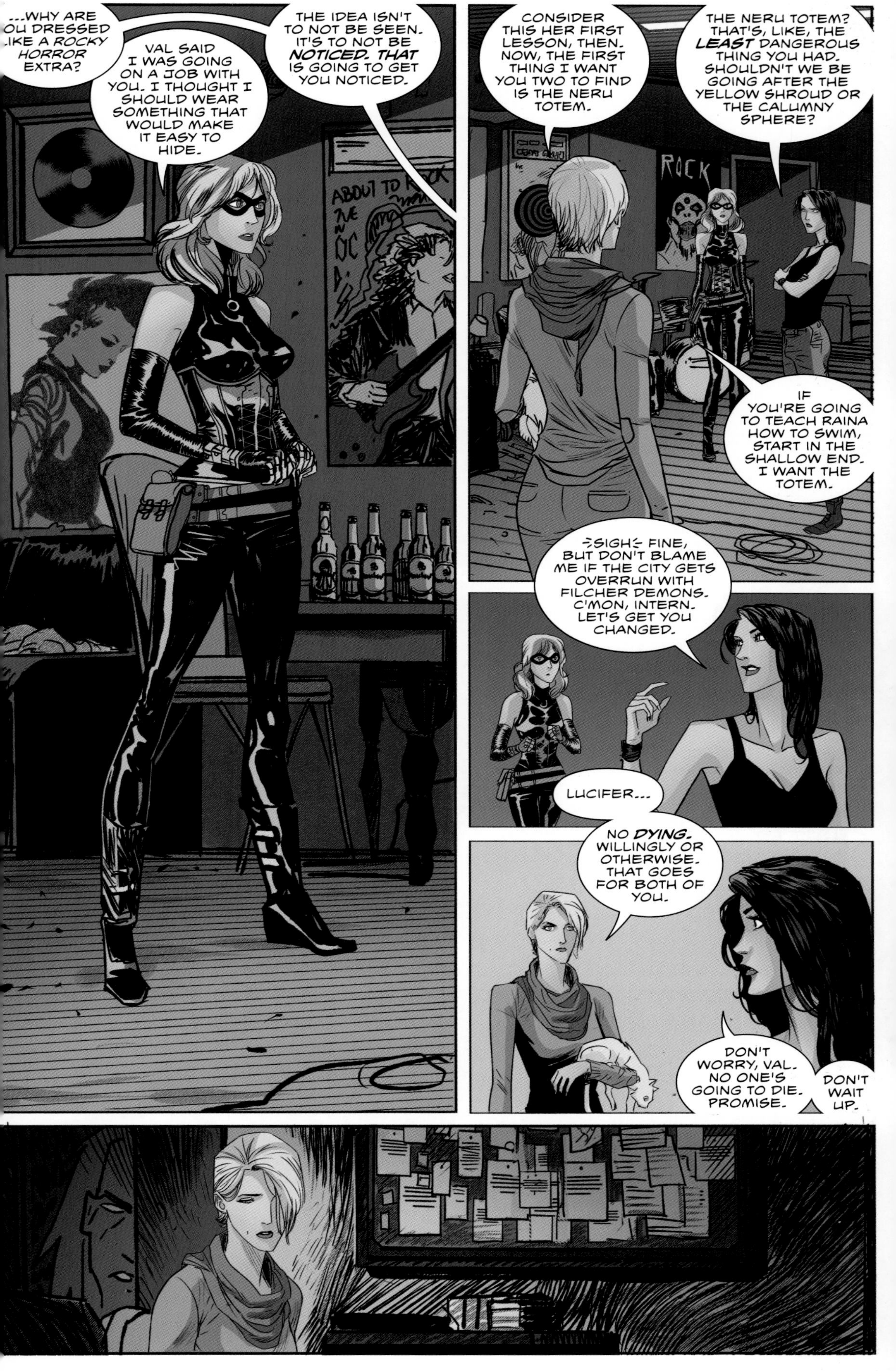
...WHY ARE
OU DRESSED
IKE A ROCKY HORROR EXTRA?
VAL SAID I WAS GOING ON A JOB WITH YOU. I THOUGHT I SHOULD WEAR SOMETHING THAT WOULD MAKE IT EASY TO HIDE.
THE IDEA ISN'T TO NOT BE SEEN. IT'S TO NOT BE NOTICED. THAT IS GOING TO GET YOU NOTICED.
CONSIDER THIS HER FIRST LESSON, THEN. NOW, THE FIRST THING I WANT YOU TWO TO FIND IS THE NERU TOTEM.
THE NERU TOTEM? THAT'S, LIKE, THE LEAST DANGEROUS THING YOU HAD. SHOULDN'T WE BE GOING AFTER THE YELLOW SHROUD OR THE CALUMNY SPHERE?
ROCK
IF YOU'RE GOING TO TEACH RAINA HOW TO SWIM, START IN THE SHALLOW END. I WANT THE TOTEM.
SIGH FINE, BUT DON'T BLAME ME IF THE CITY GETS OVERRUN WITH FILCHER DEMONS. C'MON, INTERN. LET'S GET YOU CHANGED.
LUCIFER...
NO DYING. WILLINGLY OR OTHERWISE. THAT GOES FOR BOTH OF YOU.
DON'T WORRY, VAL. NO ONE'S GOING TO DIE. PROMISE.
DON'T WAIT UP.

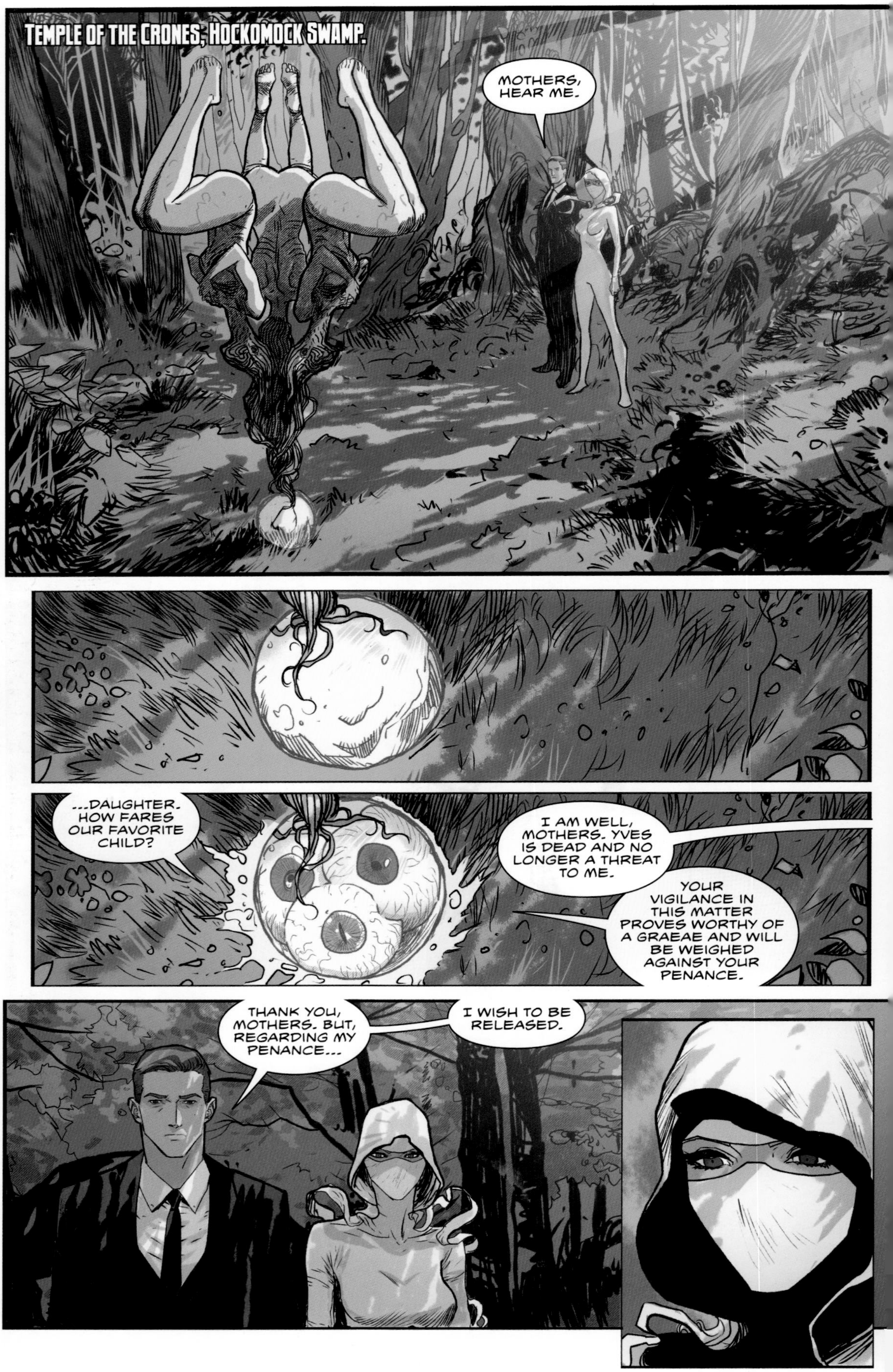
TEMPLE OF THE CRONES, HOCKOMOCK SWAMP.
MOTHERS, HEAR ME.
...DAUGHTER. HOW FARES OUR FAVORITE CHILD?
I AM WELL, MOTHERS. YVES IS DEAD AND NO LONGER A THREAT TO ME.
YOUR VIGILANCE IN THIS MATTER PROVES WORTHY OF A GRAEAE AND WILL BE WEIGHED AGAINST YOUR PENANCE.
THANK YOU, MOTHERS. BUT, REGARDING MY PENANCE...
I WISH TO BE RELEASED.

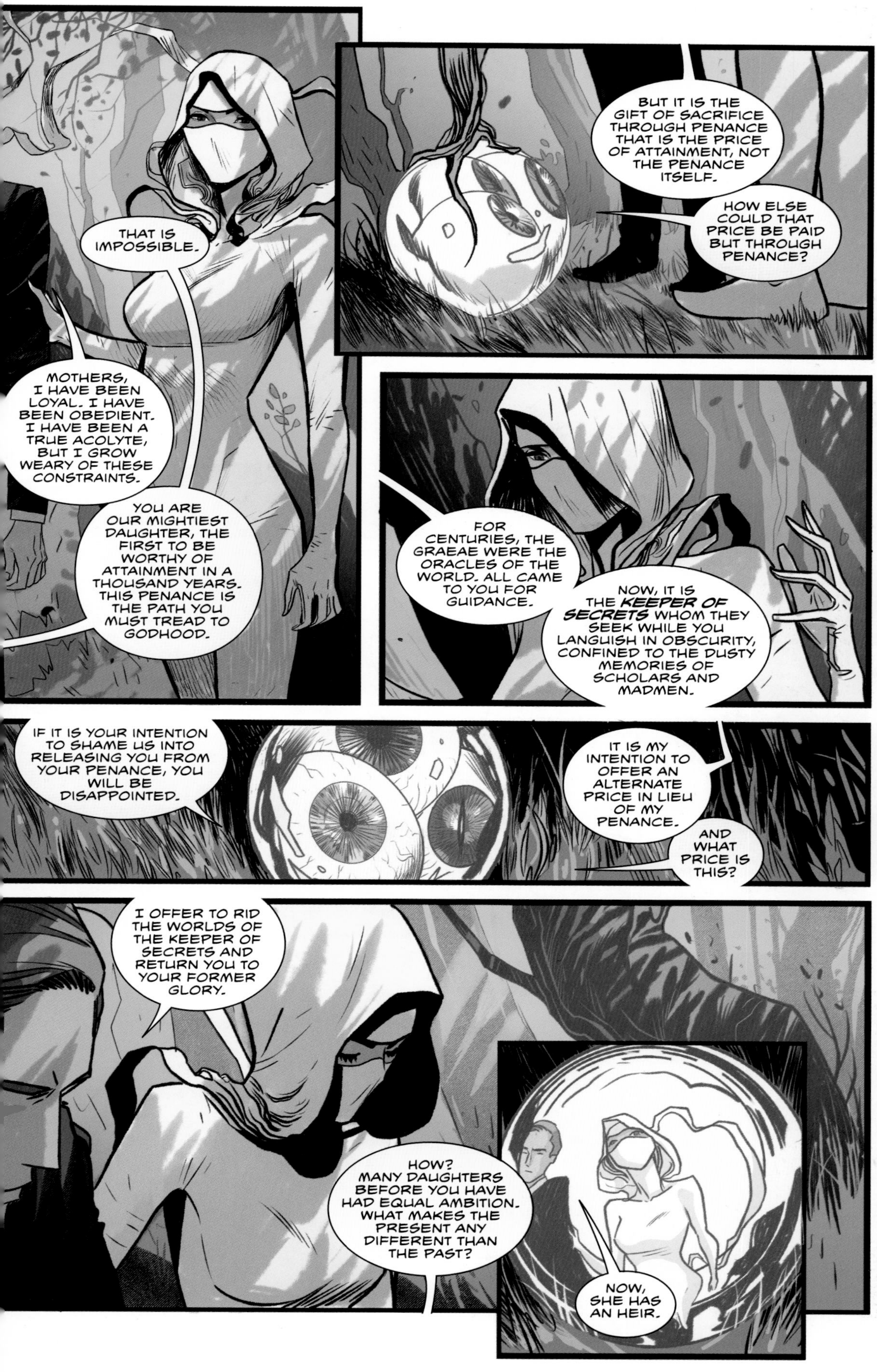
THAT IS IMPOSSIBLE.
MOTHERS, I HAVE BEEN LOYAL. I HAVE BEEN OBEDIENT. I HAVE BEEN A TRUE ACOLYTE, BUT I GROW WEARY OF THESE CONSTRAINTS.
YOU ARE OUR MIGHTIEST DAUGHTER, THE FIRST TO BE WORTHY OF ATTAINMENT IN A THOUSAND YEARS. THIS PENANCE IS THE PATH YOU MUST TREAD TO GODHOOD.
BUT IT IS THE GIFT OF SACRIFICE THROUGH PENANCE THAT IS THE PRICE OF ATTAINMENT, NOT THE PENANCE ITSELF.
HOW ELSE COULD THAT PRICE BE PAID BUT THROUGH PENANCE?
FOR CENTURIES, THE GRAEAE WERE THE ORACLES OF THE WORLD. ALL CAME TO YOU FOR GUIDANCE.
NOW, IT IS THE KEEPER OF SECRETS WHOM THEY SEEK WHILE YOU LANGUISH IN OBSCURITY, CONFINED TO THE DUSTY MEMORIES OF SCHOLARS AND MADMEN.
IF IT IS YOUR INTENTION TO SHAME US INTO RELEASING YOU FROM YOUR PENANCE, YOU WILL BE DISAPPOINTED.
IT IS MY INTENTION TO OFFER AN ALTERNATE PRICE IN LIEU OF MY PENANCE.
AND WHAT PRICE IS THIS?
I OFFER TO RID THE WORLDS OF THE KEEPER OF SECRETS AND RETURN YOU TO YOUR FORMER GLORY.
HOW? MANY DAUGHTERS BEFORE YOU HAVE HAD EQUAL AMBITION. WHAT MAKES THE PRESENT ANY DIFFERENT THAN THE PAST?
NOW, SHE HAS AN HEIR.

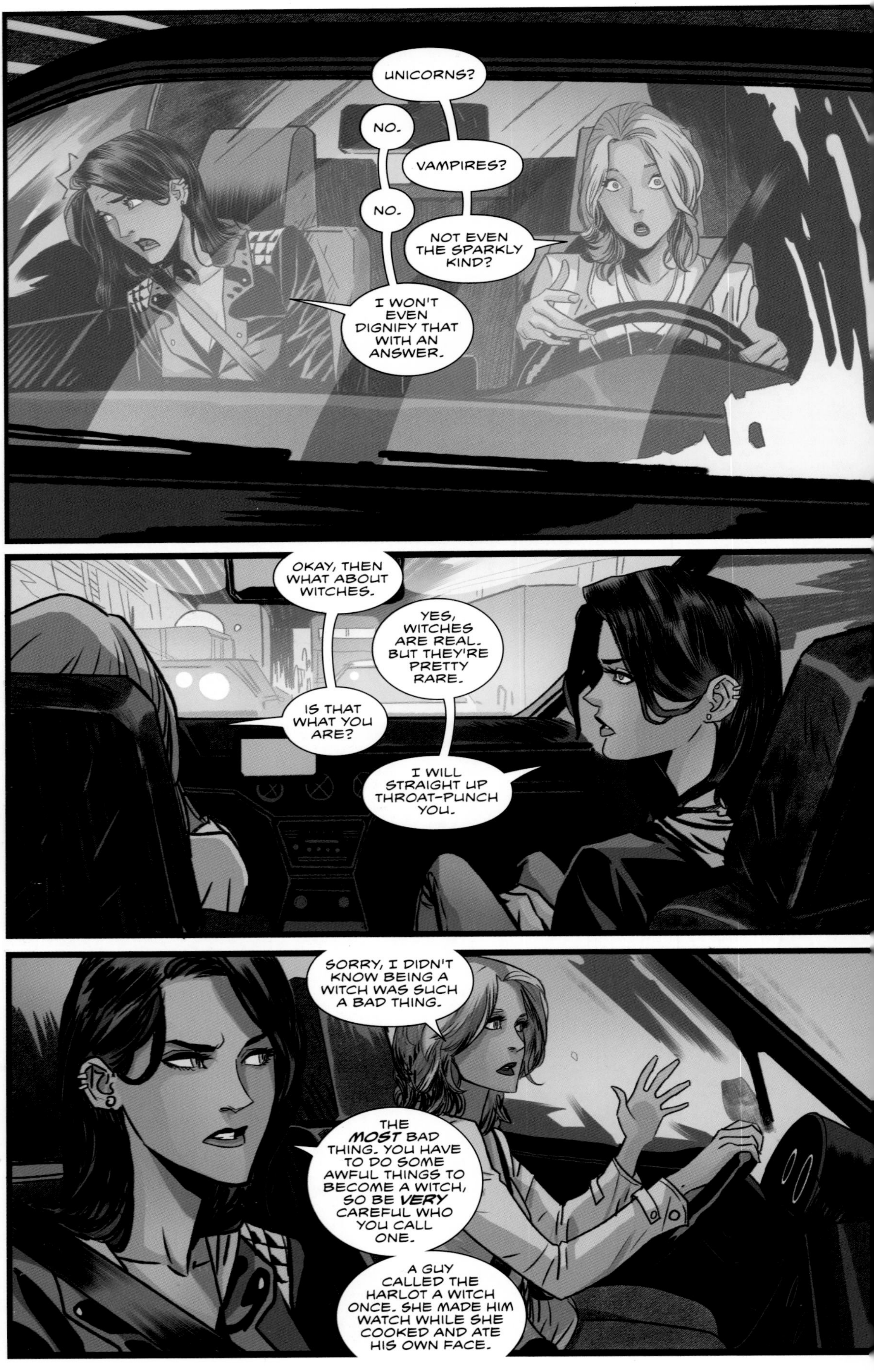
UNICORNS?
NO.
VAMPIRES?
NO.
NOT EVEN THE SPARKLY KIND?
I WON'T EVEN DIGNIFY THAT WITH AN ANSWER.
OKAY, THEN WHAT ABOUT WITCHES.
YES, WITCHES ARE REAL. BUT THEY'RE PRETTY RARE.
IS THAT WHAT YOU ARE?
I WILL STRAIGHT UP THROAT-PUNCH YOU.
SORRY, I DIDN'T KNOW BEING A WITCH WAS SUCH A BAD THING.
THE MOST BAD THING. YOU HAVE TO DO SOME AWFUL THINGS TO BECOME A WITCH, SO BE VERY CAREFUL WHO YOU CALL ONE.
A GUY CALLED THE HARLOT A WITCH ONCE. SHE MADE HIM WATCH WHILE SHE COOKED AND ATE HIS OWN FACE.

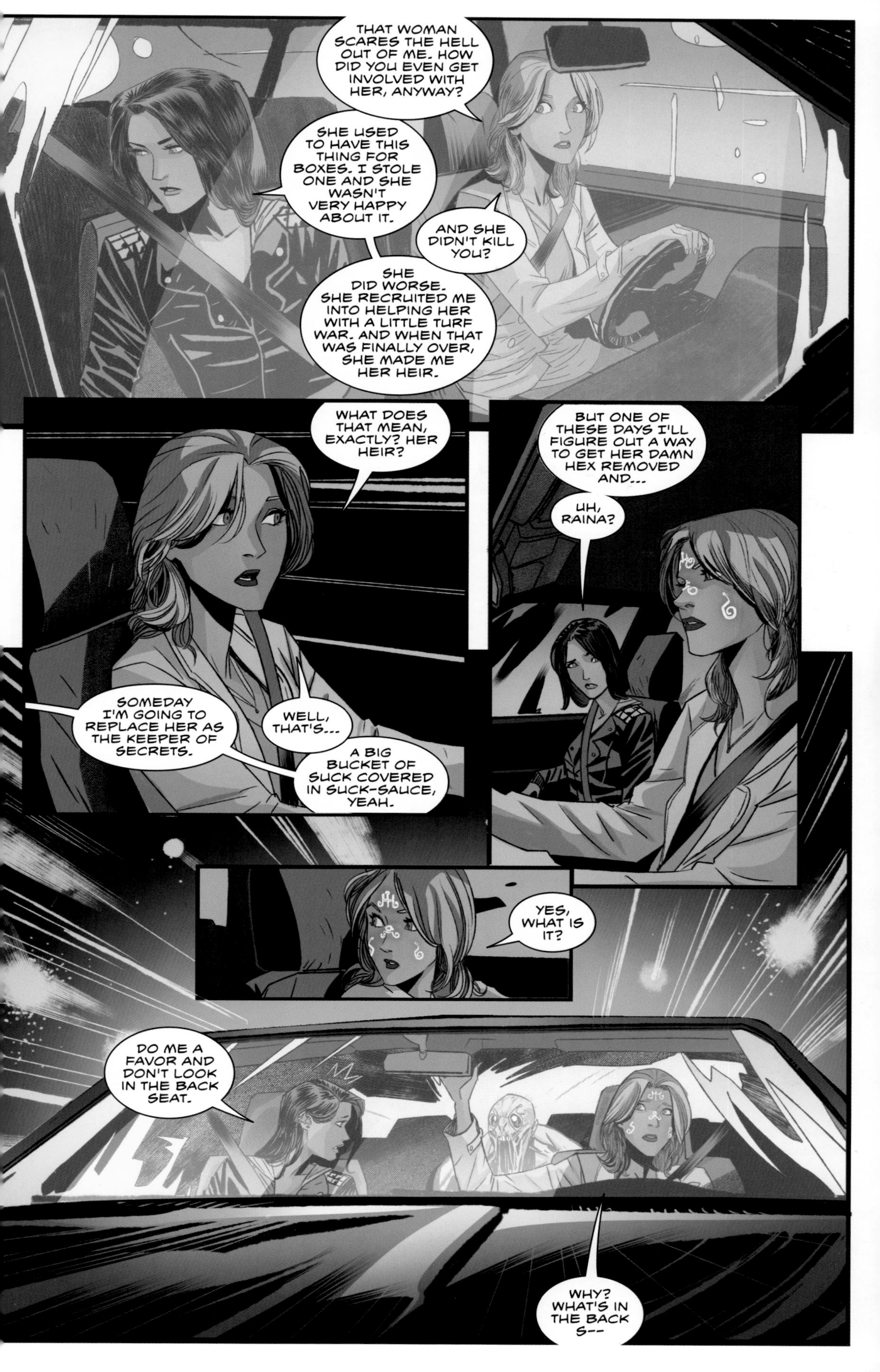
THAT WOMAN SCARES THE HELL OUT OF ME. HOW DID YOU EVEN GET INVOLVED WITH HER, ANYWAY?
SHE USED TO HAVE THIS THING FOR BOXES. I STOLE ONE AND SHE WASN'T VERY HAPPY ABOUT IT.
AND SHE DIDN'T KILL YOU?
SHE DID WORSE. SHE RECRUITED ME INTO HELPING HER WITH A LITTLE TURF WAR. AND WHEN THAT WAS FINALLY OVER, SHE MADE ME HER HEIR.
WHAT DOES THAT MEAN, EXACTLY? HER HEIR?
SOMEDAY I'M GOING TO REPLACE HER AS THE KEEPER OF SECRETS.
WELL, THAT'S...
A BIG BUCKET OF SUCK COVERED IN SUCK-SAUCE, YEAH.
BUT ONE OF THESE DAYS I'LL FIGURE OUT A WAY TO GET HER DAMN HEX REMOVED AND...
UH, RAINA?
YES, WHAT IS IT?
DO ME A FAVOR AND DON'T LOOK IN THE BACK SEAT.
WHY? WHAT'S IN THE BACK S--

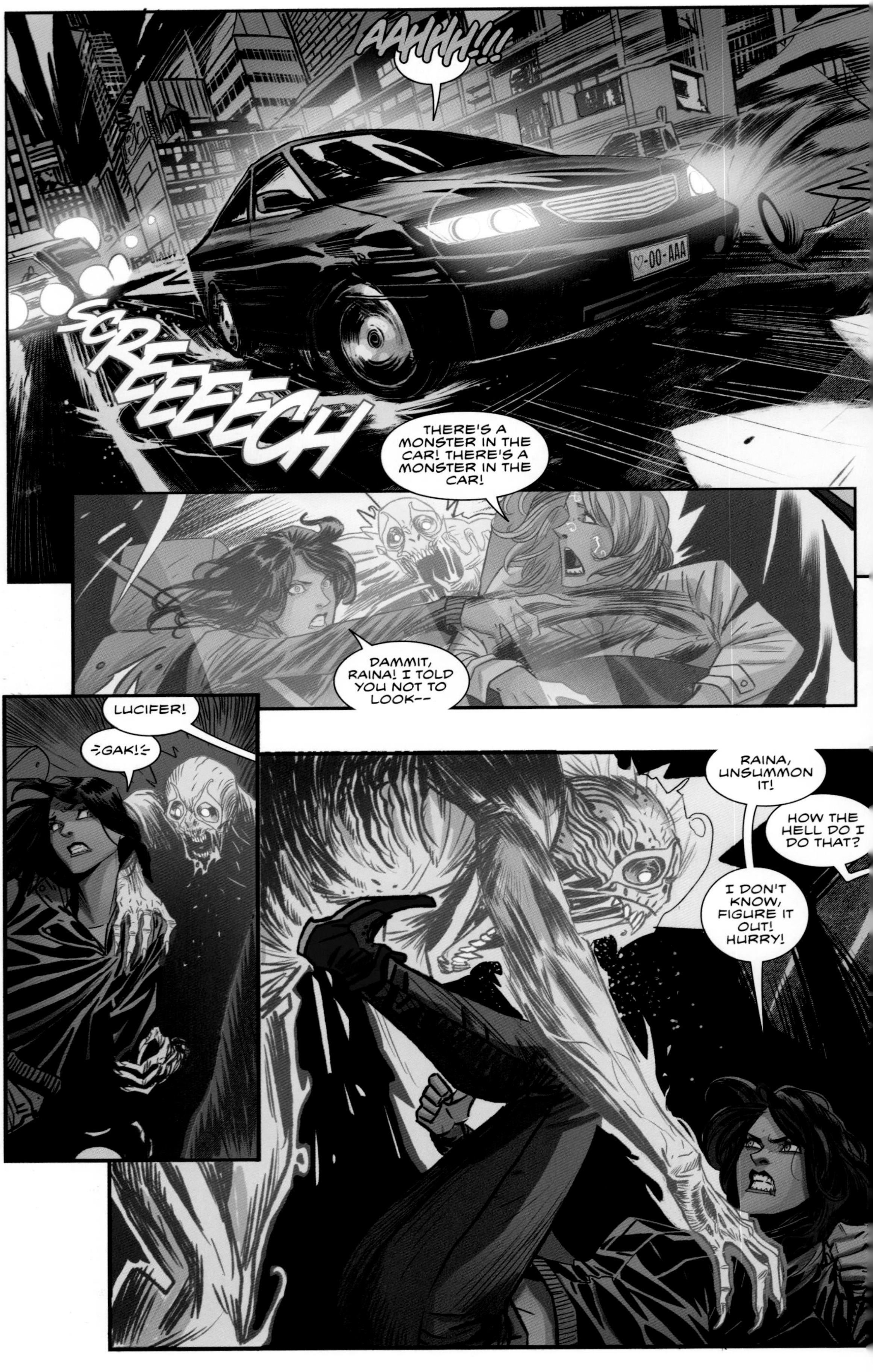
AAHHH!!!
SCREEEEECH
THERE'S A MONSTER IN THE CAR! THERE'S A MONSTER IN THE CAR!
DAMMIT, RAINA! I TOLD YOU NOT TO LOOK--
LUCIFER!
GAK!
RAINA, UNSUMMON IT!
HOW THE HELL DO I DO THAT?
I DON'T KNOW, FIGURE IT OUT! HURRY!

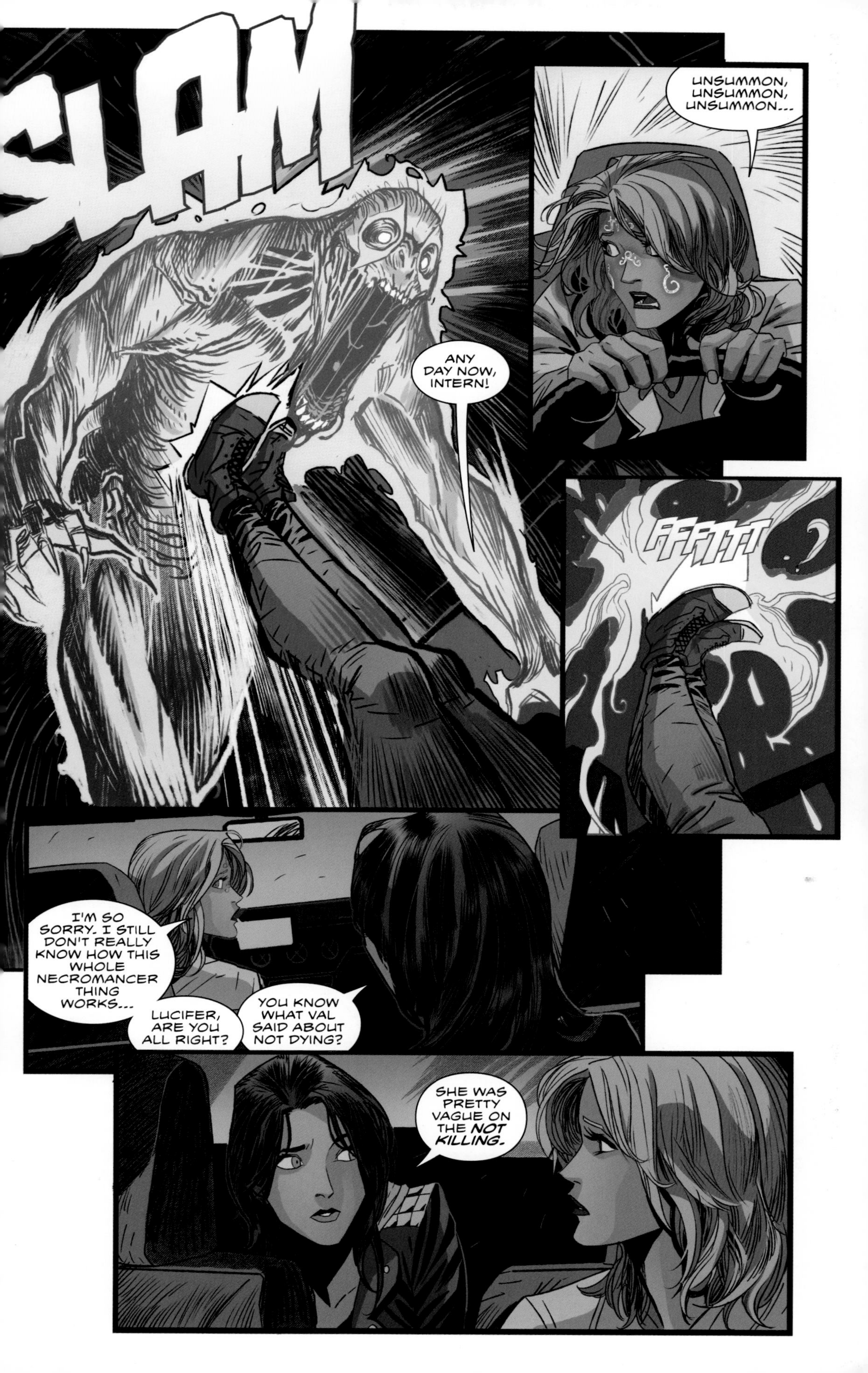
SLAM
ANY DAY NOW, INTERN!
UNSUMMON, UNSUMMON, UNSUMMON...
FFFTTT
I'M SO SORRY. I STILL DON'T REALLY KNOW HOW THIS WHOLE NECROMANCER THING WORKS...
LUCIFER, ARE YOU ALL RIGHT?
YOU KNOW WHAT VAL SAID ABOUT NOT DYING?
SHE WAS PRETTY VAGUE ON THE *NOT KILLING.*

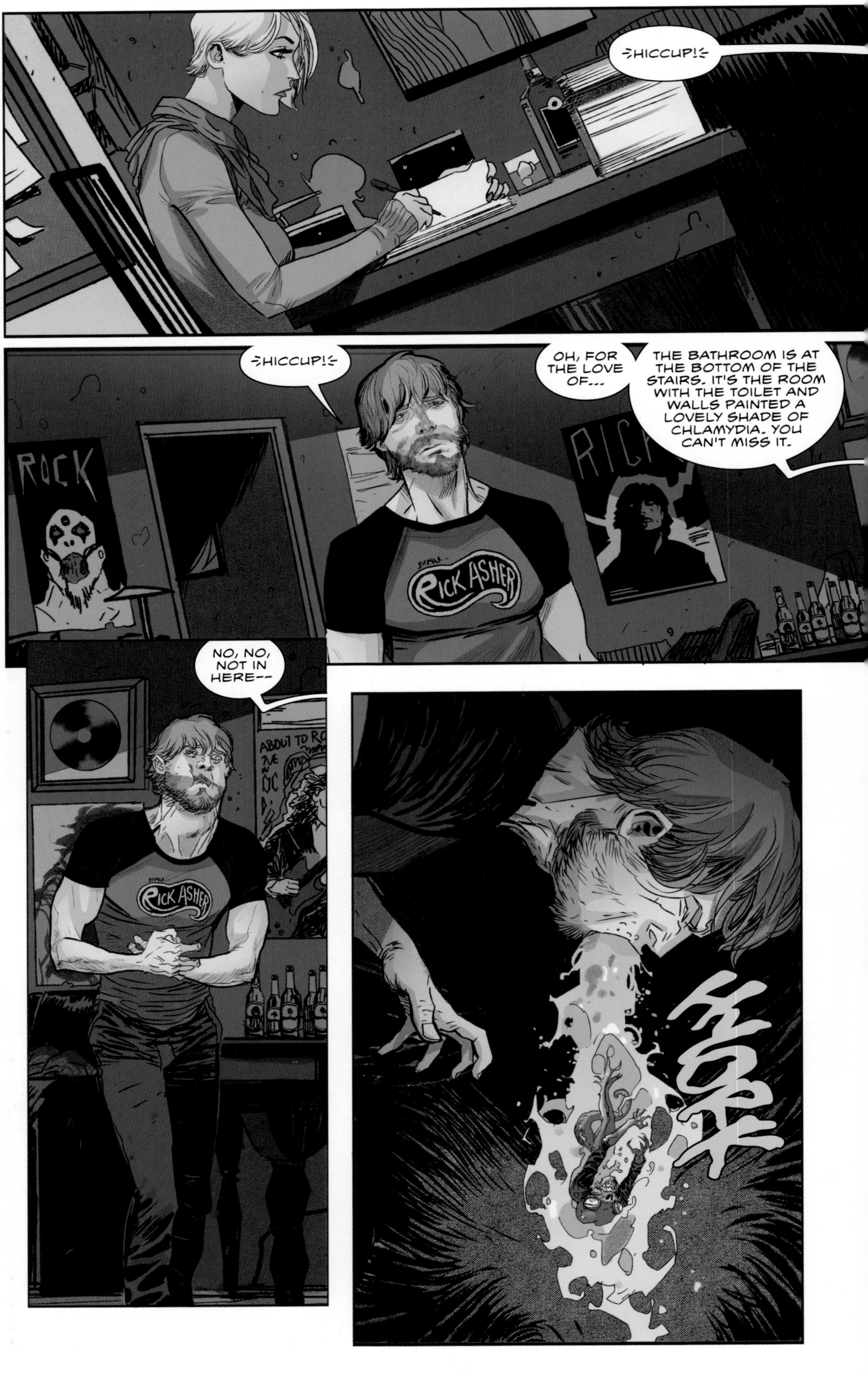
HICCUP!
HICCUP!
OH, FOR THE LOVE OF--
THE BATHROOM IS AT THE BOTTOM OF THE STAIRS. IT'S THE ROOM WITH THE TOILET AND WALLS PAINTED A LOVELY SHADE OF CHLAMYDIA. YOU CAN'T MISS IT.
ROCK
RICK ASHER
NO, NO, NOT IN HERE--
RICK ASHER

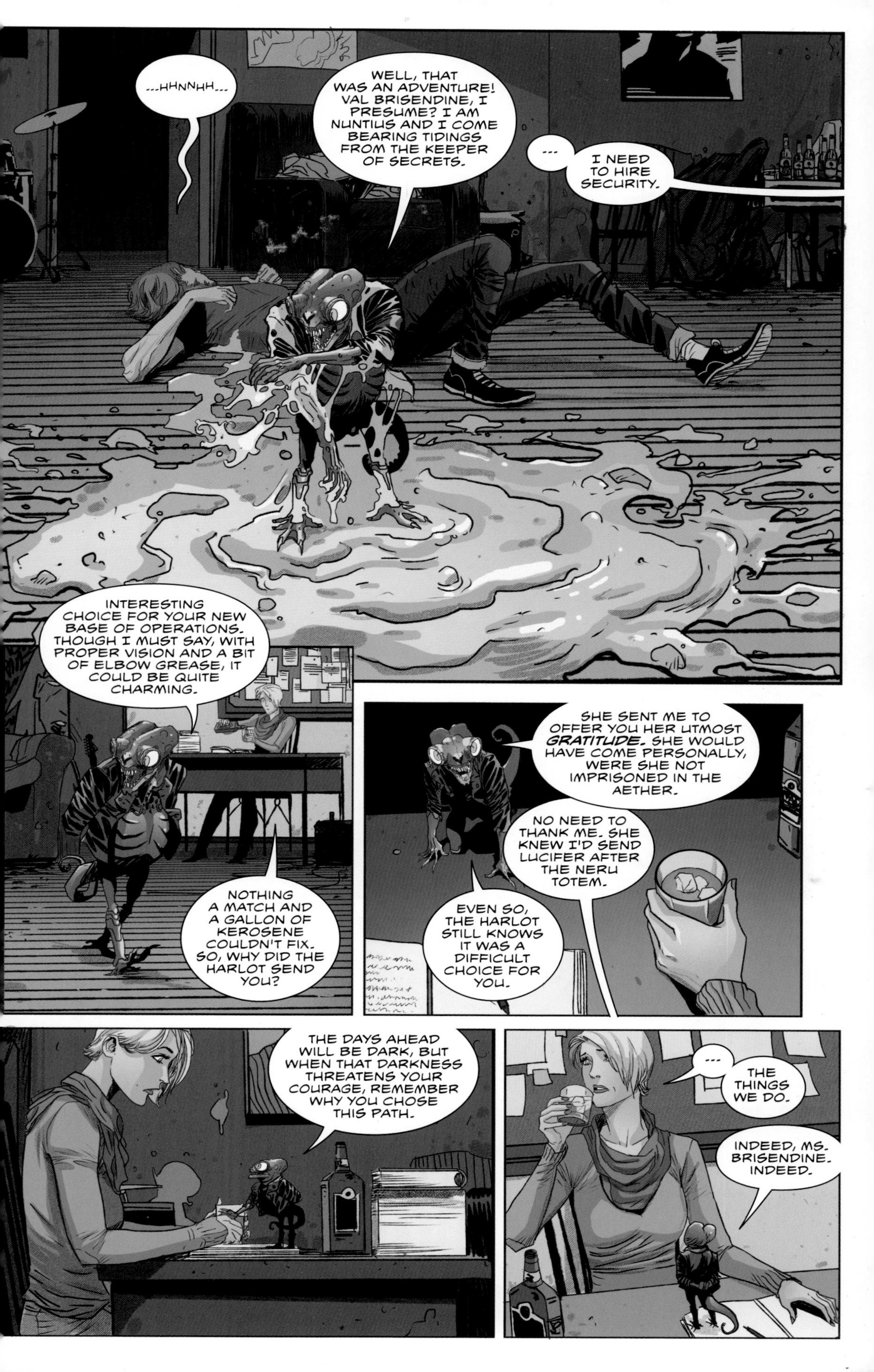

...HHNNHH...
WELL, THAT WAS AN ADVENTURE! VAL BRISENDINE, I PRESUME? I AM NUNTIUS AND I COME BEARING TIDINGS FROM THE KEEPER OF SECRETS.
...
I NEED TO HIRE SECURITY.
INTERESTING CHOICE FOR YOUR NEW BASE OF OPERATIONS. THOUGH I MUST SAY, WITH PROPER VISION AND A BIT OF ELBOW GREASE, IT COULD BE QUITE CHARMING.
NOTHING A MATCH AND A GALLON OF KEROSENE COULDN'T FIX. SO, WHY DID THE HARLOT SEND YOU?
SHE SENT ME TO OFFER YOU HER UTMOST *GRATITUDE*. SHE WOULD HAVE COME PERSONALLY, WERE SHE NOT IMPRISONED IN THE AETHER.
NO NEED TO THANK ME. SHE KNEW I'D SEND LUCIFER AFTER THE NERU TOTEM.
EVEN SO, THE HARLOT STILL KNOWS IT WAS A DIFFICULT CHOICE FOR YOU.
THE DAYS AHEAD WILL BE DARK, BUT WHEN THAT DARKNESS THREATENS YOUR COURAGE, REMEMBER WHY YOU CHOSE THIS PATH.
...
THE THINGS WE DO.
INDEED, MS. BRISENDINE. INDEED.

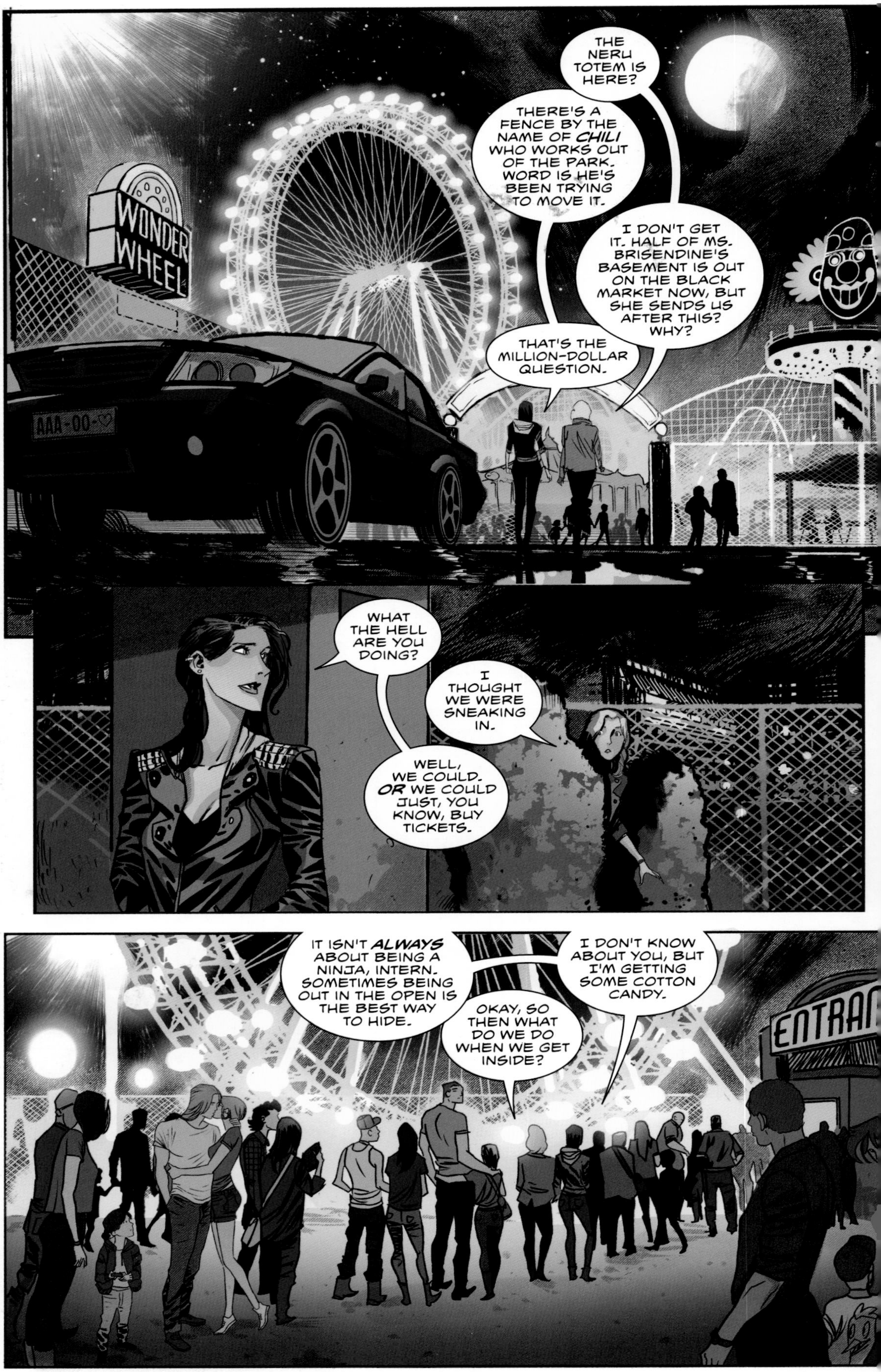
WONDER WHEEL
THE NERU TOTEM IS HERE?
THERE'S A FENCE BY THE NAME OF *CHILI* WHO WORKS OUT OF THE PARK. WORD IS HE'S BEEN TRYING TO MOVE IT.
I DON'T GET IT. HALF OF MS. BRISENDINE'S BASEMENT IS OUT ON THE BLACK MARKET NOW, BUT SHE SENDS US AFTER THIS? WHY?
THAT'S THE MILLION-DOLLAR QUESTION.
WHAT THE HELL ARE YOU DOING?
I THOUGHT WE WERE SNEAKING IN.
WELL, WE COULD. *OR* WE COULD JUST, YOU KNOW, BUY TICKETS.
IT ISN'T *ALWAYS* ABOUT BEING A NINJA, INTERN. SOMETIMES BEING OUT IN THE OPEN IS THE BEST WAY TO HIDE.
I DON'T KNOW ABOUT YOU, BUT I'M GETTING SOME COTTON CANDY.
OKAY, SO THEN WHAT DO WE DO WHEN WE GET INSIDE?
ENTRAN

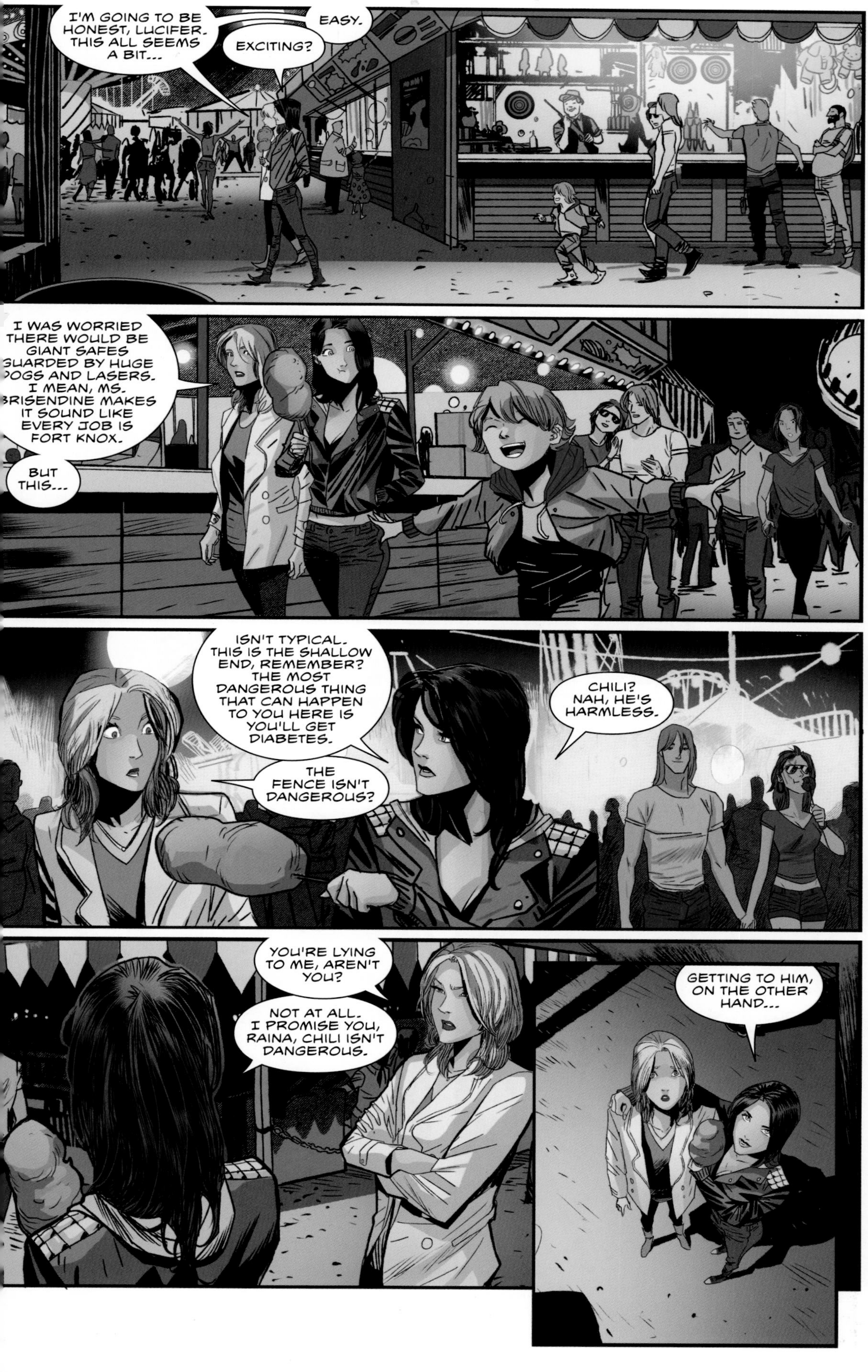
I'M GOING TO BE HONEST, LUCIFER. THIS ALL SEEMS A BIT...
EXCITING?
EASY.
I WAS WORRIED THERE WOULD BE GIANT SAFES GUARDED BY HUGE DOGS AND LASERS. I MEAN, MS. BRISENDINE MAKES IT SOUND LIKE EVERY JOB IS FORT KNOX.
BUT THIS...
ISN'T TYPICAL. THIS IS THE SHALLOW END, REMEMBER? THE MOST DANGEROUS THING THAT CAN HAPPEN TO YOU HERE IS YOU'LL GET DIABETES.
THE FENCE ISN'T DANGEROUS?
CHILI? NAH, HE'S HARMLESS.
YOU'RE LYING TO ME, AREN'T YOU?
NOT AT ALL. I PROMISE YOU, RAINA, CHILI ISN'T DANGEROUS.
GETTING TO HIM, ON THE OTHER HAND...

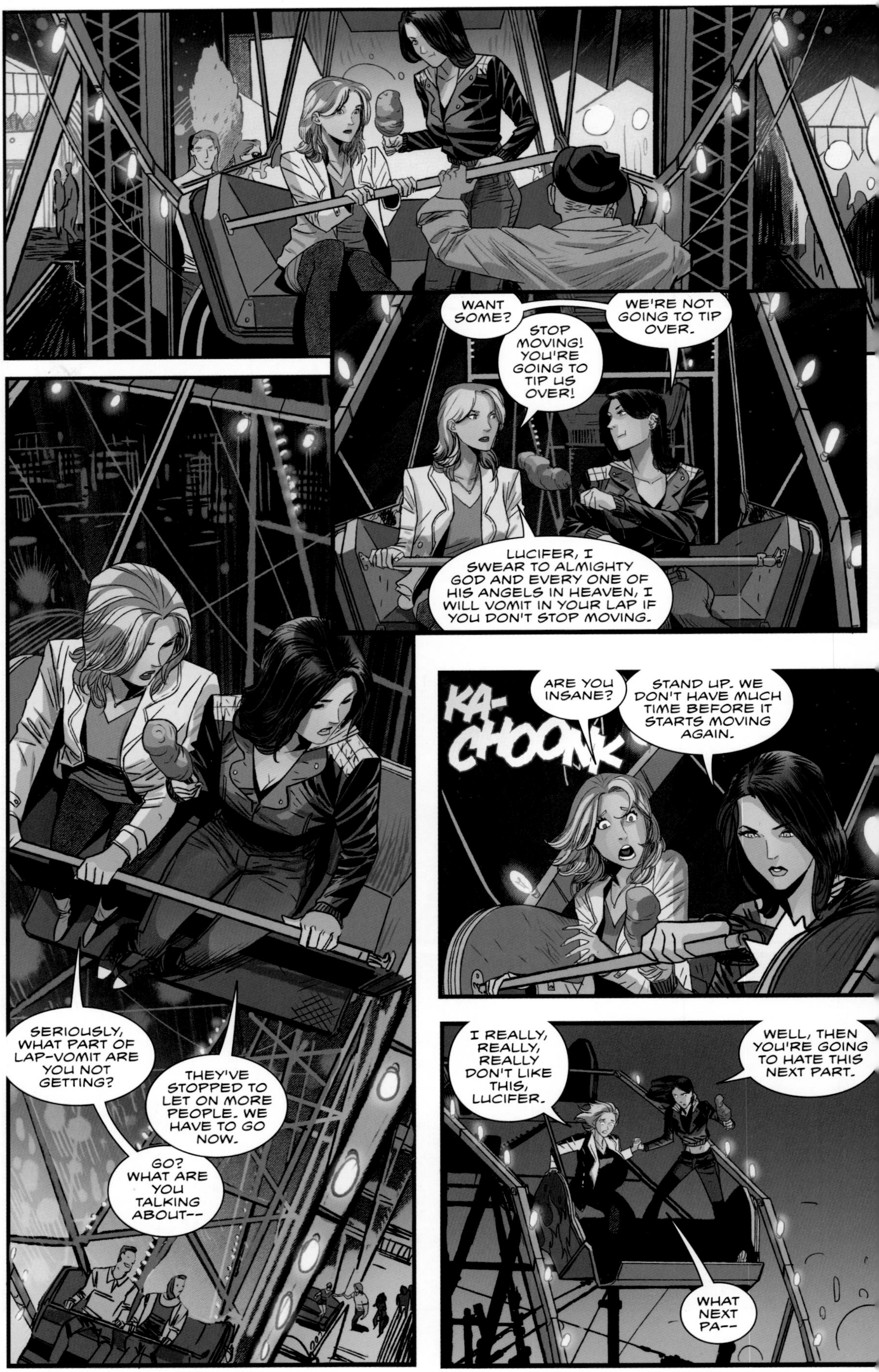
WANT SOME?
STOP MOVING! YOU'RE GOING TO TIP US OVER!
WE'RE NOT GOING TO TIP OVER.
LUCIFER, I SWEAR TO ALMIGHTY GOD AND EVERY ONE OF HIS ANGELS IN HEAVEN, I WILL VOMIT IN YOUR LAP IF YOU DON'T STOP MOVING.
SERIOUSLY, WHAT PART OF LAP-VOMIT ARE YOU NOT GETTING?
THEY'VE STOPPED TO LET ON MORE PEOPLE. WE HAVE TO GO NOW.
GO? WHAT ARE YOU TALKING ABOUT--
KA-CHOONK
ARE YOU INSANE?
STAND UP. WE DON'T HAVE MUCH TIME BEFORE IT STARTS MOVING AGAIN.
I REALLY, REALLY, REALLY DON'T LIKE THIS, LUCIFER.
WELL, THEN YOU'RE GOING TO HATE THIS NEXT PART.
WHAT NEXT PA--

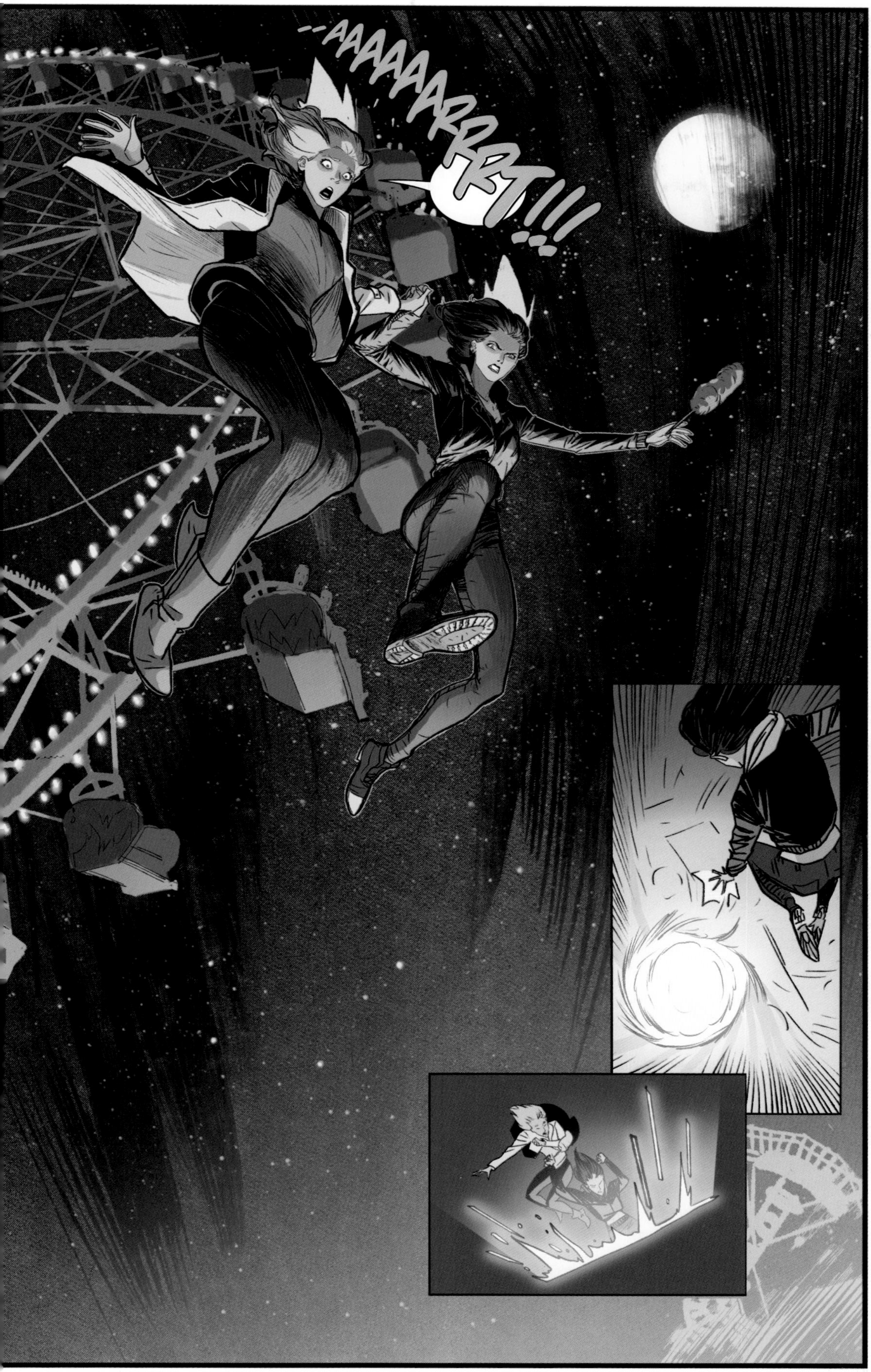
--AAAAAARRRRT!!!!

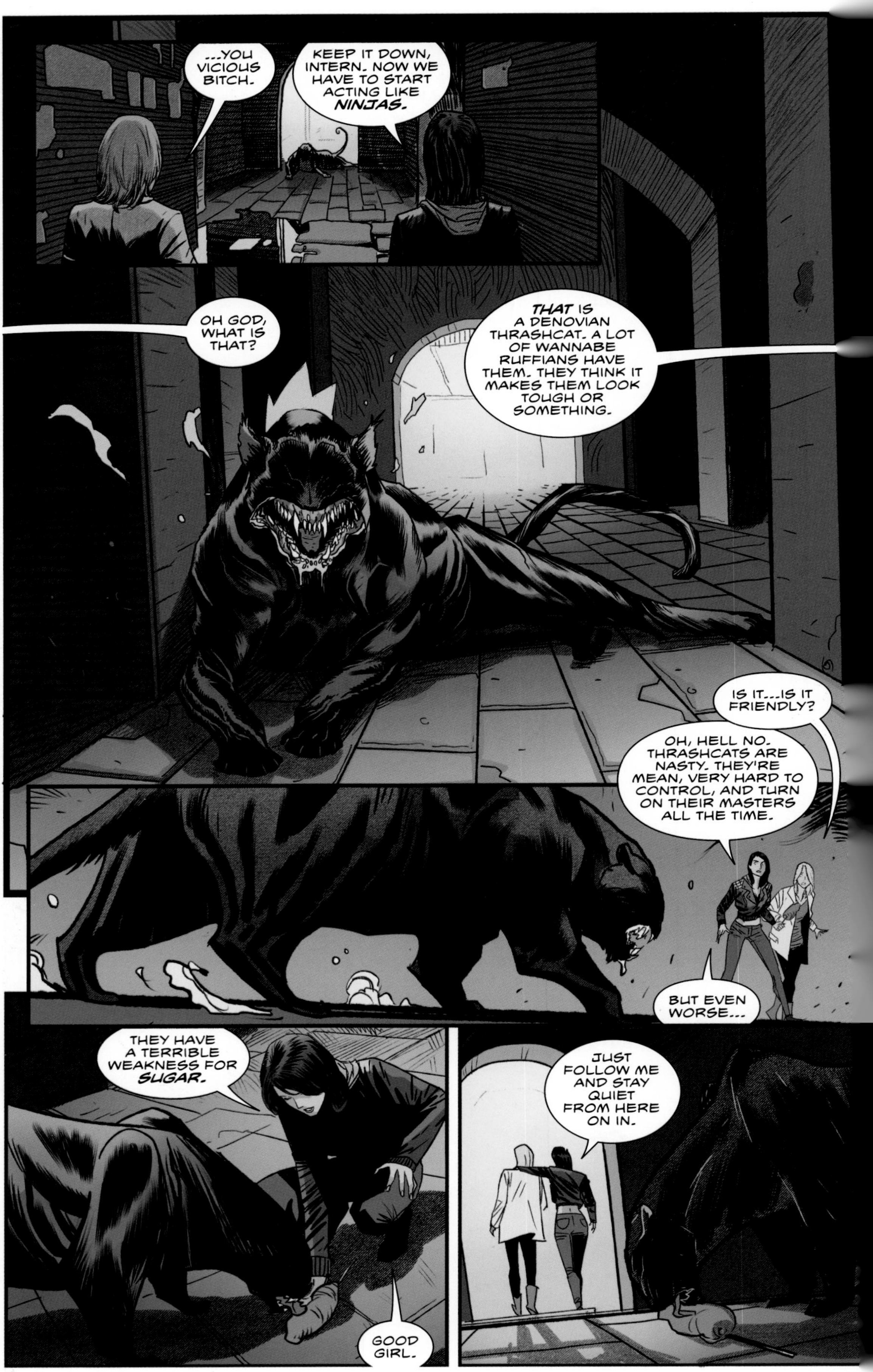
...YOU VICIOUS BITCH.
KEEP IT DOWN, INTERN. NOW WE HAVE TO START ACTING LIKE NINJAS.
OH GOD, WHAT IS THAT?
THAT IS A DENOVIAN THRASHCAT. A LOT OF WANNABE RUFFIANS HAVE THEM. THEY THINK IT MAKES THEM LOOK TOUGH OR SOMETHING.
IS IT...IS IT FRIENDLY?
OH, HELL NO. THRASHCATS ARE NASTY. THEY'RE MEAN, VERY HARD TO CONTROL, AND TURN ON THEIR MASTERS ALL THE TIME.
BUT EVEN WORSE...
THEY HAVE A TERRIBLE WEAKNESS FOR SUGAR.
GOOD GIRL.
JUST FOLLOW ME AND STAY QUIET FROM HERE ON IN.

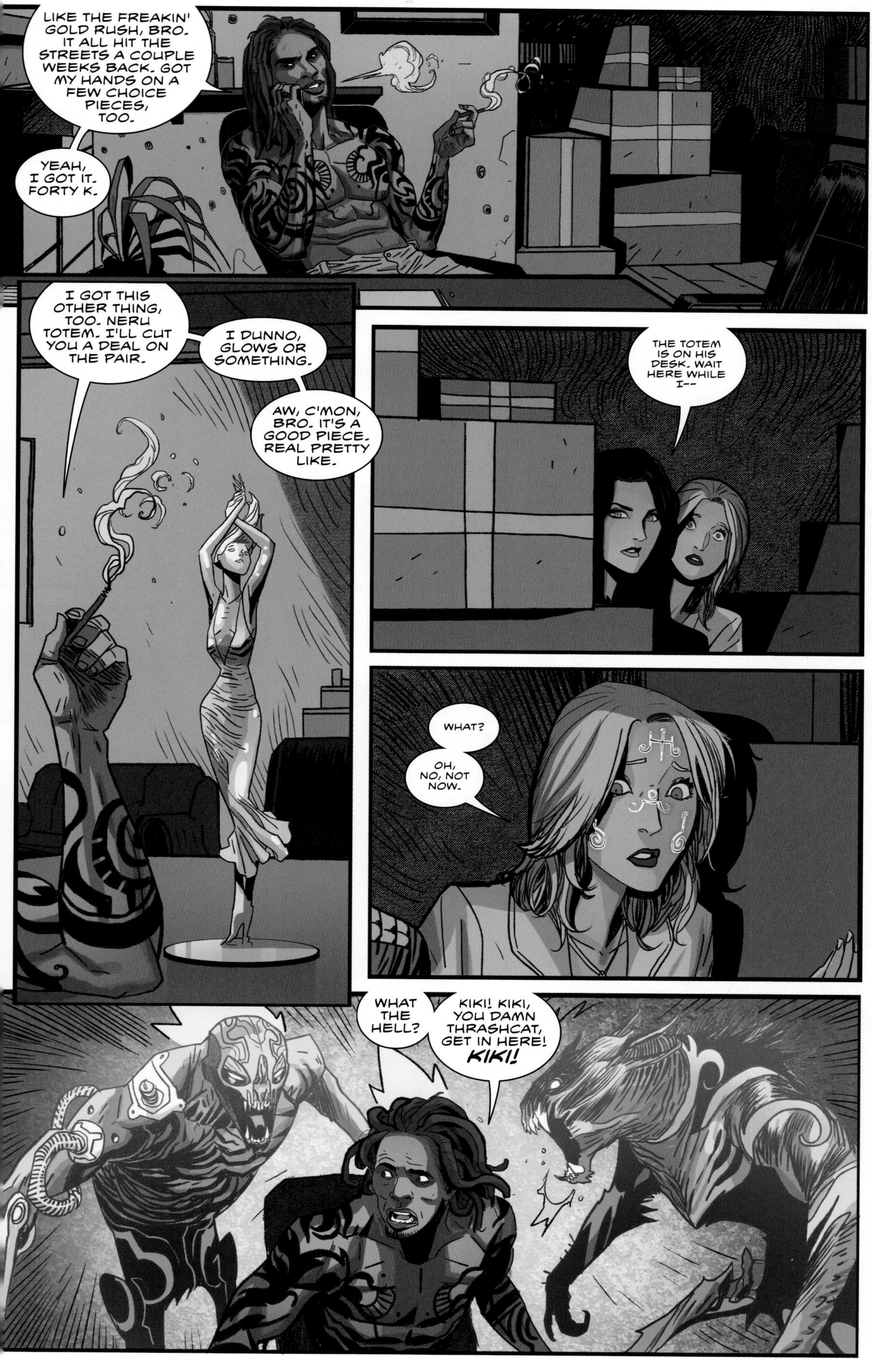
LIKE THE FREAKIN' GOLD RUSH, BRO. IT ALL HIT THE STREETS A COUPLE WEEKS BACK. GOT MY HANDS ON A FEW CHOICE PIECES, TOO.
YEAH, I GOT IT. FORTY K.
I GOT THIS OTHER THING, TOO. NERU TOTEM. I'LL CUT YOU A DEAL ON THE PAIR.
I DUNNO, GLOWS OR SOMETHING.
AW, C'MON, BRO. IT'S A GOOD PIECE. REAL PRETTY LIKE.
THE TOTEM IS ON HIS DESK. WAIT HERE WHILE I--
WHAT?
OH, NO, NOT NOW.
WHAT THE HELL?
KIKI! KIKI, YOU DAMN THRASHCAT, GET IN HERE! KIKI!

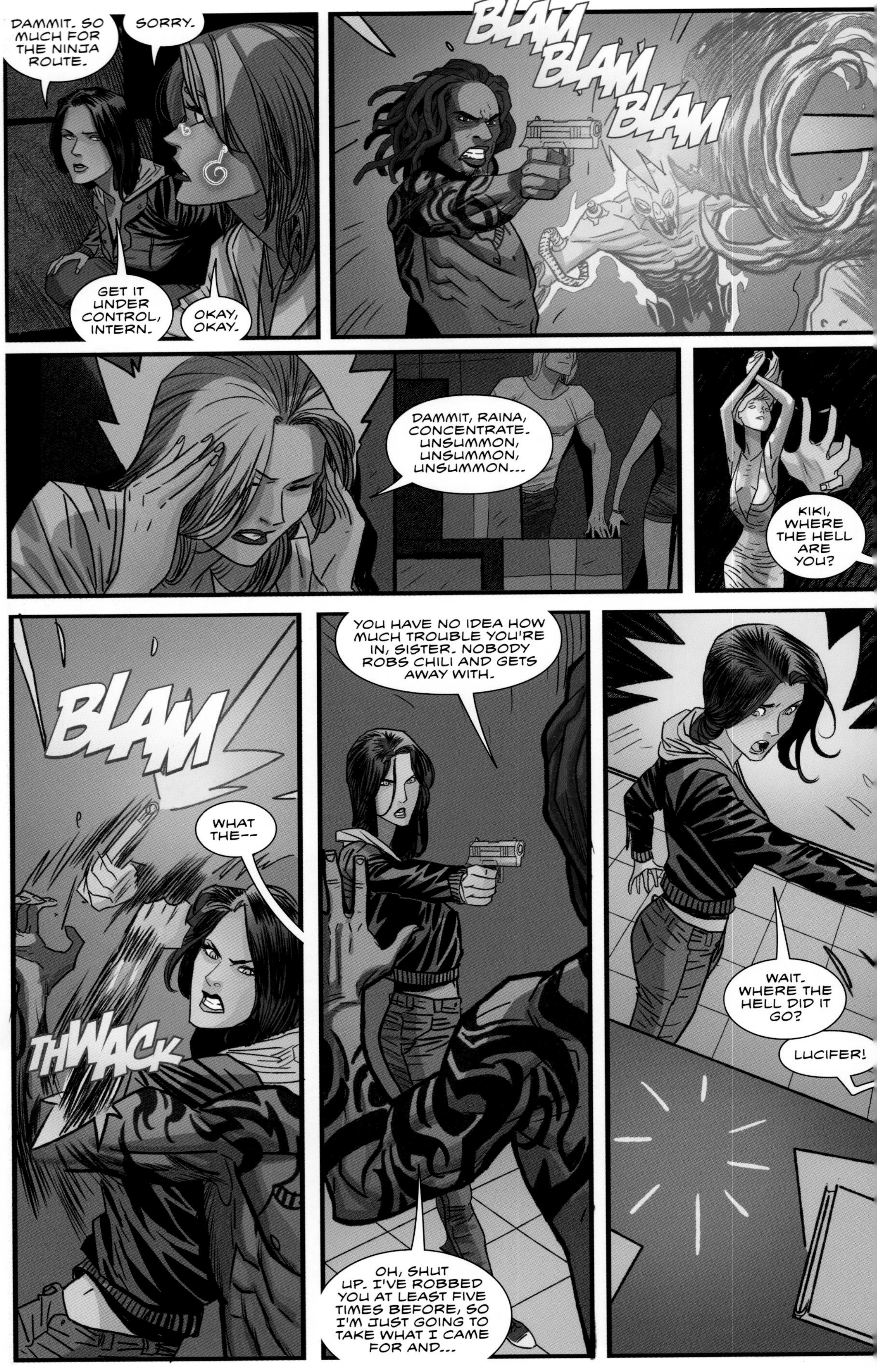
DAMMIT. SO MUCH FOR THE NINJA ROUTE.
SORRY.
GET IT UNDER CONTROL, INTERN.
OKAY, OKAY.
BLAM BLAM BLAM
DAMMIT, RAINA, CONCENTRATE. UNSUMMON, UNSUMMON, UNSUMMON...
KIKI, WHERE THE HELL ARE YOU?
BLAM
WHAT THE--
THWACK
YOU HAVE NO IDEA HOW MUCH TROUBLE YOU'RE IN, SISTER. NOBODY ROBS CHILI AND GETS AWAY WITH.
OH, SHUT UP. I'VE ROBBED YOU AT LEAST FIVE TIMES BEFORE, SO I'M JUST GOING TO TAKE WHAT I CAME FOR AND...
WAIT. WHERE THE HELL DID IT GO?
LUCIFER!

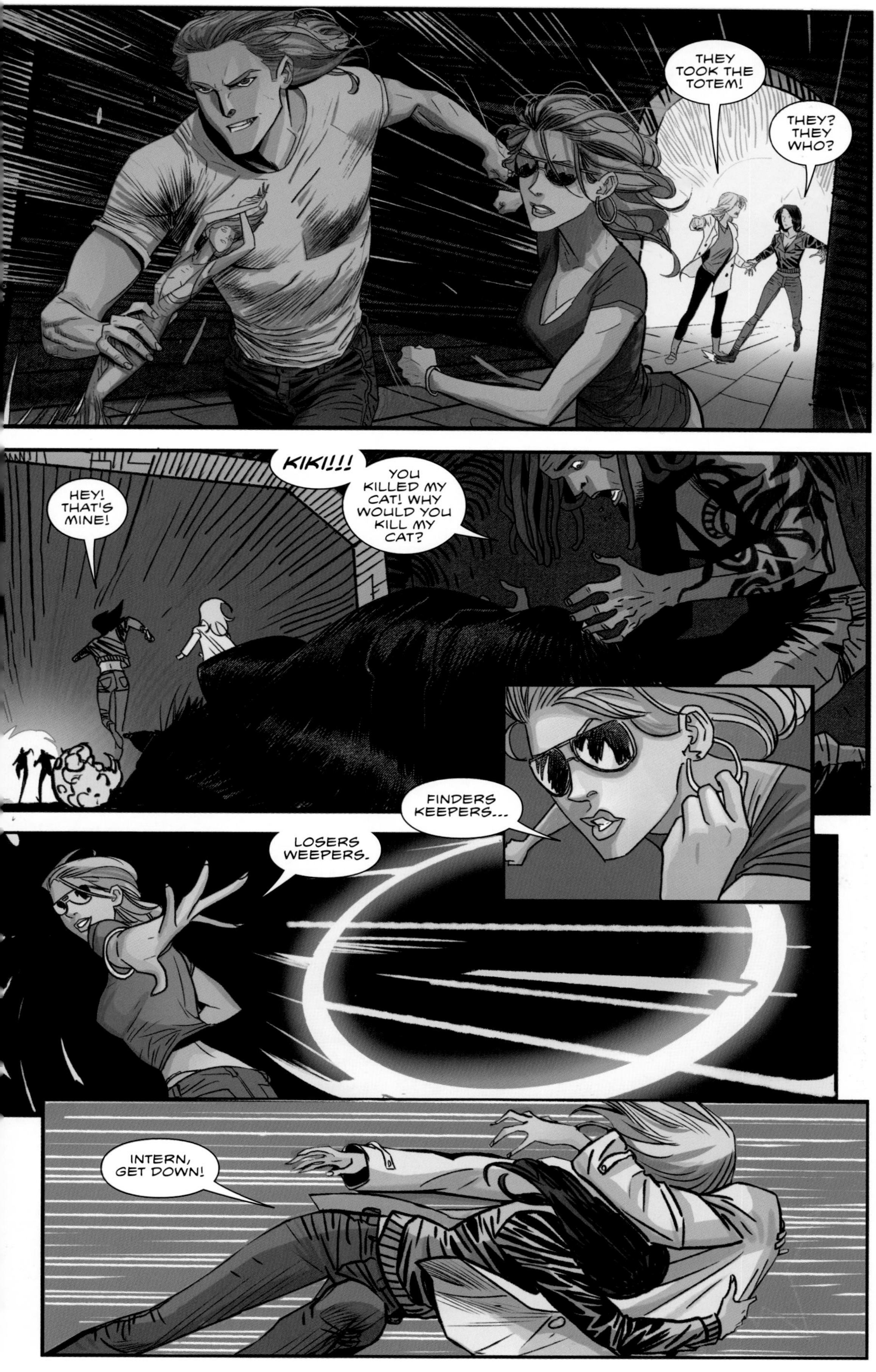
THEY TOOK THE TOTEM!
THEY? THEY WHO?
HEY! THAT'S MINE!
KIKI!!!
YOU KILLED MY CAT! WHY WOULD YOU KILL MY CAT?
FINDERS KEEPERS...
LOSERS WEEPERS.
INTERN, GET DOWN!

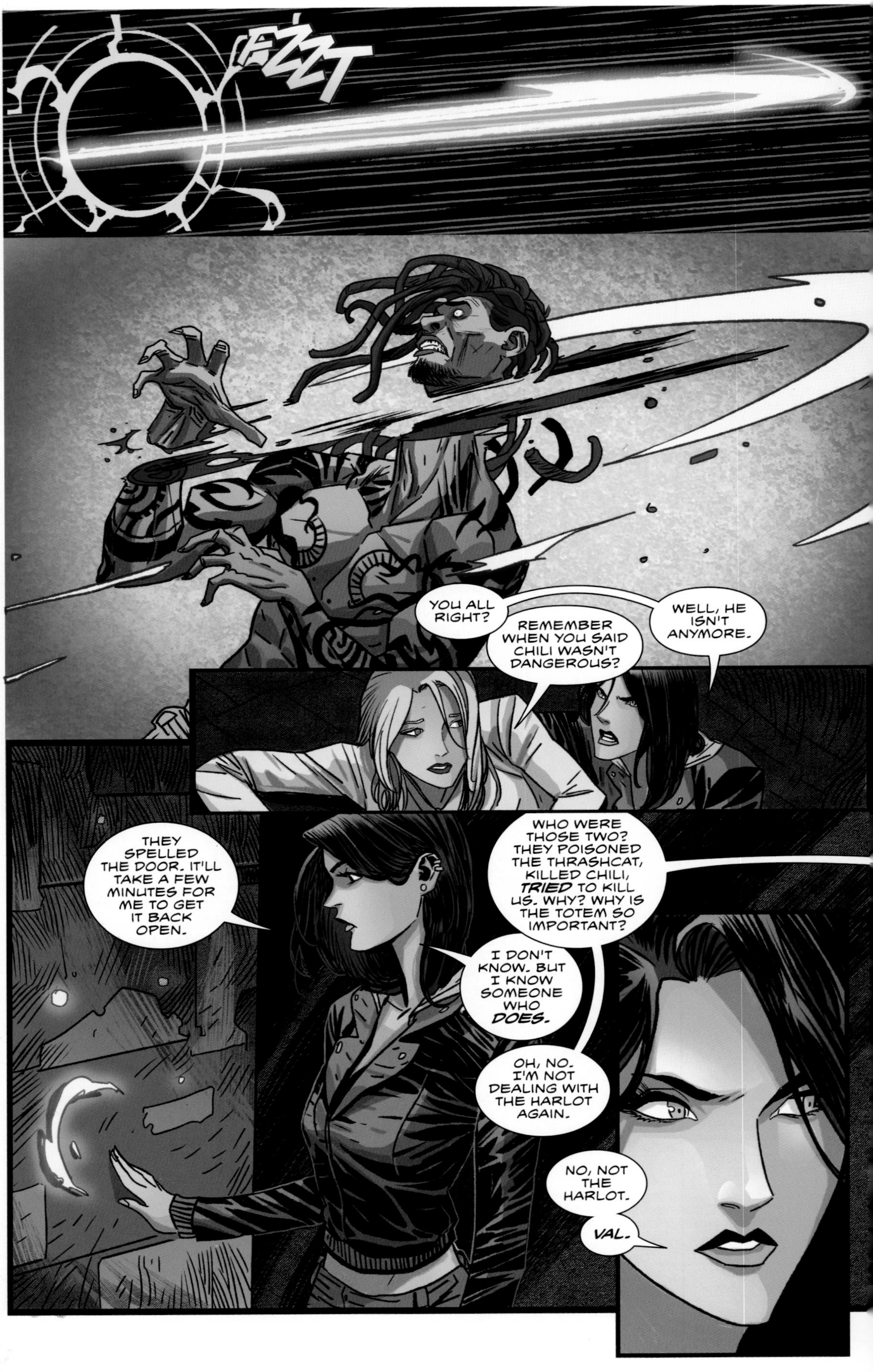
FZZZT
YOU ALL RIGHT?
REMEMBER WHEN YOU SAID CHILI WASN'T DANGEROUS?
WELL, HE ISN'T ANYMORE.
THEY SPELLED THE DOOR. IT'LL TAKE A FEW MINUTES FOR ME TO GET IT BACK OPEN.
WHO WERE THOSE TWO? THEY POISONED THE THRASHCAT, KILLED CHILI, TRIED TO KILL US. WHY? WHY IS THE TOTEM SO IMPORTANT?
I DON'T KNOW. BUT I KNOW SOMEONE WHO DOES.
OH, NO. I'M NOT DEALING WITH THE HARLOT AGAIN.
NO, NOT THE HARLOT.
VAL.

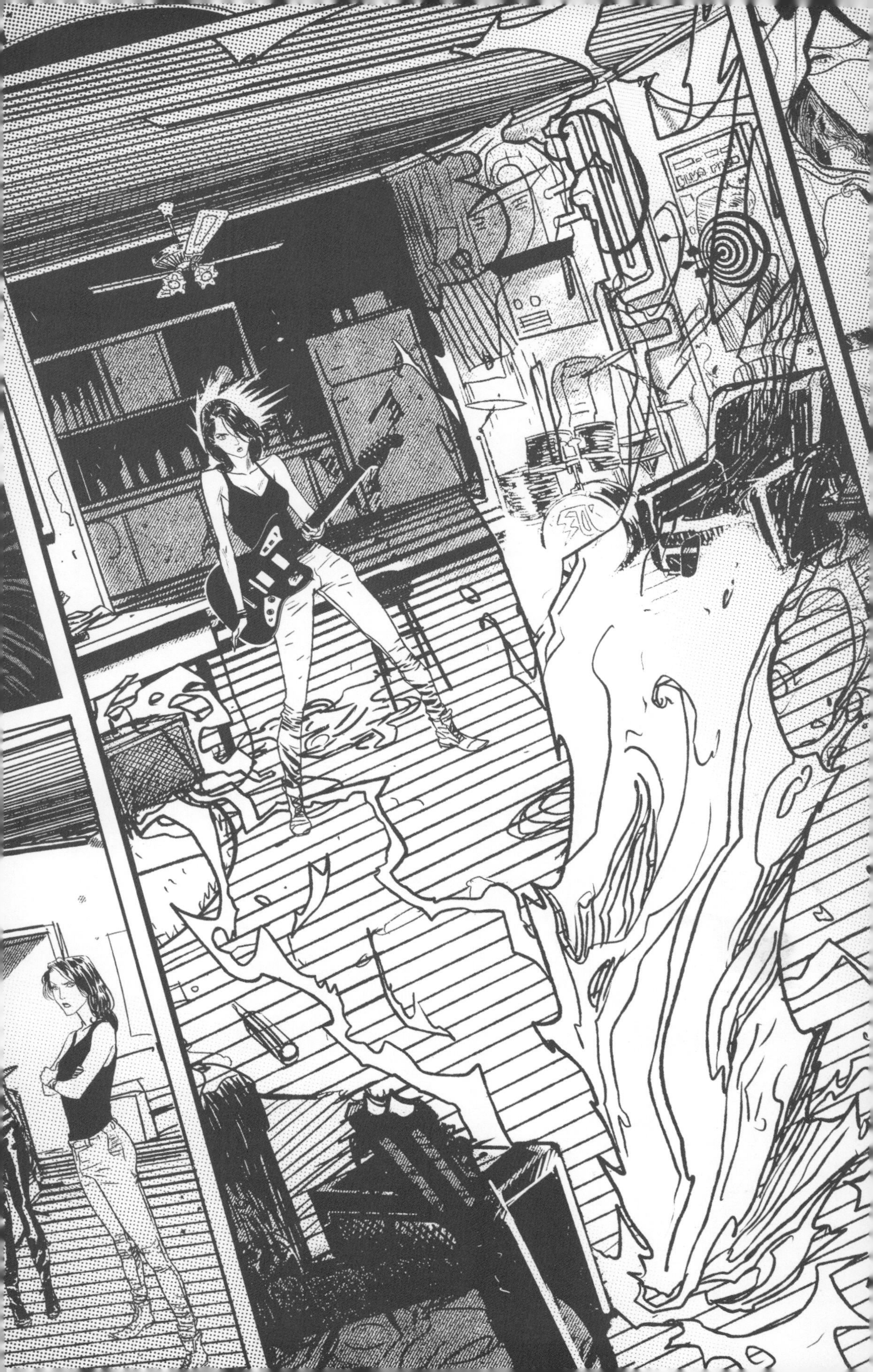

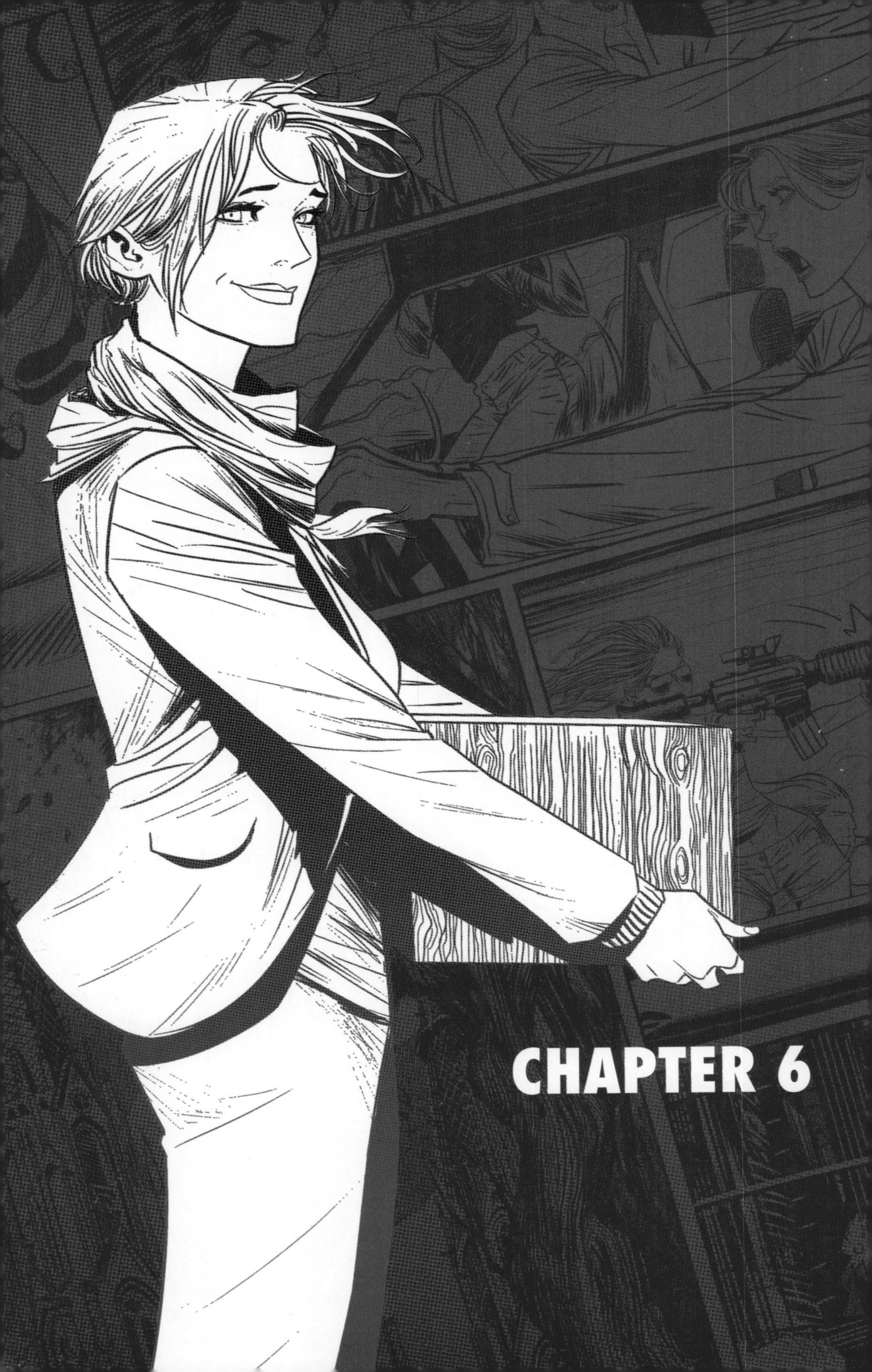

CHAPTER 6

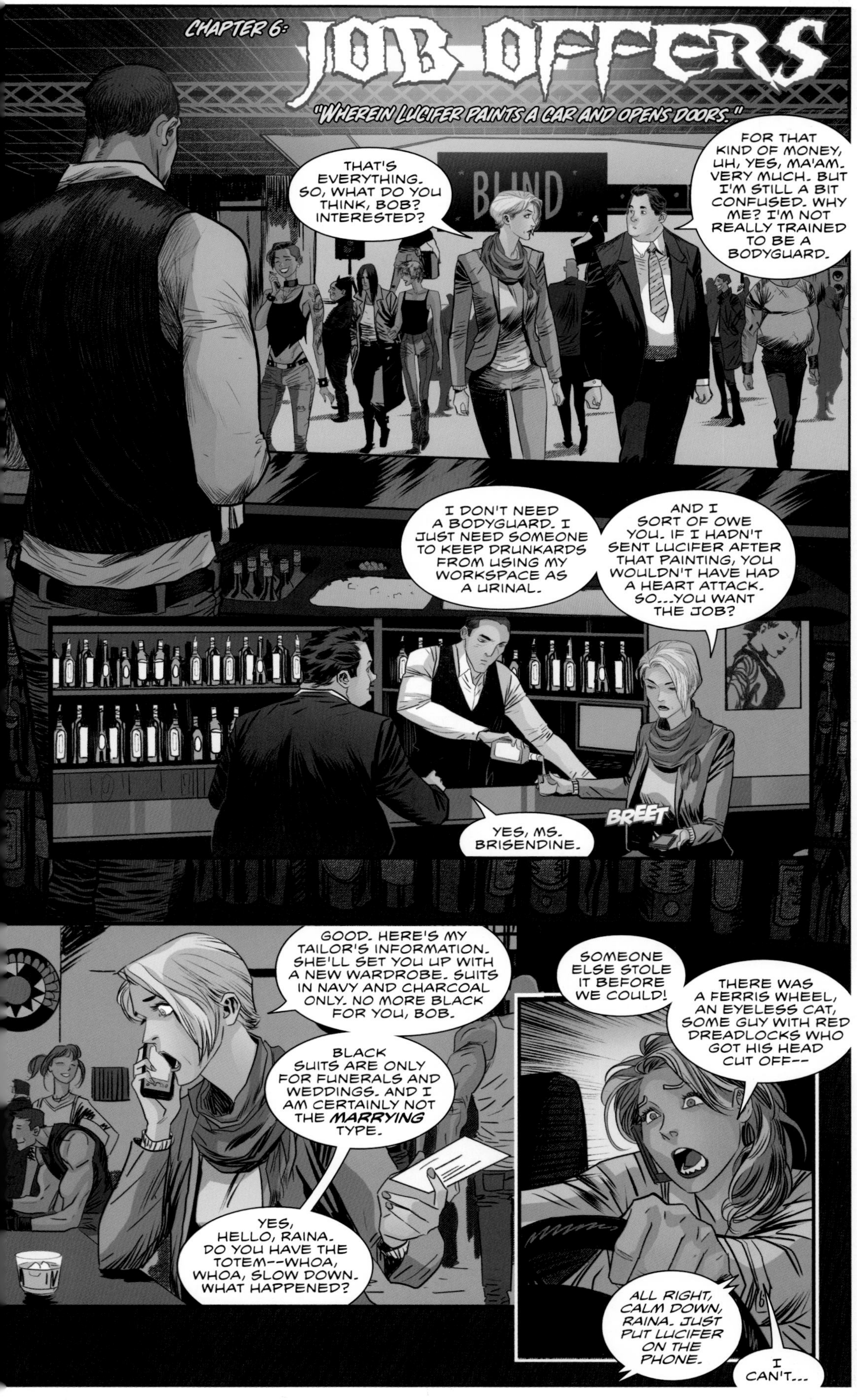
CHAPTER 6: JOB OFFERS
"WHEREIN LUCIFER PAINTS A CAR AND OPENS DOORS."
BLIND
THAT'S EVERYTHING. SO, WHAT DO YOU THINK, BOB? INTERESTED?
FOR THAT KIND OF MONEY, UH, YES, MA'AM. VERY MUCH. BUT I'M STILL A BIT CONFUSED. WHY ME? I'M NOT REALLY TRAINED TO BE A BODYGUARD.
I DON'T NEED A BODYGUARD. I JUST NEED SOMEONE TO KEEP DRUNKARDS FROM USING MY WORKSPACE AS A URINAL.
AND I SORT OF OWE YOU. IF I HADN'T SENT LUCIFER AFTER THAT PAINTING, YOU WOULDN'T HAVE HAD A HEART ATTACK. SO...YOU WANT THE JOB?
YES, MS. BRISENDINE.
BREET
GOOD. HERE'S MY TAILOR'S INFORMATION. SHE'LL SET YOU UP WITH A NEW WARDROBE. SUITS IN NAVY AND CHARCOAL ONLY. NO MORE BLACK FOR YOU, BOB.
BLACK SUITS ARE ONLY FOR FUNERALS AND WEDDINGS. AND I AM CERTAINLY NOT THE MARRYING TYPE.
YES, HELLO, RAINA. DO YOU HAVE THE TOTEM--WHOA, WHOA, SLOW DOWN. WHAT HAPPENED?
SOMEONE ELSE STOLE IT BEFORE WE COULD!
THERE WAS A FERRIS WHEEL, AN EYELESS CAT, SOME GUY WITH RED DREADLOCKS WHO GOT HIS HEAD CUT OFF--
ALL RIGHT, CALM DOWN, RAINA. JUST PUT LUCIFER ON THE PHONE.
I CAN'T...

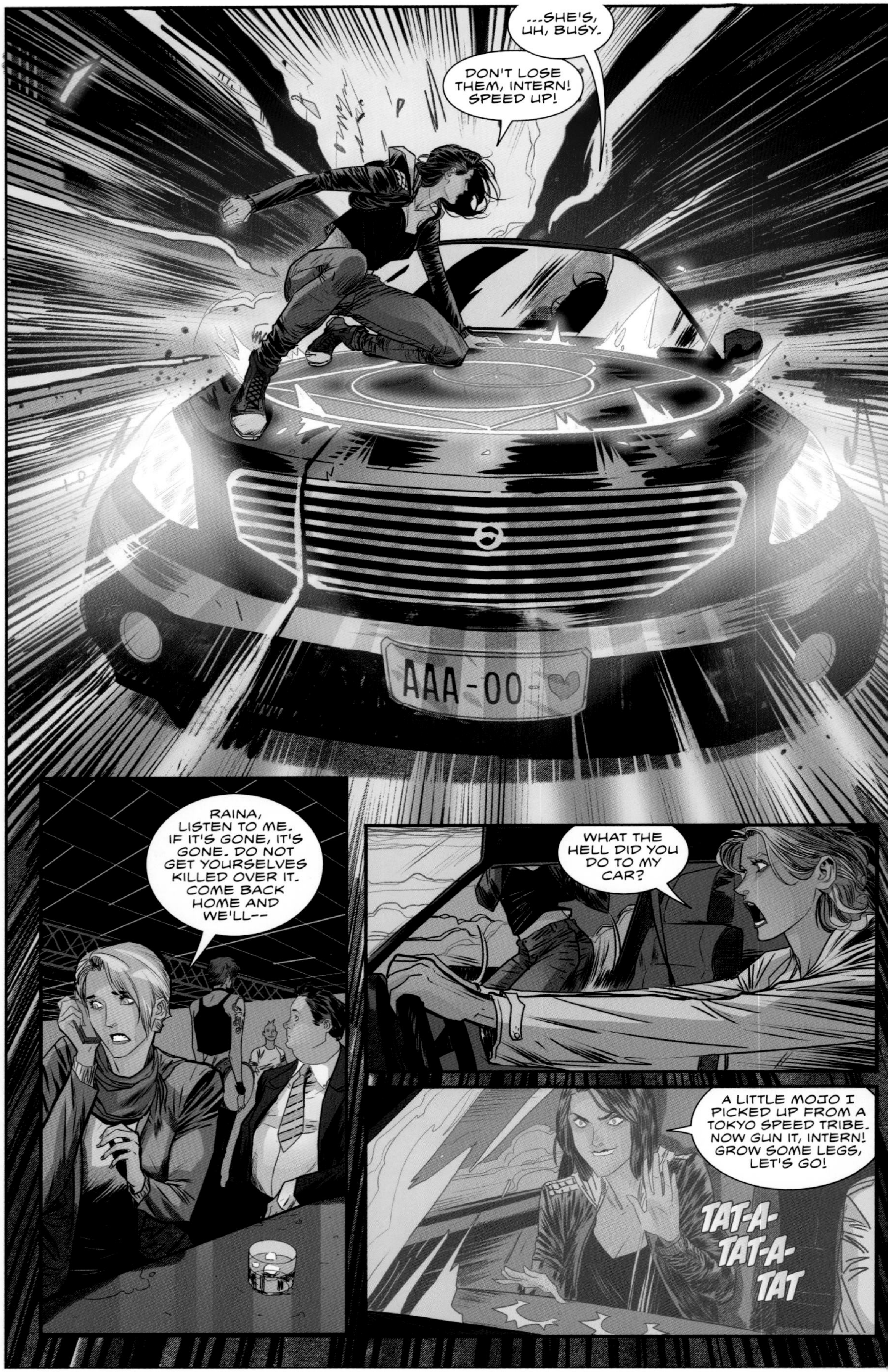

...SHE'S, UH, BUSY.
DON'T LOSE THEM, INTERN! SPEED UP!
AAA-00-
RAINA, LISTEN TO ME. IF IT'S GONE, IT'S GONE. DO NOT GET YOURSELVES KILLED OVER IT. COME BACK HOME AND WE'LL--
WHAT THE HELL DID YOU DO TO MY CAR?
A LITTLE MOJO I PICKED UP FROM A TOKYO SPEED TRIBE. NOW GUN IT, INTERN! GROW SOME LEGS, LET'S GO!
TAT-A-TAT-A-TAT

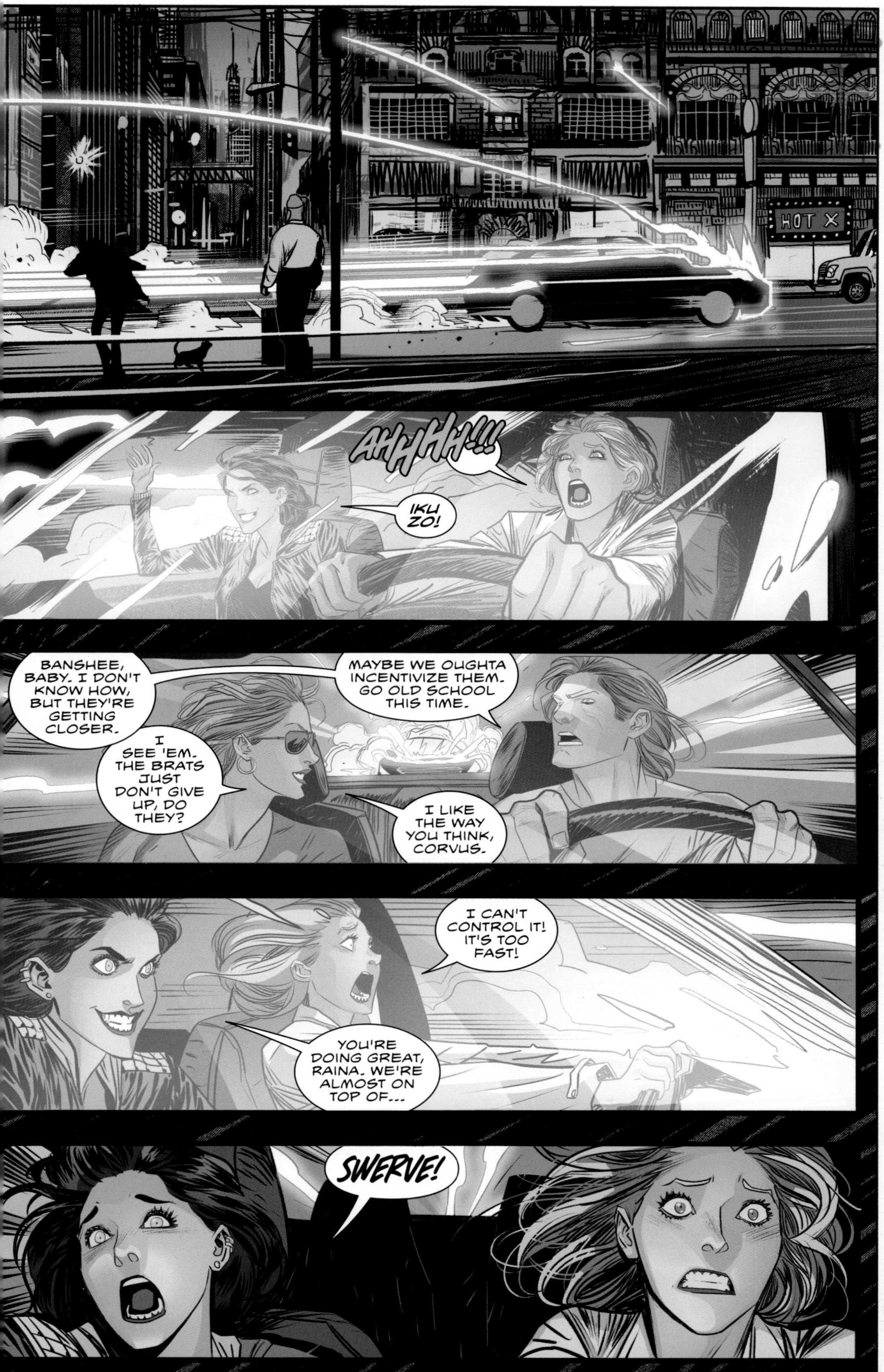
HOT X
AHHHH!!!
IKU ZO!
BANSHEE, BABY. I DON'T KNOW HOW, BUT THEY'RE GETTING CLOSER.
I SEE 'EM. THE BRATS JUST DON'T GIVE UP, DO THEY?
MAYBE WE OUGHTA INCENTIVIZE THEM. GO OLD SCHOOL THIS TIME.
I LIKE THE WAY YOU THINK, CORVUS.
I CAN'T CONTROL IT! IT'S TOO FAST!
YOU'RE DOING GREAT, RAINA. WE'RE ALMOST ON TOP OF...
SWERVE!

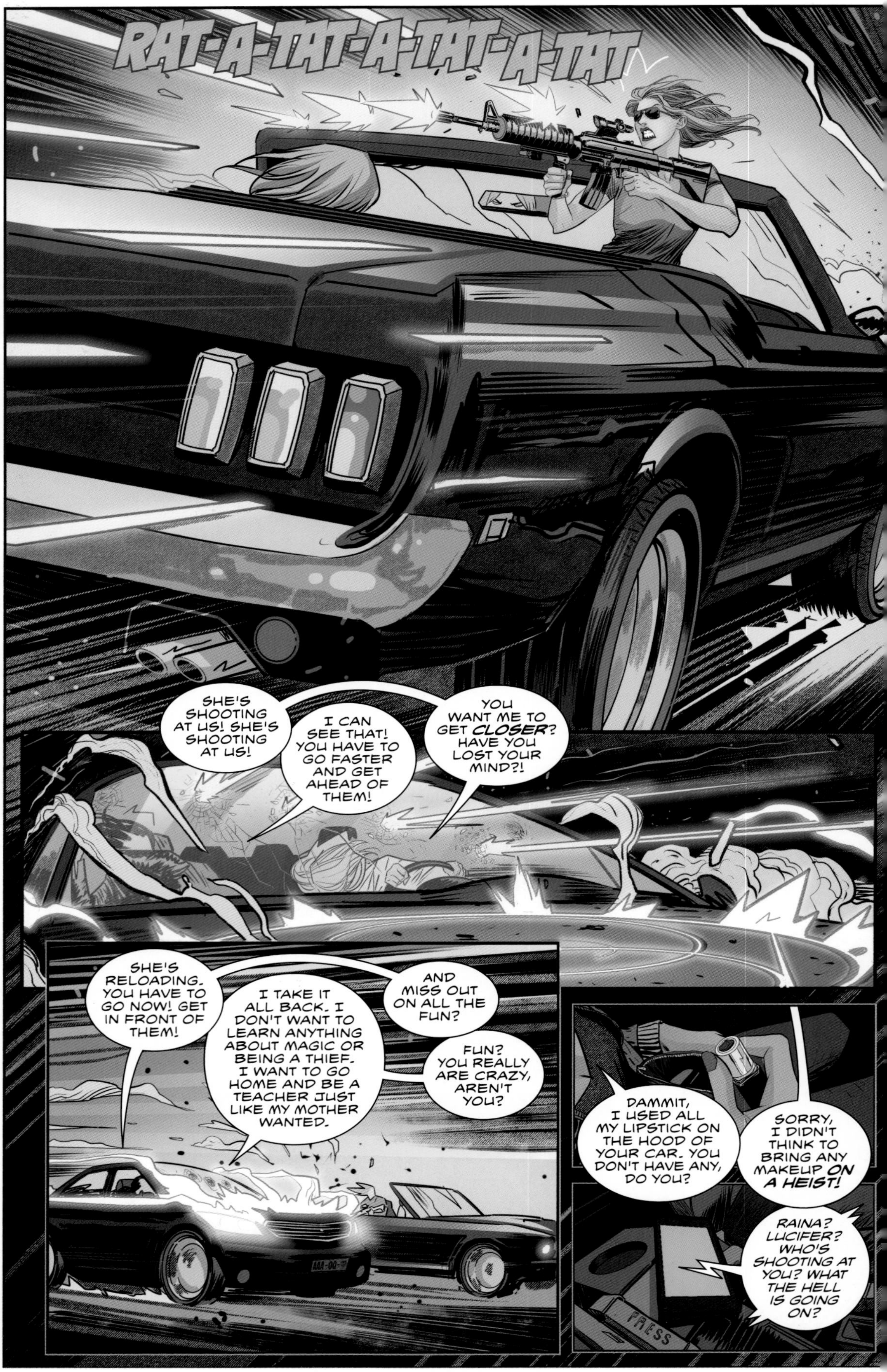

RAT-A-TAT-A-TAT-A-TAT
SHE'S SHOOTING AT US! SHE'S SHOOTING AT US!
I CAN SEE THAT! YOU HAVE TO GO FASTER AND GET AHEAD OF THEM!
YOU WANT ME TO GET CLOSER? HAVE YOU LOST YOUR MIND?!
SHE'S RELOADING. YOU HAVE TO GO NOW! GET IN FRONT OF THEM!
AND MISS OUT ON ALL THE FUN?
I TAKE IT ALL BACK. I DON'T WANT TO LEARN ANYTHING ABOUT MAGIC OR BEING A THIEF. I WANT TO GO HOME AND BE A TEACHER JUST LIKE MY MOTHER WANTED.
FUN? YOU REALLY ARE CRAZY, AREN'T YOU?
DAMMIT, I USED ALL MY LIPSTICK ON THE HOOD OF YOUR CAR. YOU DON'T HAVE ANY, DO YOU?
SORRY, I DIDN'T THINK TO BRING ANY MAKEUP ON A HEIST!
RAINA? LUCIFER? WHO'S SHOOTING AT YOU? WHAT THE HELL IS GOING ON?
PRESS

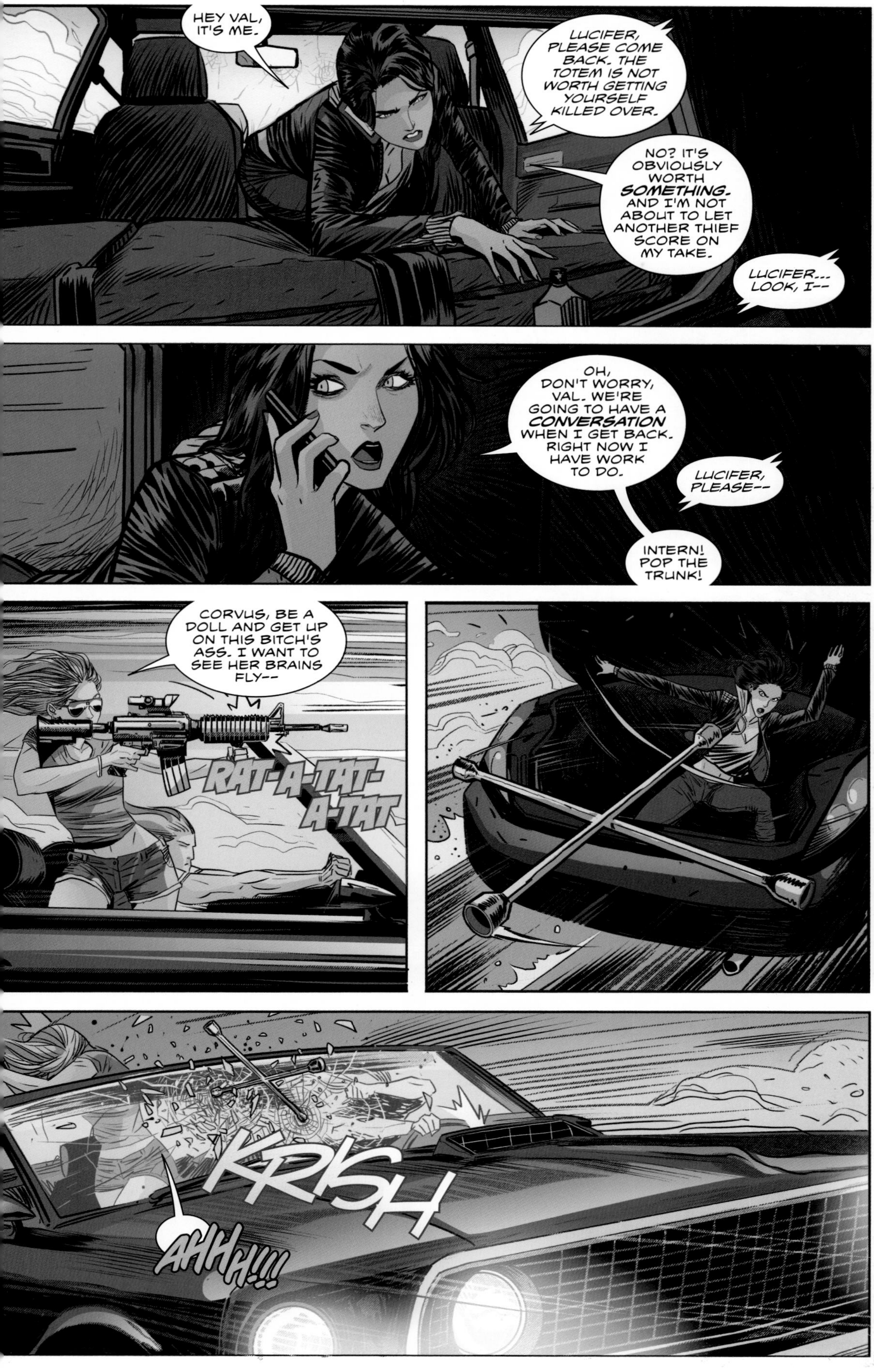
HEY VAL, IT'S ME.
LUCIFER, PLEASE COME BACK. THE TOTEM IS NOT WORTH GETTING YOURSELF KILLED OVER.
NO? IT'S OBVIOUSLY WORTH SOMETHING. AND I'M NOT ABOUT TO LET ANOTHER THIEF SCORE ON MY TAKE.
LUCIFER... LOOK, I--
OH, DON'T WORRY, VAL. WE'RE GOING TO HAVE A CONVERSATION WHEN I GET BACK. RIGHT NOW I HAVE WORK TO DO.
LUCIFER, PLEASE--
INTERN! POP THE TRUNK!
CORVUS, BE A DOLL AND GET UP ON THIS BITCH'S ASS. I WANT TO SEE HER BRAINS FLY--
RAT-A-TAT-A-TAT
KRISH
AHHH!!!

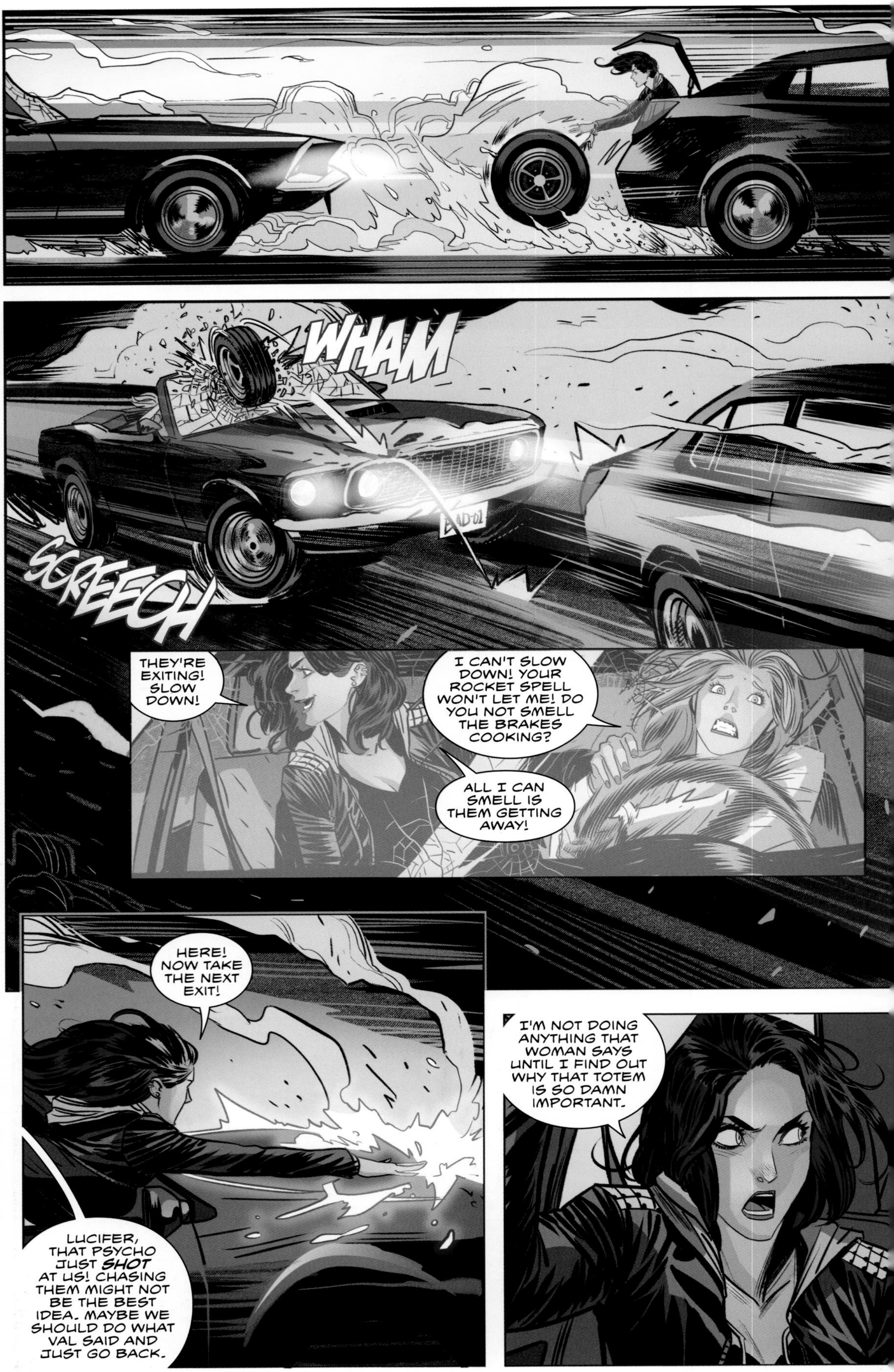
WHAM
SCREEECH
THEY'RE EXITING! SLOW DOWN!
I CAN'T SLOW DOWN! YOUR ROCKET SPELL WON'T LET ME! DO YOU NOT SMELL THE BRAKES COOKING?
ALL I CAN SMELL IS THEM GETTING AWAY!
HERE! NOW TAKE THE NEXT EXIT!
LUCIFER, THAT PSYCHO JUST *SHOT* AT US! CHASING THEM MIGHT NOT BE THE BEST IDEA. MAYBE WE SHOULD DO WHAT VAL SAID AND JUST GO BACK.
I'M NOT DOING ANYTHING THAT WOMAN SAYS UNTIL I FIND OUT WHY THAT TOTEM IS SO DAMN IMPORTANT.

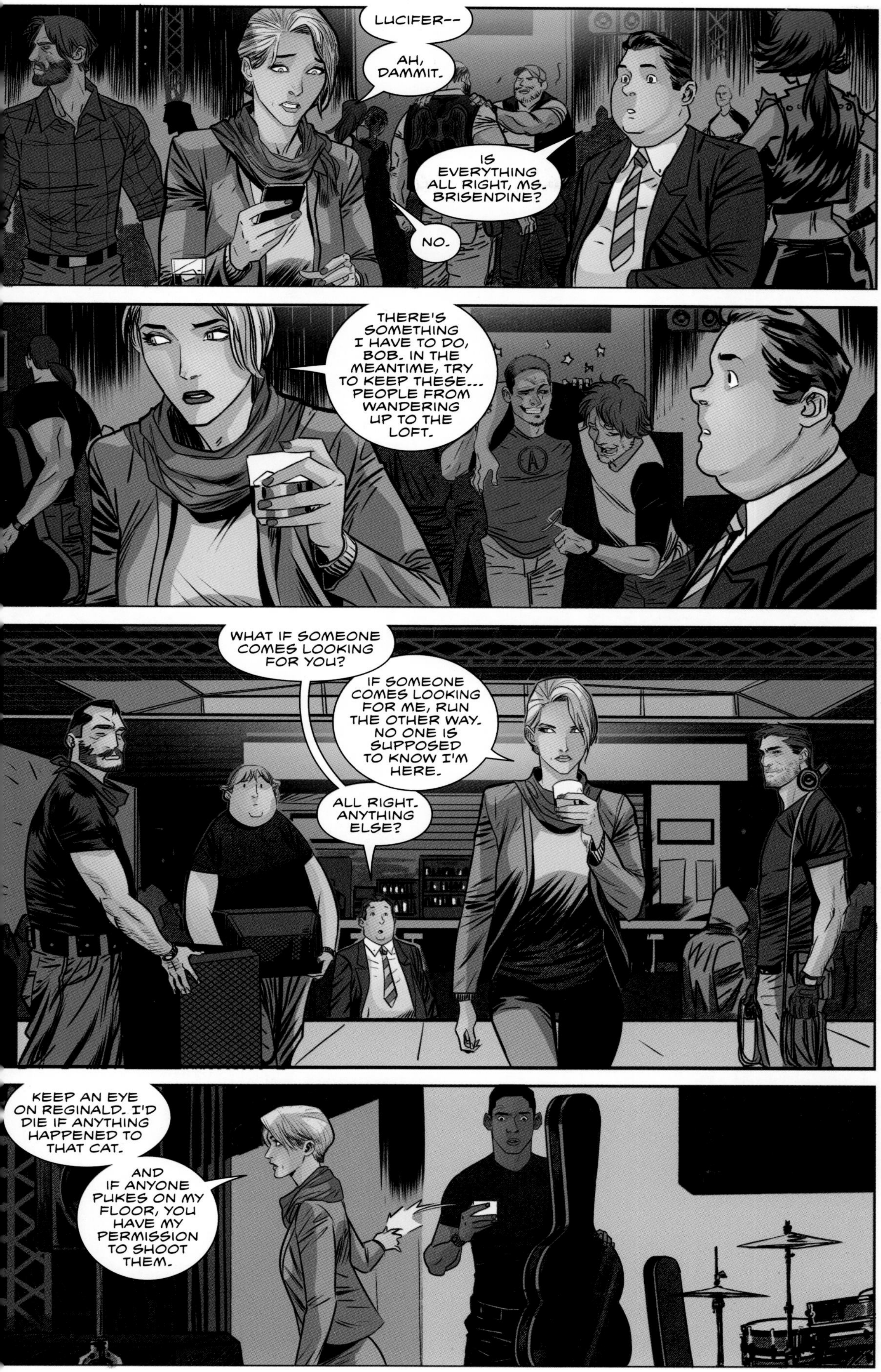
LUCIFER--
AH, DAMMIT.
IS EVERYTHING ALL RIGHT, MS. BRISENDINE?
NO.
THERE'S SOMETHING I HAVE TO DO, BOB. IN THE MEANTIME, TRY TO KEEP THESE... PEOPLE FROM WANDERING UP TO THE LOFT.
WHAT IF SOMEONE COMES LOOKING FOR YOU?
IF SOMEONE COMES LOOKING FOR ME, RUN THE OTHER WAY. NO ONE IS SUPPOSED TO KNOW I'M HERE.
ALL RIGHT. ANYTHING ELSE?
KEEP AN EYE ON REGINALD. I'D DIE IF ANYTHING HAPPENED TO THAT CAT.
AND IF ANYONE PUKES ON MY FLOOR, YOU HAVE MY PERMISSION TO SHOOT THEM.

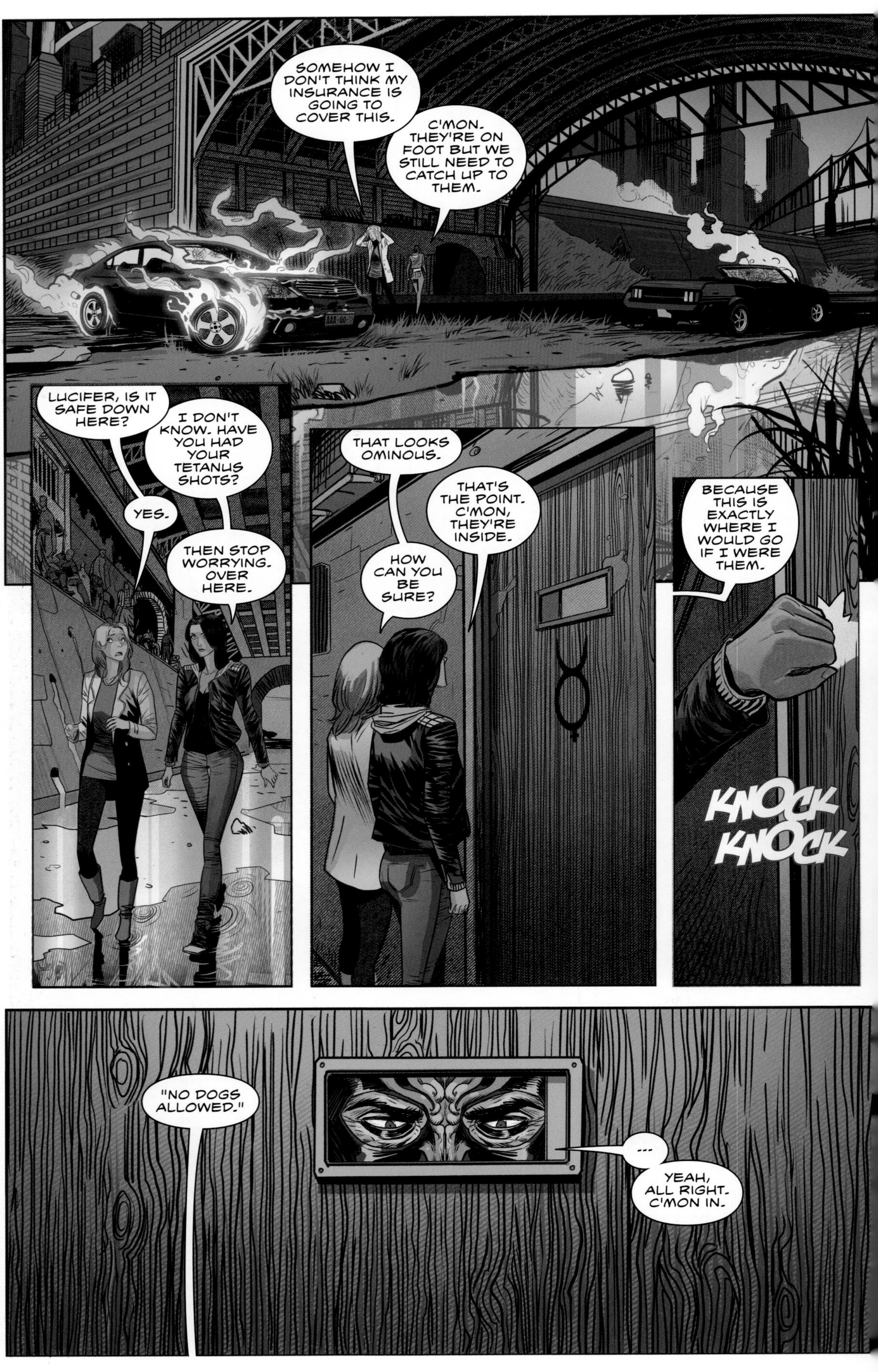
SOMEHOW I DON'T THINK MY INSURANCE IS GOING TO COVER THIS.
C'MON. THEY'RE ON FOOT BUT WE STILL NEED TO CATCH UP TO THEM.
LUCIFER, IS IT SAFE DOWN HERE?
I DON'T KNOW. HAVE YOU HAD YOUR TETANUS SHOTS?
YES.
THEN STOP WORRYING. OVER HERE.
THAT LOOKS OMINOUS.
THAT'S THE POINT. C'MON, THEY'RE INSIDE.
HOW CAN YOU BE SURE?
BECAUSE THIS IS EXACTLY WHERE I WOULD GO IF I WERE THEM.
KNOCK KNOCK
"NO DOGS ALLOWED."
...
YEAH, ALL RIGHT. C'MON IN.

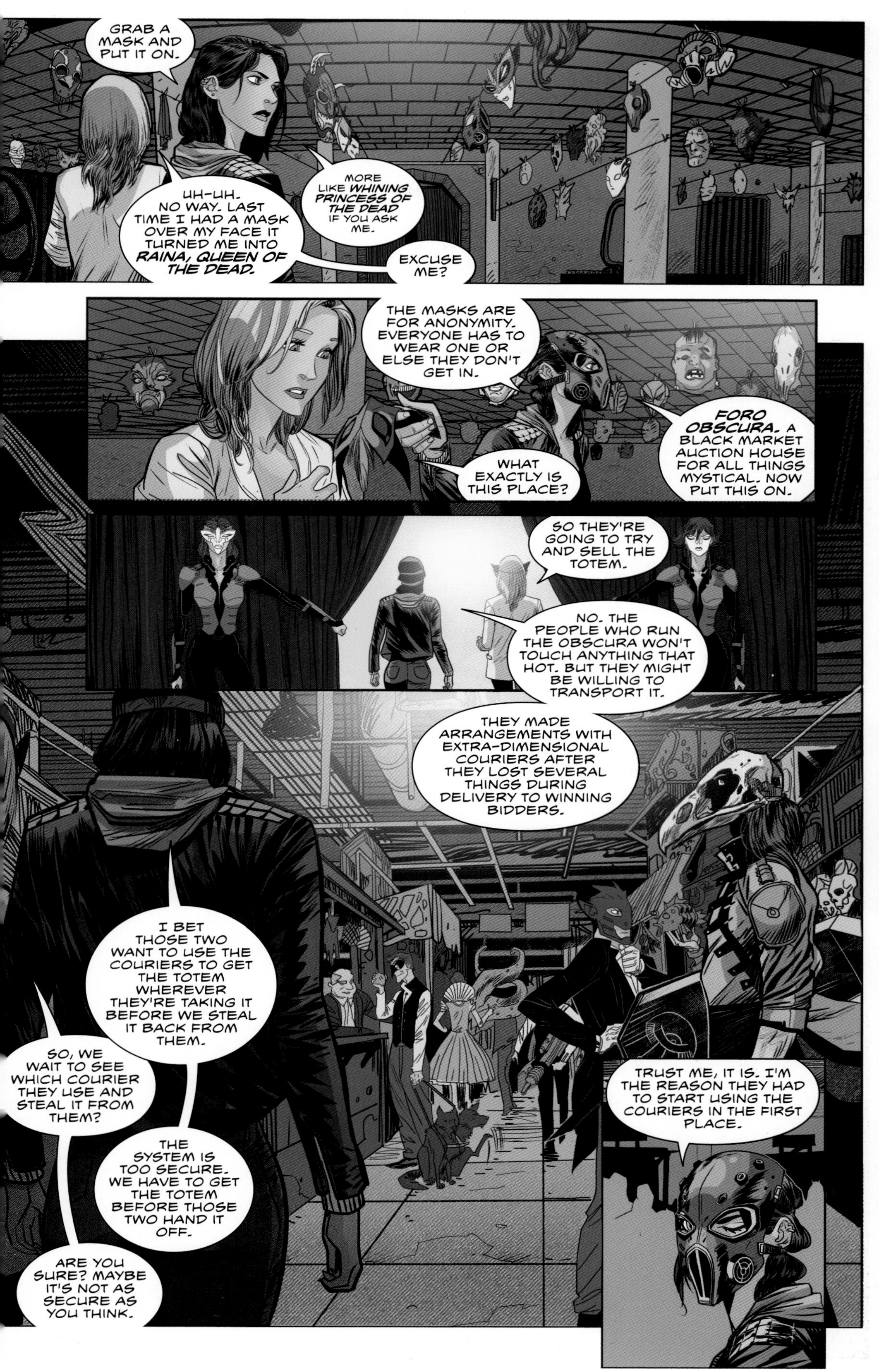
GRAB A MASK AND PUT IT ON.
UH-UH. NO WAY. LAST TIME I HAD A MASK OVER MY FACE IT TURNED ME INTO RAINA, QUEEN OF THE DEAD.
MORE LIKE WHINING PRINCESS OF THE DEAD IF YOU ASK ME.
EXCUSE ME?
THE MASKS ARE FOR ANONYMITY. EVERYONE HAS TO WEAR ONE OR ELSE THEY DON'T GET IN.
WHAT EXACTLY IS THIS PLACE?
FORO OBSCURA. A BLACK MARKET AUCTION HOUSE FOR ALL THINGS MYSTICAL. NOW PUT THIS ON.
SO THEY'RE GOING TO TRY AND SELL THE TOTEM.
NO. THE PEOPLE WHO RUN THE OBSCURA WON'T TOUCH ANYTHING THAT HOT. BUT THEY MIGHT BE WILLING TO TRANSPORT IT.
THEY MADE ARRANGEMENTS WITH EXTRA-DIMENSIONAL COURIERS AFTER THEY LOST SEVERAL THINGS DURING DELIVERY TO WINNING BIDDERS.
I BET THOSE TWO WANT TO USE THE COURIERS TO GET THE TOTEM WHEREVER THEY'RE TAKING IT BEFORE WE STEAL IT BACK FROM THEM.
SO, WE WAIT TO SEE WHICH COURIER THEY USE AND STEAL IT FROM THEM?
THE SYSTEM IS TOO SECURE. WE HAVE TO GET THE TOTEM BEFORE THOSE TWO HAND IT OFF.
ARE YOU SURE? MAYBE IT'S NOT AS SECURE AS YOU THINK.
TRUST ME, IT IS. I'M THE REASON THEY HAD TO START USING THE COURIERS IN THE FIRST PLACE.

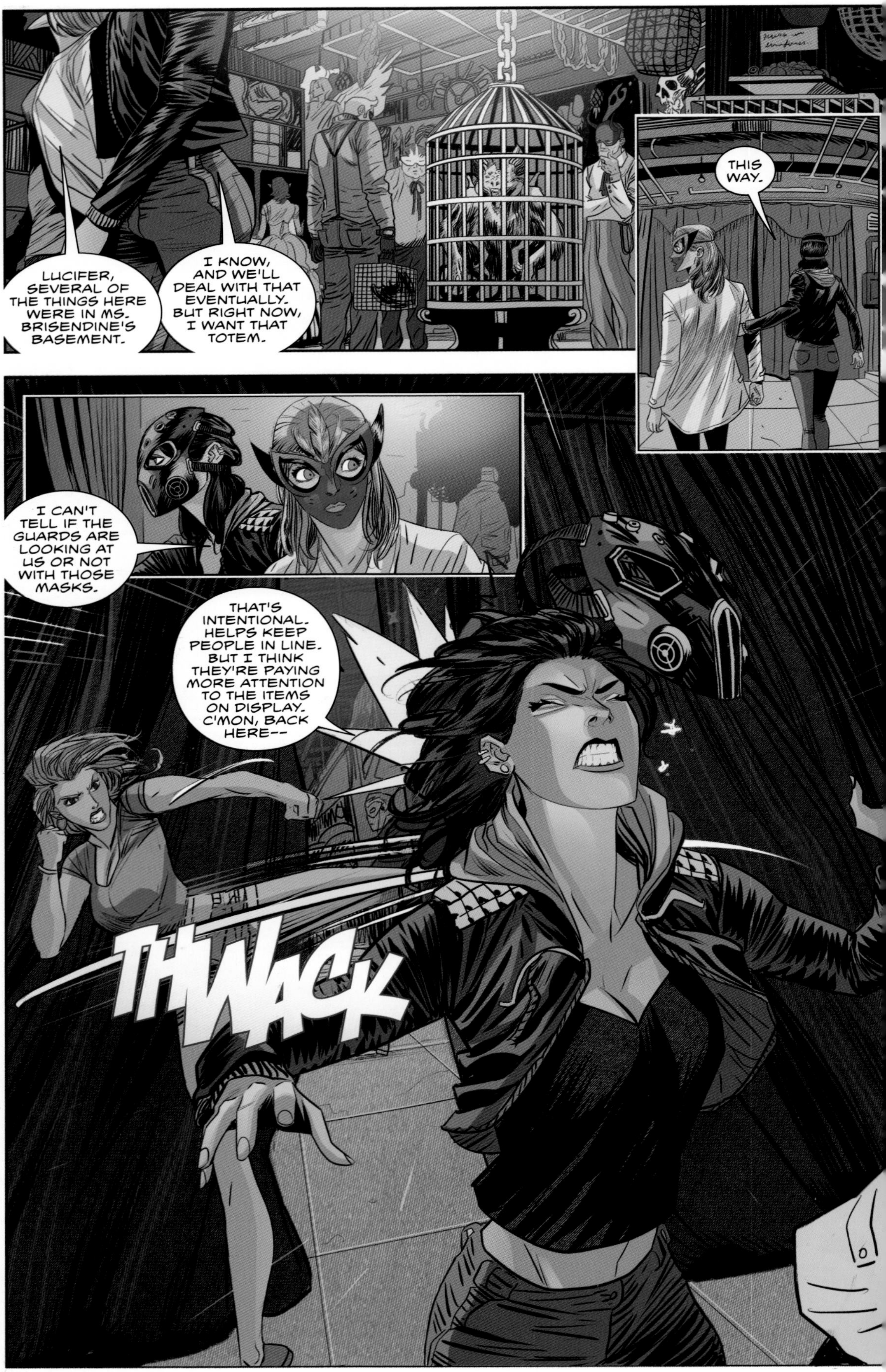
LUCIFER, SEVERAL OF THE THINGS HERE WERE IN MS. BRISENDINE'S BASEMENT.
I KNOW, AND WE'LL DEAL WITH THAT EVENTUALLY. BUT RIGHT NOW, I WANT THAT TOTEM.
THIS WAY.
I CAN'T TELL IF THE GUARDS ARE LOOKING AT US OR NOT WITH THOSE MASKS.
THAT'S INTENTIONAL. HELPS KEEP PEOPLE IN LINE. BUT I THINK THEY'RE PAYING MORE ATTENTION TO THE ITEMS ON DISPLAY. C'MON, BACK HERE--
THWACK

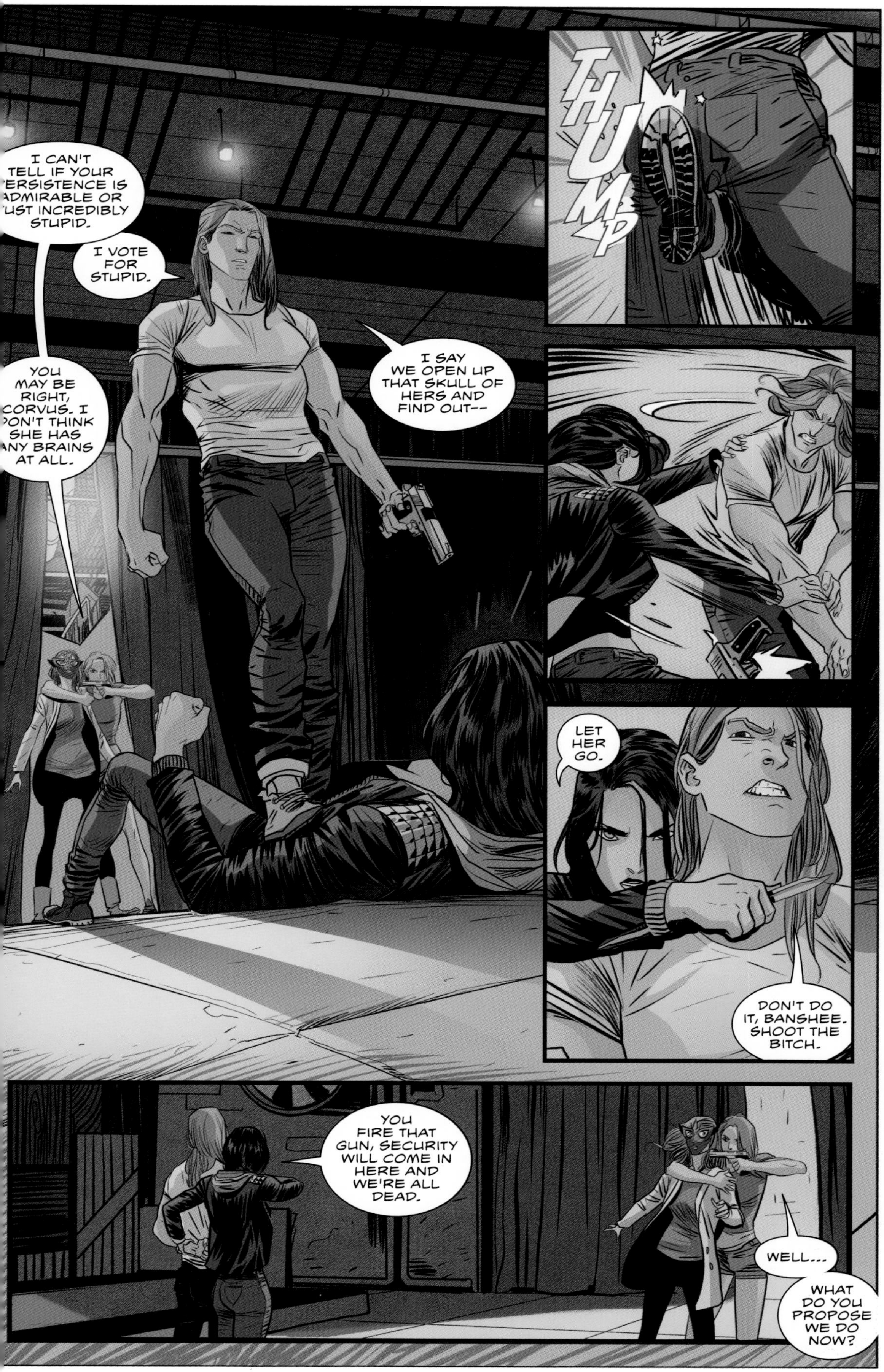
I CAN'T TELL IF YOUR PERSISTENCE IS ADMIRABLE OR JUST INCREDIBLY STUPID.
I VOTE FOR STUPID.
YOU MAY BE RIGHT, CORVUS. I DON'T THINK SHE HAS ANY BRAINS AT ALL.
I SAY WE OPEN UP THAT SKULL OF HERS AND FIND OUT--
THUMP
LET HER GO.
DON'T DO IT, BANSHEE. SHOOT THE BITCH.
YOU FIRE THAT GUN, SECURITY WILL COME IN HERE AND WE'RE ALL DEAD.
WELL...
WHAT DO YOU PROPOSE WE DO NOW?

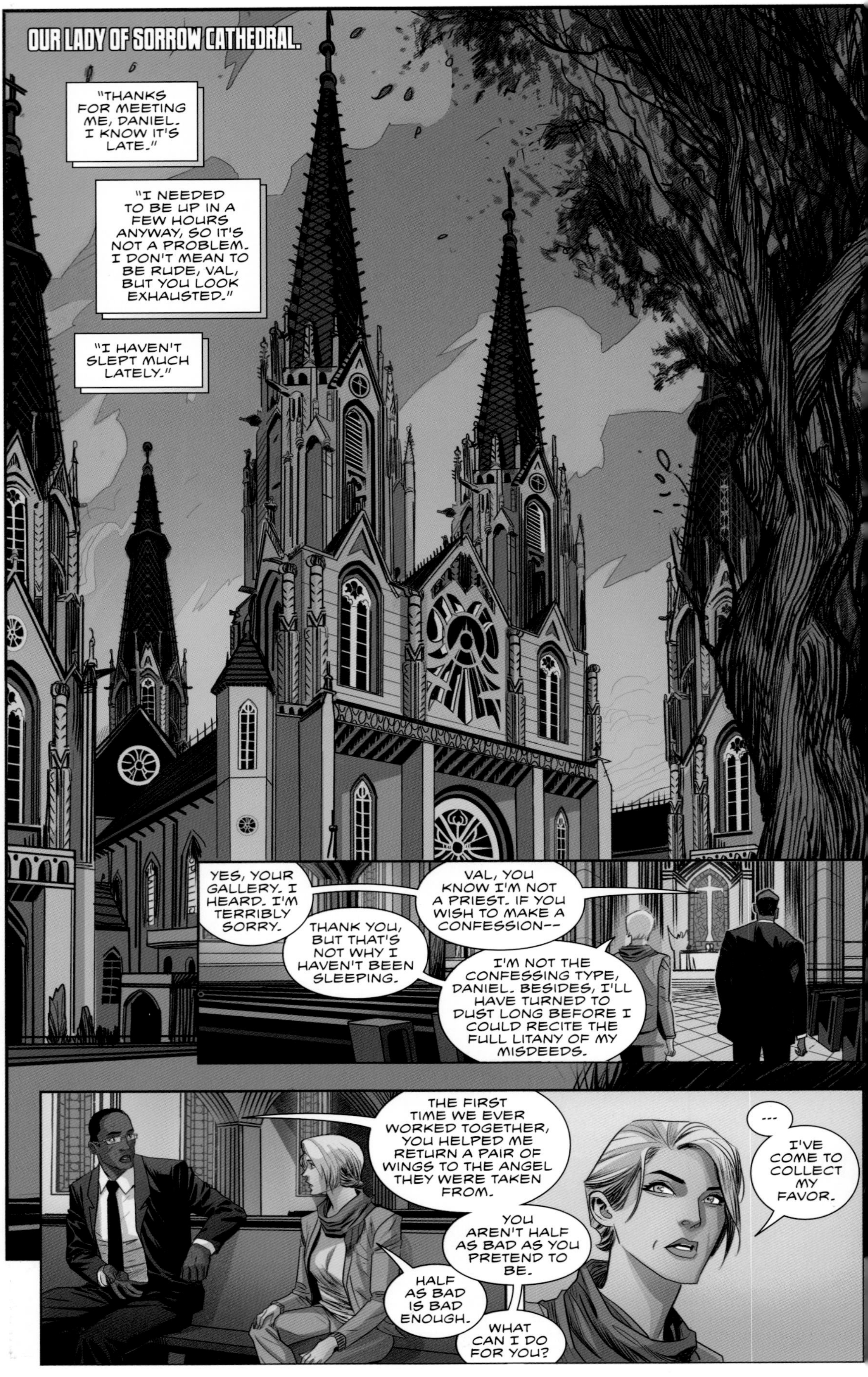
OUR LADY OF SORROW CATHEDRAL.
"THANKS FOR MEETING ME, DANIEL. I KNOW IT'S LATE."
"I NEEDED TO BE UP IN A FEW HOURS ANYWAY, SO IT'S NOT A PROBLEM. I DON'T MEAN TO BE RUDE, VAL, BUT YOU LOOK EXHAUSTED."
"I HAVEN'T SLEPT MUCH LATELY."
YES, YOUR GALLERY. I HEARD. I'M TERRIBLY SORRY.
THANK YOU, BUT THAT'S NOT WHY I HAVEN'T BEEN SLEEPING.
VAL, YOU KNOW I'M NOT A PRIEST. IF YOU WISH TO MAKE A CONFESSION--
I'M NOT THE CONFESSING TYPE, DANIEL. BESIDES, I'LL HAVE TURNED TO DUST LONG BEFORE I COULD RECITE THE FULL LITANY OF MY MISDEEDS.
THE FIRST TIME WE EVER WORKED TOGETHER, YOU HELPED ME RETURN A PAIR OF WINGS TO THE ANGEL THEY WERE TAKEN FROM.
YOU AREN'T HALF AS BAD AS YOU PRETEND TO BE.
HALF AS BAD IS BAD ENOUGH.
WHAT CAN I DO FOR YOU?
...
I'VE COME TO COLLECT MY FAVOR.

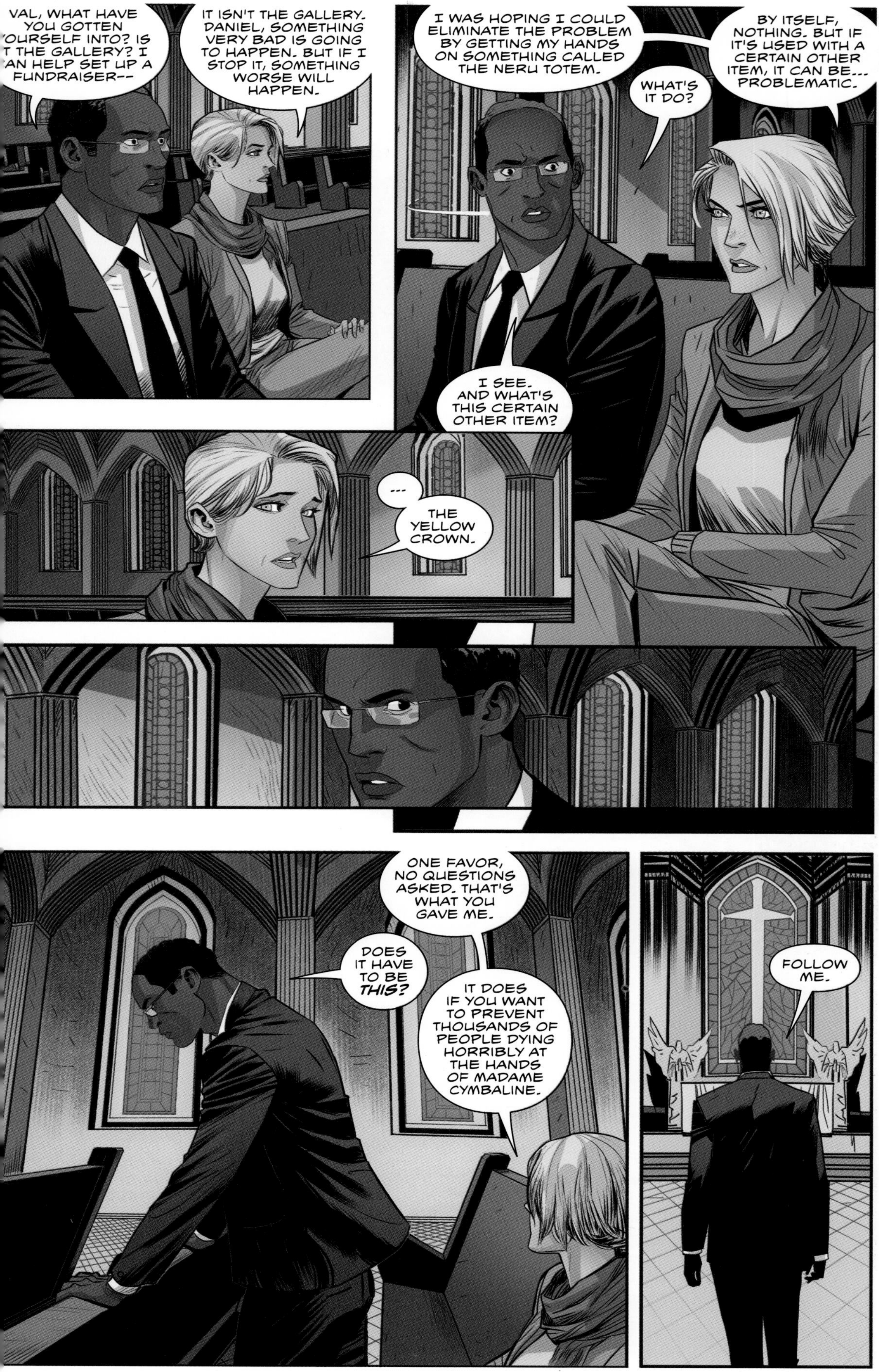
VAL, WHAT HAVE YOU GOTTEN YOURSELF INTO? IS IT THE GALLERY? I CAN HELP SET UP A FUNDRAISER--
IT ISN'T THE GALLERY. DANIEL, SOMETHING VERY BAD IS GOING TO HAPPEN. BUT IF I STOP IT, SOMETHING WORSE WILL HAPPEN.
I WAS HOPING I COULD ELIMINATE THE PROBLEM BY GETTING MY HANDS ON SOMETHING CALLED THE NERU TOTEM.
WHAT'S IT DO?
BY ITSELF, NOTHING. BUT IF IT'S USED WITH A CERTAIN OTHER ITEM, IT CAN BE... PROBLEMATIC.
I SEE. AND WHAT'S THIS CERTAIN OTHER ITEM?
...
THE YELLOW CROWN.
ONE FAVOR, NO QUESTIONS ASKED. THAT'S WHAT YOU GAVE ME.
DOES IT HAVE TO BE *THIS?*
IT DOES IF YOU WANT TO PREVENT THOUSANDS OF PEOPLE DYING HORRIBLY AT THE HANDS OF MADAME CYMBALINE.
FOLLOW ME.

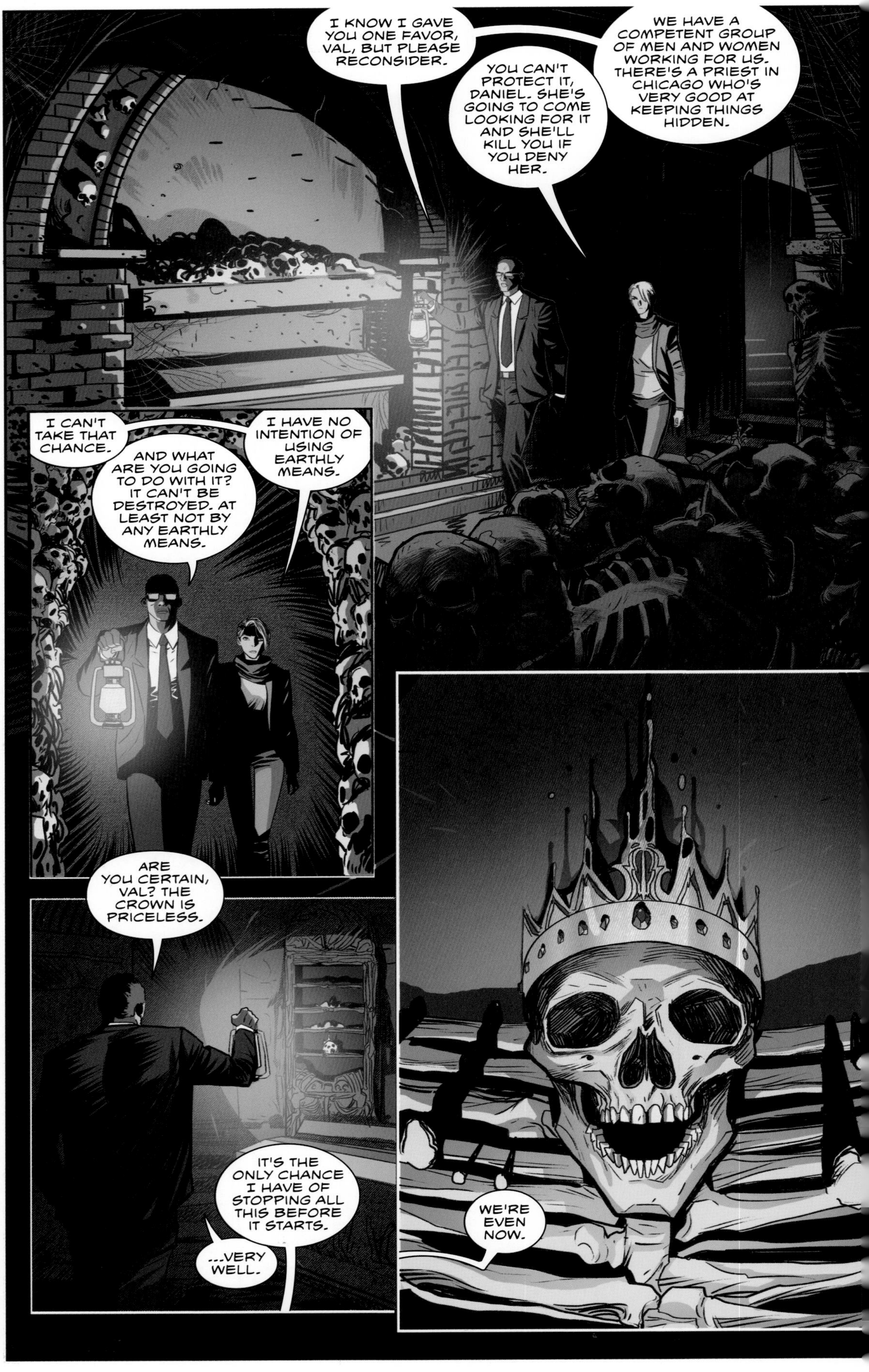
I KNOW I GAVE YOU ONE FAVOR, VAL, BUT PLEASE RECONSIDER.
WE HAVE A COMPETENT GROUP OF MEN AND WOMEN WORKING FOR US. THERE'S A PRIEST IN CHICAGO WHO'S VERY GOOD AT KEEPING THINGS HIDDEN.
YOU CAN'T PROTECT IT, DANIEL. SHE'S GOING TO COME LOOKING FOR IT AND SHE'LL KILL YOU IF YOU DENY HER.
I CAN'T TAKE THAT CHANCE.
AND WHAT ARE YOU GOING TO DO WITH IT? IT CAN'T BE DESTROYED. AT LEAST NOT BY ANY EARTHLY MEANS.
I HAVE NO INTENTION OF USING EARTHLY MEANS.
ARE YOU CERTAIN, VAL? THE CROWN IS PRICELESS.
IT'S THE ONLY CHANCE I HAVE OF STOPPING ALL THIS BEFORE IT STARTS.
...VERY WELL.
WE'RE EVEN NOW.

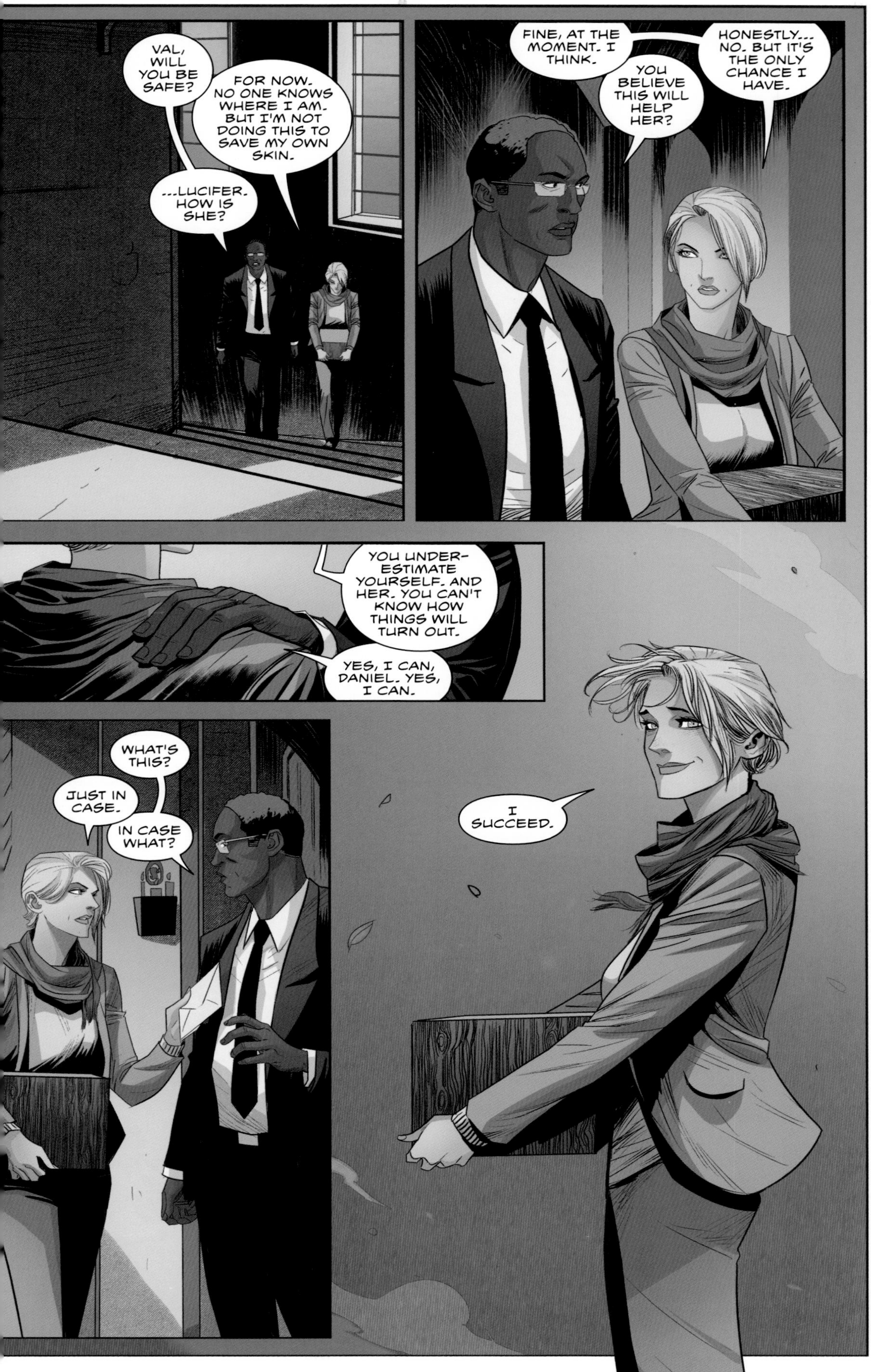
VAL, WILL YOU BE SAFE?
FOR NOW. NO ONE KNOWS WHERE I AM. BUT I'M NOT DOING THIS TO SAVE MY OWN SKIN.
...LUCIFER. HOW IS SHE?
FINE, AT THE MOMENT. I THINK.
YOU BELIEVE THIS WILL HELP HER?
HONESTLY... NO. BUT IT'S THE ONLY CHANCE I HAVE.
YOU UNDER-ESTIMATE YOURSELF. AND HER. YOU CAN'T KNOW HOW THINGS WILL TURN OUT.
YES, I CAN, DANIEL. YES, I CAN.
WHAT'S THIS?
JUST IN CASE.
IN CASE WHAT?
I SUCCEED.

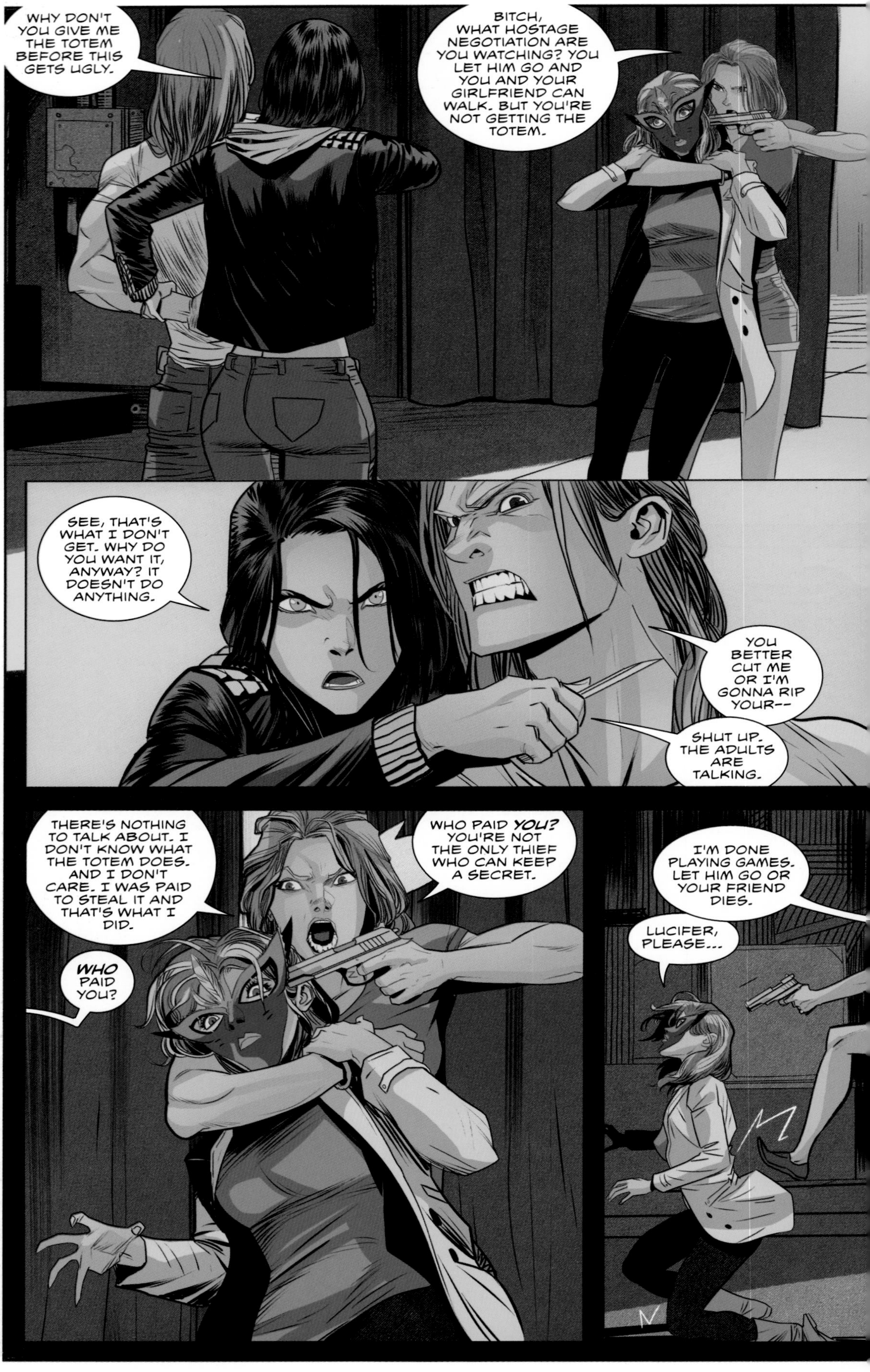
WHY DON'T YOU GIVE ME THE TOTEM BEFORE THIS GETS UGLY.
BITCH, WHAT HOSTAGE NEGOTIATION ARE YOU WATCHING? YOU LET HIM GO AND YOU AND YOUR GIRLFRIEND CAN WALK. BUT YOU'RE NOT GETTING THE TOTEM.
SEE, THAT'S WHAT I DON'T GET. WHY DO YOU WANT IT, ANYWAY? IT DOESN'T DO ANYTHING.
YOU BETTER CUT ME OR I'M GONNA RIP YOUR--
SHUT UP. THE ADULTS ARE TALKING.
THERE'S NOTHING TO TALK ABOUT. I DON'T KNOW WHAT THE TOTEM DOES. AND I DON'T CARE. I WAS PAID TO STEAL IT AND THAT'S WHAT I DID.
WHO PAID YOU?
WHO PAID *YOU?* YOU'RE NOT THE ONLY THIEF WHO CAN KEEP A SECRET.
I'M DONE PLAYING GAMES. LET HIM GO OR YOUR FRIEND DIES.
LUCIFER, PLEASE...

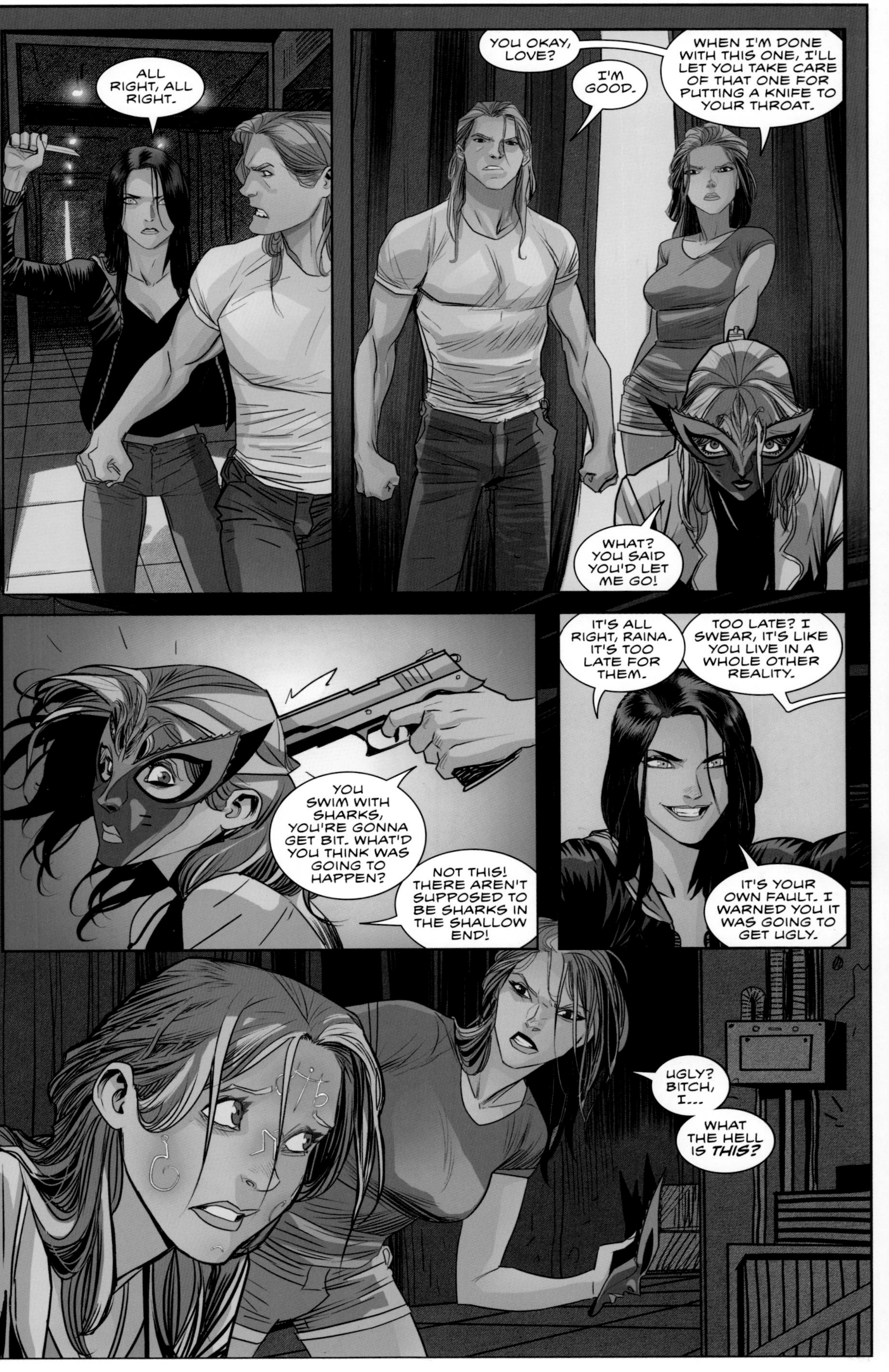
ALL RIGHT, ALL RIGHT.
YOU OKAY, LOVE?
I'M GOOD.
WHEN I'M DONE WITH THIS ONE, I'LL LET YOU TAKE CARE OF THAT ONE FOR PUTTING A KNIFE TO YOUR THROAT.
WHAT? YOU SAID YOU'D LET ME GO!
YOU SWIM WITH SHARKS, YOU'RE GONNA GET BIT. WHAT'D YOU THINK WAS GOING TO HAPPEN?
NOT THIS! THERE AREN'T SUPPOSED TO BE SHARKS IN THE SHALLOW END!
IT'S ALL RIGHT, RAINA. IT'S TOO LATE FOR THEM.
TOO LATE? I SWEAR, IT'S LIKE YOU LIVE IN A WHOLE OTHER REALITY.
IT'S YOUR OWN FAULT. I WARNED YOU IT WAS GOING TO GET UGLY.
UGLY? BITCH, I...
WHAT THE HELL IS *THIS?*

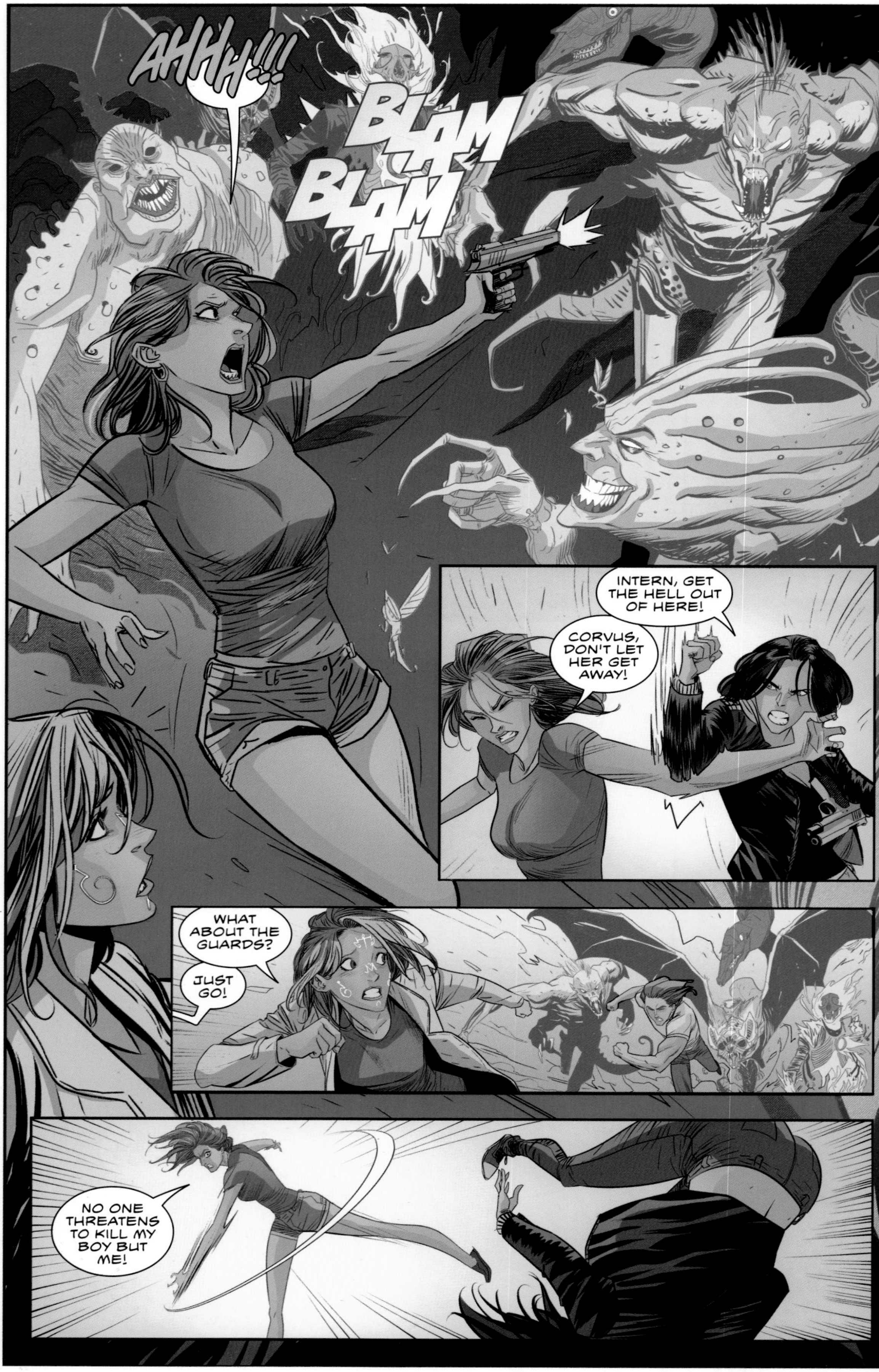
AHHH!!!
BLAM
BLAM
INTERN, GET THE HELL OUT OF HERE!
CORVUS, DON'T LET HER GET AWAY!
WHAT ABOUT THE GUARDS?
JUST GO!
NO ONE THREATENS TO KILL MY BOY BUT ME!

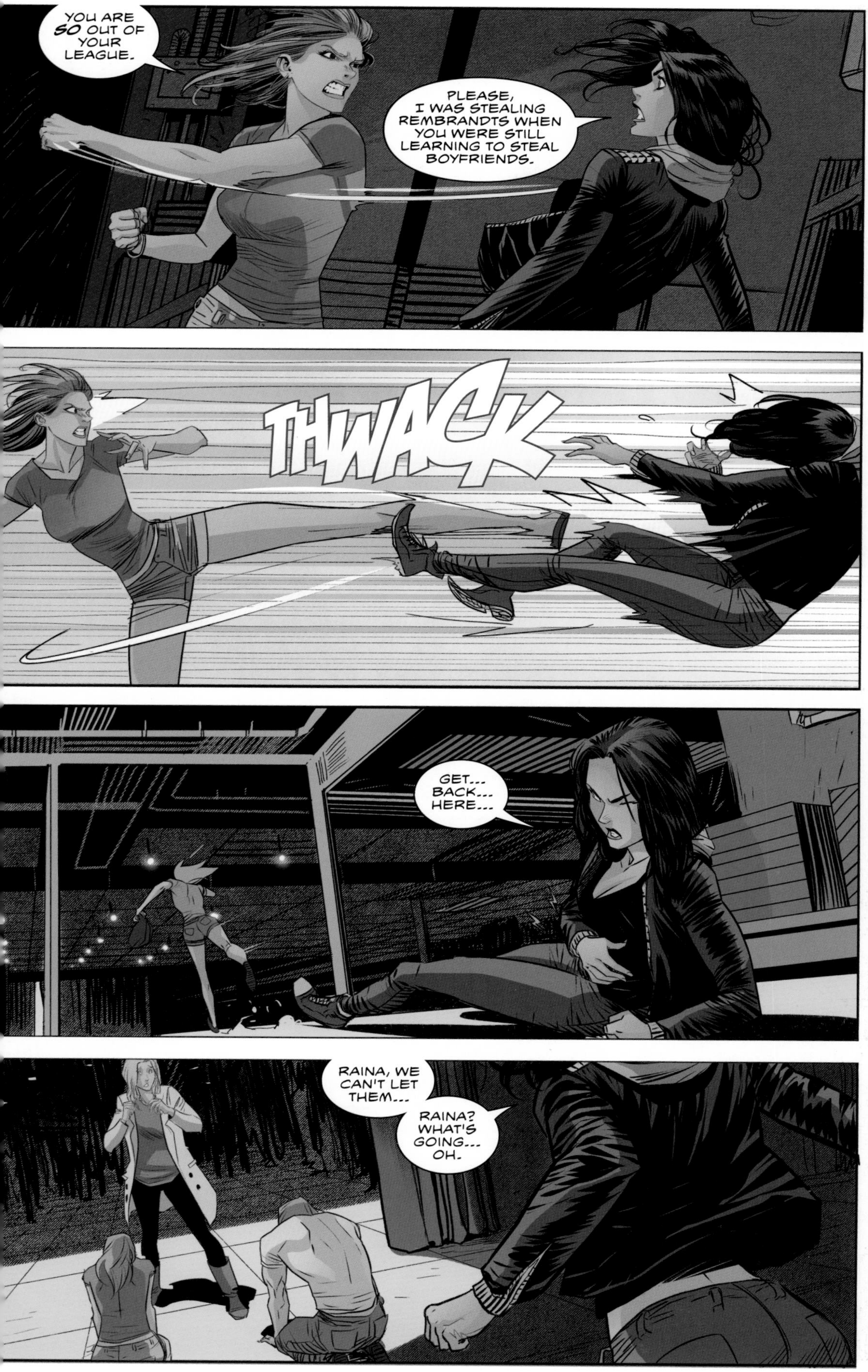
YOU ARE SO OUT OF YOUR LEAGUE.
PLEASE, I WAS STEALING REMBRANDTS WHEN YOU WERE STILL LEARNING TO STEAL BOYFRIENDS.
THWACK
GET... BACK... HERE...
RAINA, WE CAN'T LET THEM...
RAINA? WHAT'S GOING... OH.

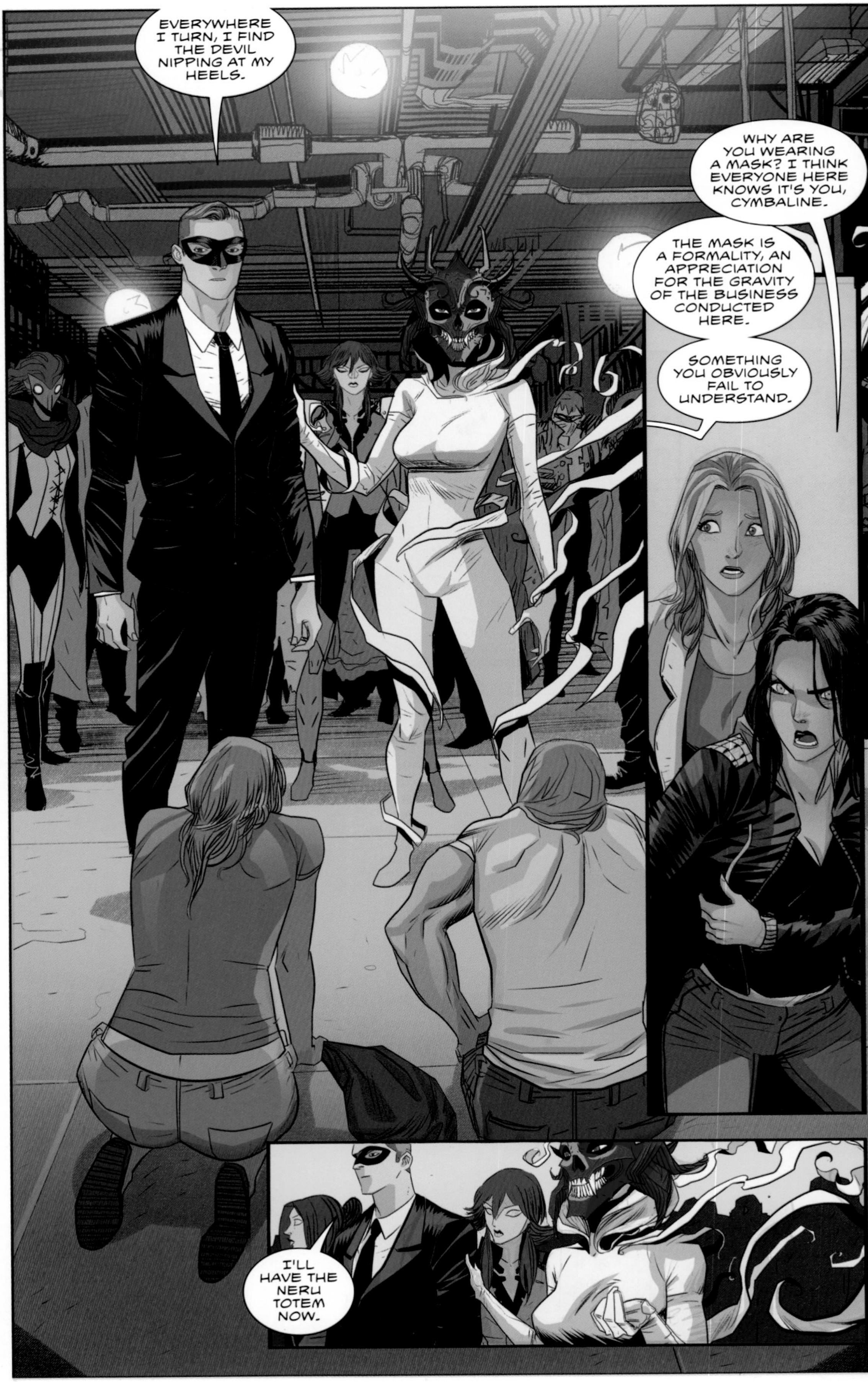
EVERYWHERE I TURN, I FIND THE DEVIL NIPPING AT MY HEELS.
WHY ARE YOU WEARING A MASK? I THINK EVERYONE HERE KNOWS IT'S YOU, CYMBALINE.
THE MASK IS A FORMALITY, AN APPRECIATION FOR THE GRAVITY OF THE BUSINESS CONDUCTED HERE.
SOMETHING YOU OBVIOUSLY FAIL TO UNDERSTAND.
I'LL HAVE THE NERU TOTEM NOW.

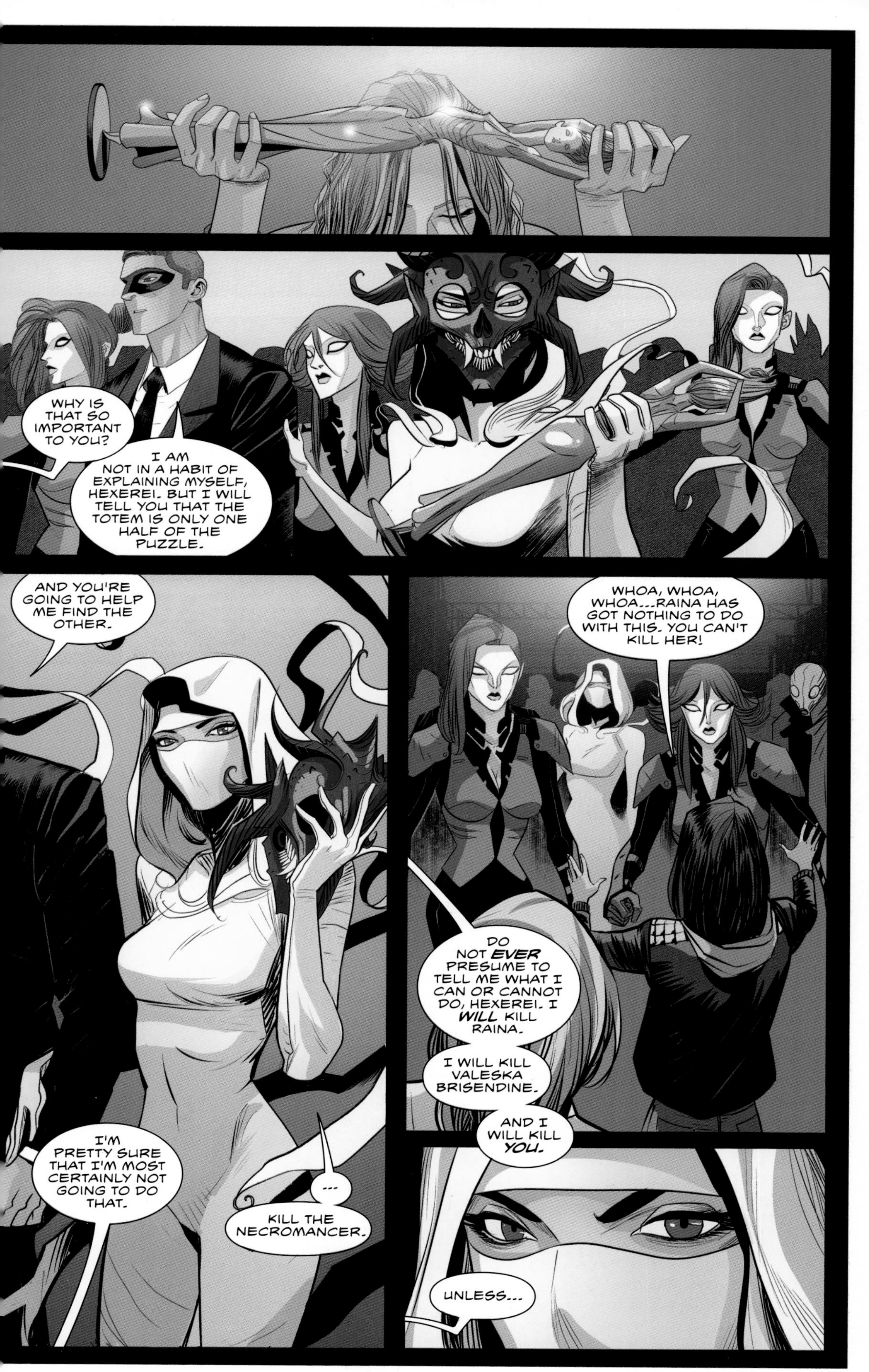
WHY IS THAT SO IMPORTANT TO YOU?
I AM NOT IN A HABIT OF EXPLAINING MYSELF, HEXEREI. BUT I WILL TELL YOU THAT THE TOTEM IS ONLY ONE HALF OF THE PUZZLE.
AND YOU'RE GOING TO HELP ME FIND THE OTHER.
I'M PRETTY SURE THAT I'M MOST CERTAINLY NOT GOING TO DO THAT.
...
KILL THE NECROMANCER.
WHOA, WHOA, WHOA...RAINA HAS GOT NOTHING TO DO WITH THIS. YOU CAN'T KILL HER!
DO NOT EVER PRESUME TO TELL ME WHAT I CAN OR CANNOT DO, HEXEREI. I WILL KILL RAINA.
I WILL KILL VALESKA BRISENDINE.
AND I WILL KILL YOU.
UNLESS...

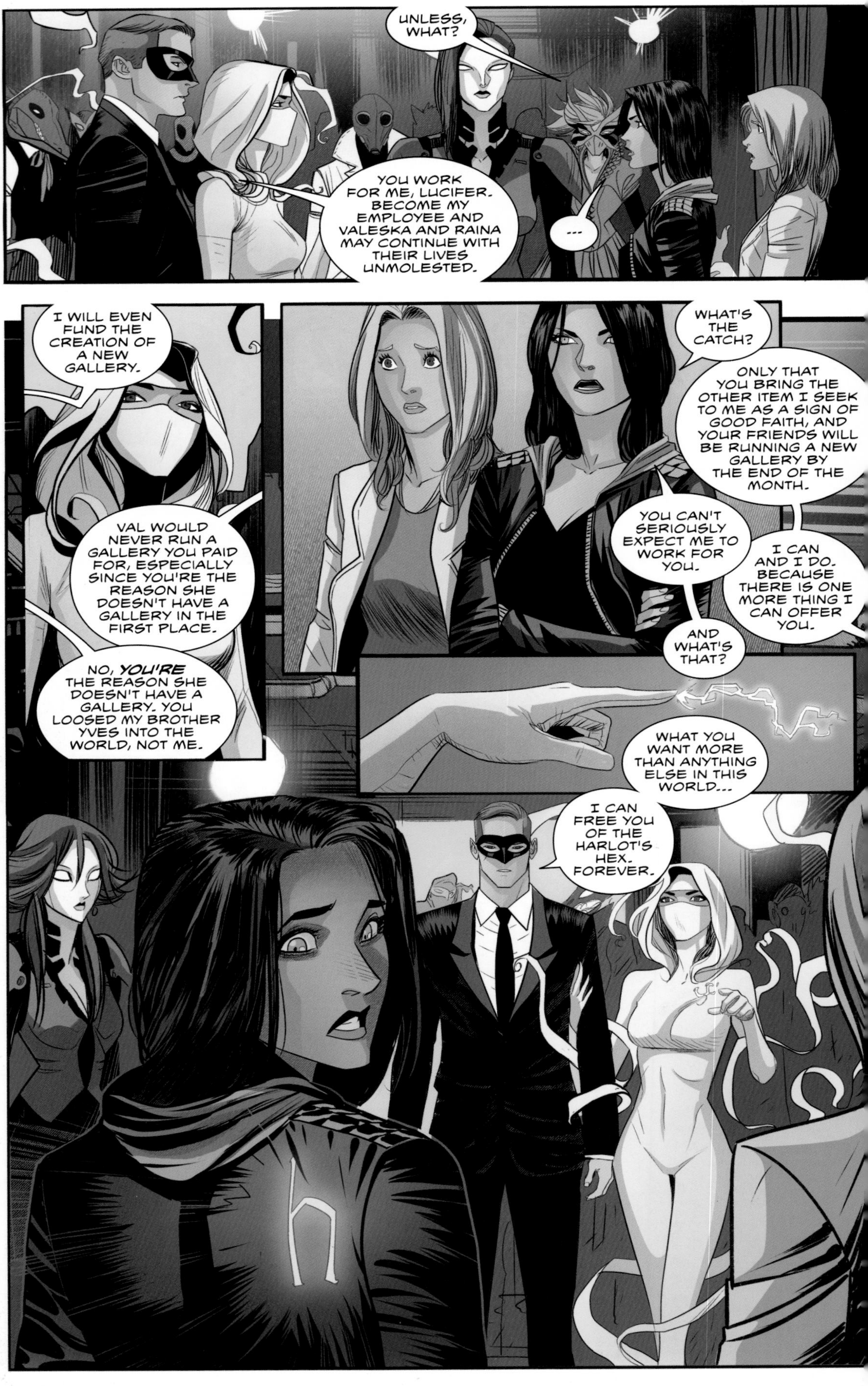
UNLESS, WHAT?
YOU WORK FOR ME, LUCIFER. BECOME MY EMPLOYEE AND VALESKA AND RAINA MAY CONTINUE WITH THEIR LIVES UNMOLESTED.
...
I WILL EVEN FUND THE CREATION OF A NEW GALLERY.
WHAT'S THE CATCH?
ONLY THAT YOU BRING THE OTHER ITEM I SEEK TO ME AS A SIGN OF GOOD FAITH, AND YOUR FRIENDS WILL BE RUNNING A NEW GALLERY BY THE END OF THE MONTH.
VAL WOULD NEVER RUN A GALLERY YOU PAID FOR, ESPECIALLY SINCE YOU'RE THE REASON SHE DOESN'T HAVE A GALLERY IN THE FIRST PLACE.
NO, *YOU'RE* THE REASON SHE DOESN'T HAVE A GALLERY. YOU LOOSED MY BROTHER YVES INTO THE WORLD, NOT ME.
YOU CAN'T SERIOUSLY EXPECT ME TO WORK FOR YOU.
I CAN AND I DO. BECAUSE THERE IS ONE MORE THING I CAN OFFER YOU.
AND WHAT'S THAT?
WHAT YOU WANT MORE THAN ANYTHING ELSE IN THIS WORLD...
I CAN FREE YOU OF THE HARLOT'S HEX. FOREVER.

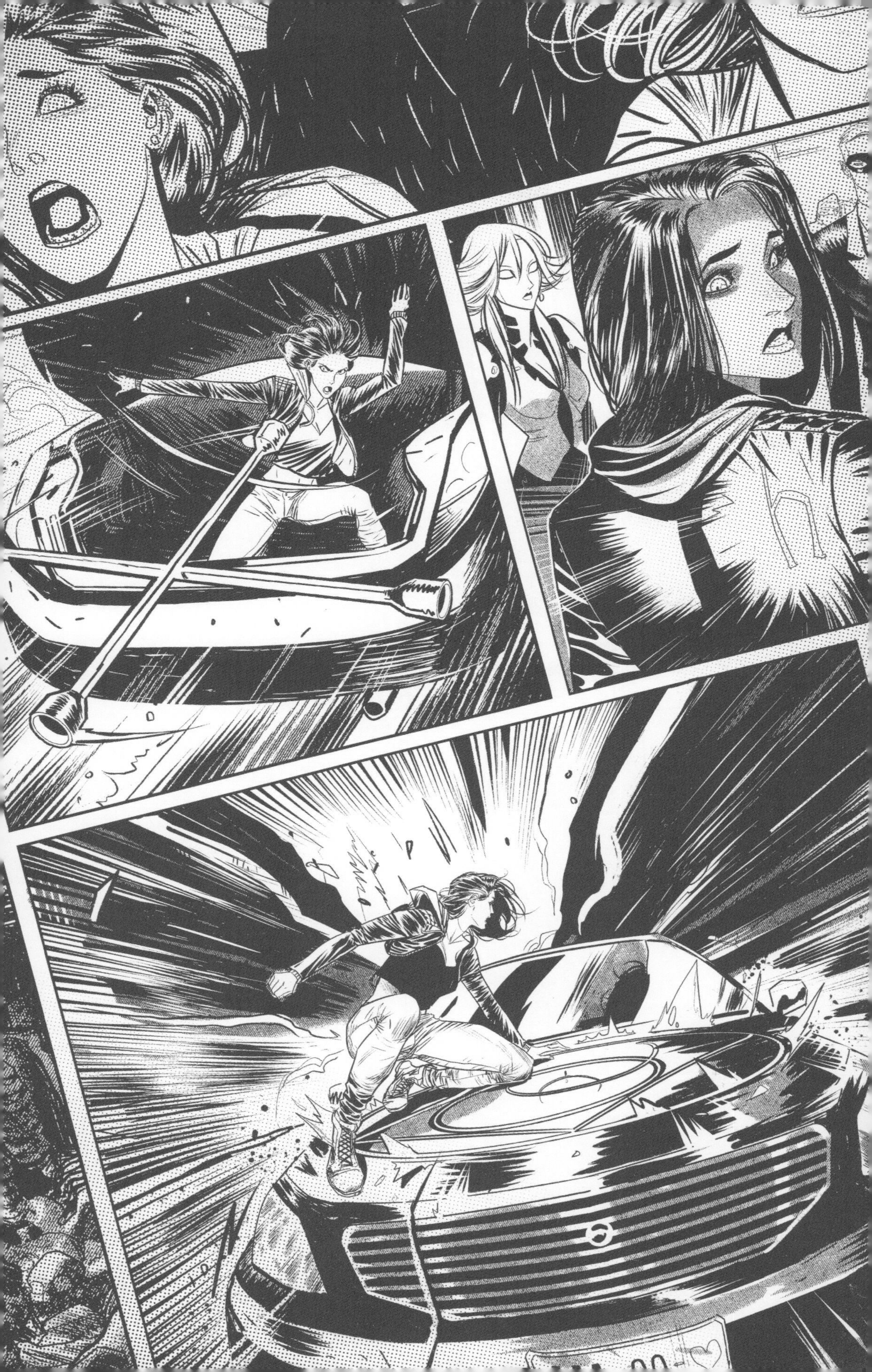

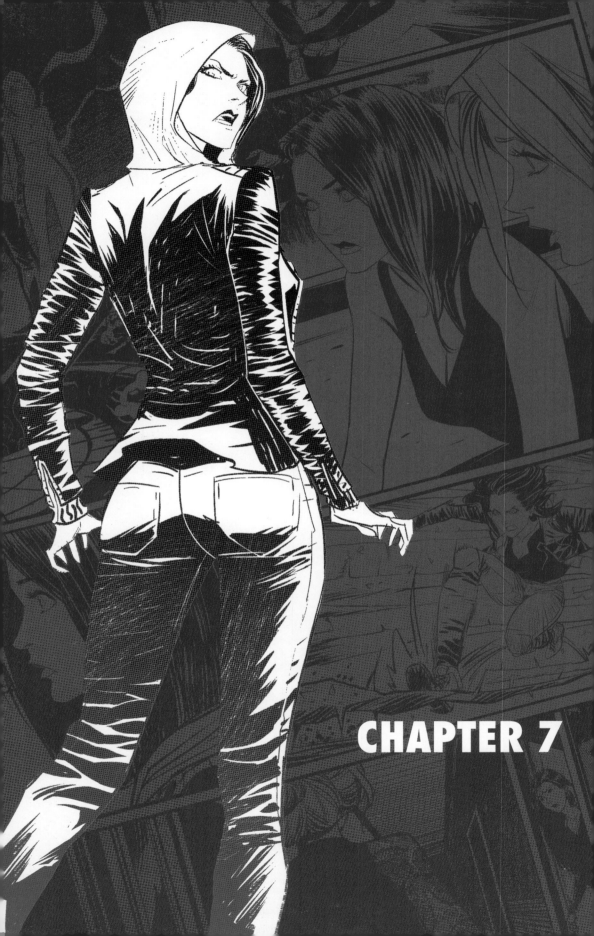

CHAPTER 7

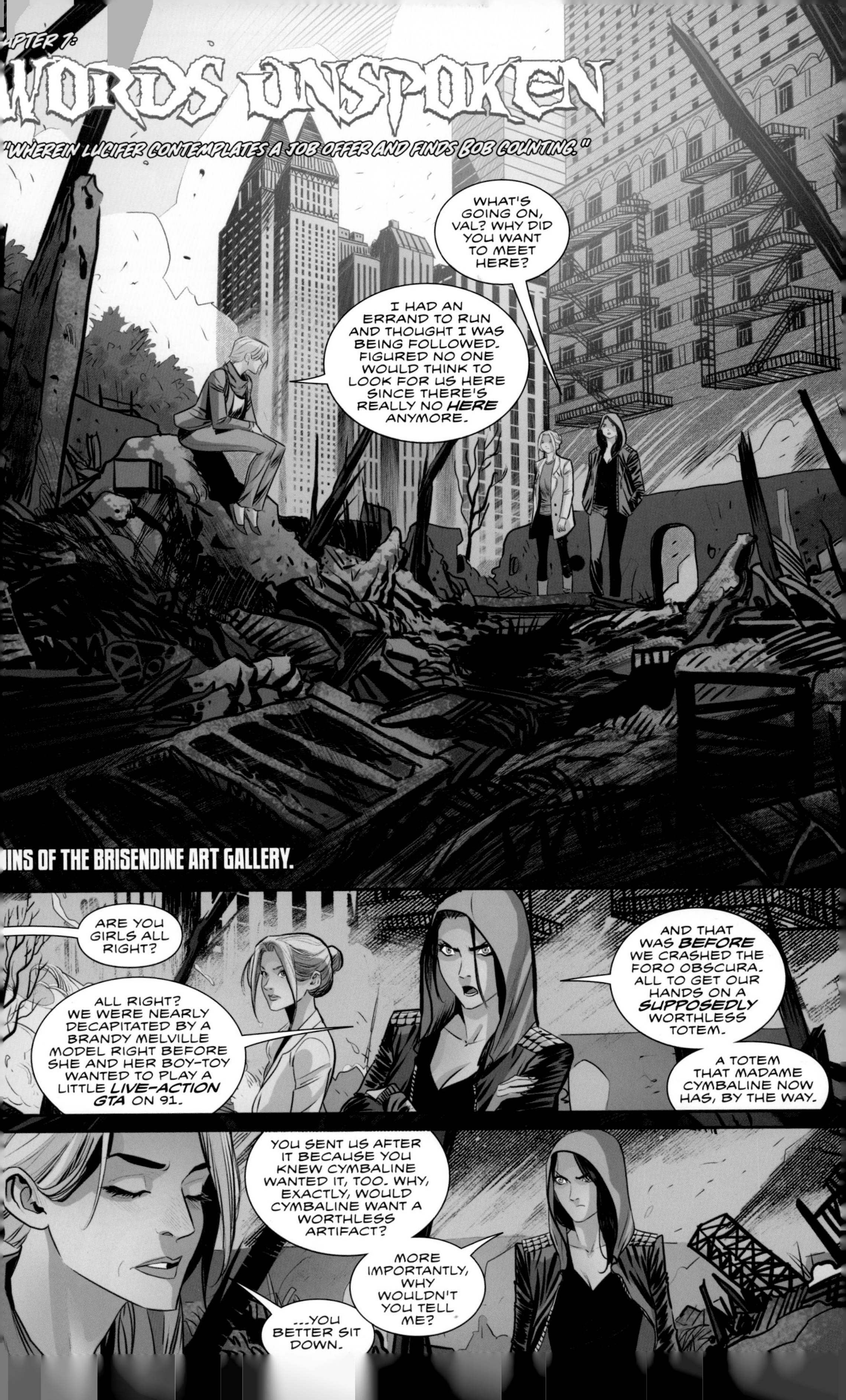
APTER 7:
WORDS UNSPOKEN
"WHEREIN LUCIFER CONTEMPLATES A JOB OFFER AND FINDS BOB COUNTING."
WHAT'S GOING ON, VAL? WHY DID YOU WANT TO MEET HERE?
I HAD AN ERRAND TO RUN AND THOUGHT I WAS BEING FOLLOWED. FIGURED NO ONE WOULD THINK TO LOOK FOR US HERE SINCE THERE'S REALLY NO HERE ANYMORE.
INS OF THE BRISENDINE ART GALLERY.
ARE YOU GIRLS ALL RIGHT?
ALL RIGHT? WE WERE NEARLY DECAPITATED BY A BRANDY MELVILLE MODEL RIGHT BEFORE SHE AND HER BOY-TOY WANTED TO PLAY A LITTLE LIVE-ACTION GTA ON 91.
AND THAT WAS BEFORE WE CRASHED THE FORO OBSCURA. ALL TO GET OUR HANDS ON A SUPPOSEDLY WORTHLESS TOTEM.
A TOTEM THAT MADAME CYMBALINE NOW HAS, BY THE WAY.
YOU SENT US AFTER IT BECAUSE YOU KNEW CYMBALINE WANTED IT, TOO. WHY, EXACTLY, WOULD CYMBALINE WANT A WORTHLESS ARTIFACT?
MORE IMPORTANTLY, WHY WOULDN'T YOU TELL ME?
...YOU BETTER SIT DOWN.

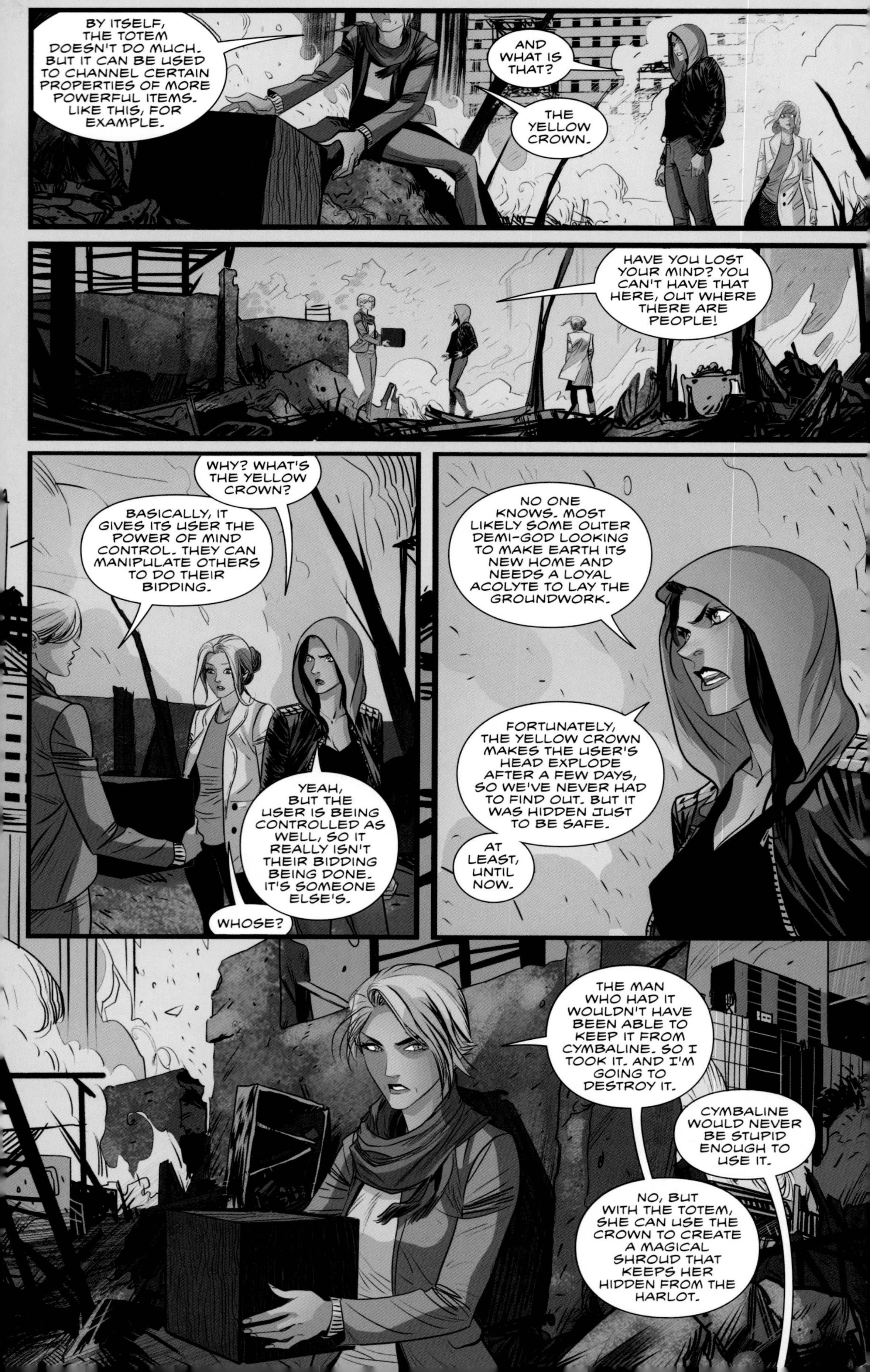
BY ITSELF, THE TOTEM DOESN'T DO MUCH. BUT IT CAN BE USED TO CHANNEL CERTAIN PROPERTIES OF MORE POWERFUL ITEMS. LIKE THIS, FOR EXAMPLE.
AND WHAT IS THAT?
THE YELLOW CROWN.
HAVE YOU LOST YOUR MIND? YOU CAN'T HAVE THAT HERE, OUT WHERE THERE ARE PEOPLE!
WHY? WHAT'S THE YELLOW CROWN?
BASICALLY, IT GIVES ITS USER THE POWER OF MIND CONTROL. THEY CAN MANIPULATE OTHERS TO DO THEIR BIDDING.
YEAH, BUT THE USER IS BEING CONTROLLED AS WELL, SO IT REALLY ISN'T THEIR BIDDING BEING DONE. IT'S SOMEONE ELSE'S.
WHOSE?
NO ONE KNOWS. MOST LIKELY SOME OUTER DEMI-GOD LOOKING TO MAKE EARTH ITS NEW HOME AND NEEDS A LOYAL ACOLYTE TO LAY THE GROUNDWORK.
FORTUNATELY, THE YELLOW CROWN MAKES THE USER'S HEAD EXPLODE AFTER A FEW DAYS, SO WE'VE NEVER HAD TO FIND OUT. BUT IT WAS HIDDEN JUST TO BE SAFE.
AT LEAST, UNTIL NOW.
THE MAN WHO HAD IT WOULDN'T HAVE BEEN ABLE TO KEEP IT FROM CYMBALINE. SO I TOOK IT. AND I'M GOING TO DESTROY IT.
CYMBALINE WOULD NEVER BE STUPID ENOUGH TO USE IT.
NO, BUT WITH THE TOTEM, SHE CAN USE THE CROWN TO CREATE A MAGICAL SHROUD THAT KEEPS HER HIDDEN FROM THE HARLOT.

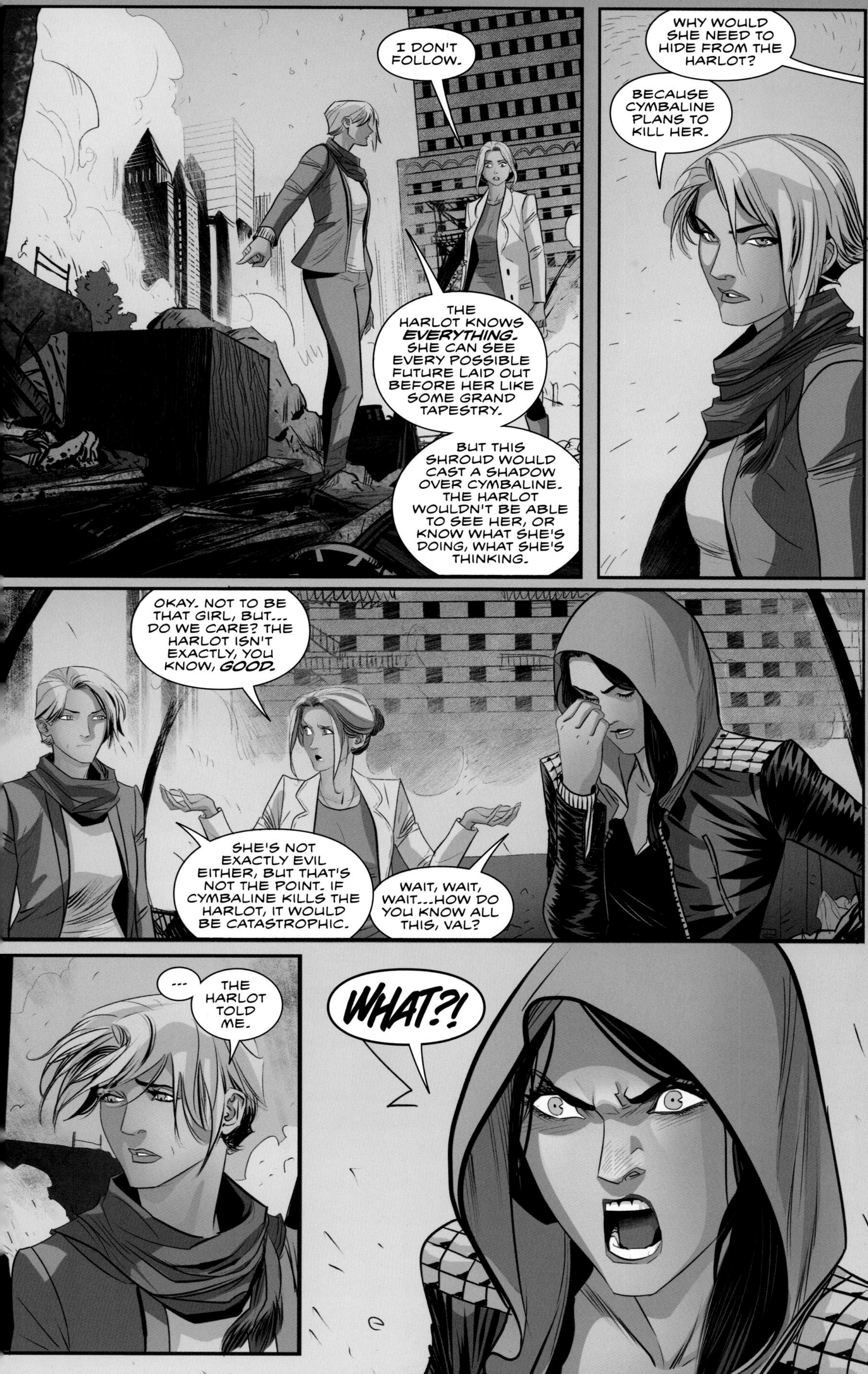
I DON'T FOLLOW.
THE HARLOT KNOWS EVERYTHING. SHE CAN SEE EVERY POSSIBLE FUTURE LAID OUT BEFORE HER LIKE SOME GRAND TAPESTRY.
BUT THIS SHROUD WOULD CAST A SHADOW OVER CYMBALINE. THE HARLOT WOULDN'T BE ABLE TO SEE HER, OR KNOW WHAT SHE'S DOING, WHAT SHE'S THINKING.
WHY WOULD SHE NEED TO HIDE FROM THE HARLOT?
BECAUSE CYMBALINE PLANS TO KILL HER.
OKAY. NOT TO BE THAT GIRL, BUT... DO WE CARE? THE HARLOT ISN'T EXACTLY, YOU KNOW, GOOD.
SHE'S NOT EXACTLY EVIL EITHER, BUT THAT'S NOT THE POINT. IF CYMBALINE KILLS THE HARLOT, IT WOULD BE CATASTROPHIC.
WAIT, WAIT, WAIT...HOW DO YOU KNOW ALL THIS, VAL?
...
THE HARLOT TOLD ME.
WHAT?!

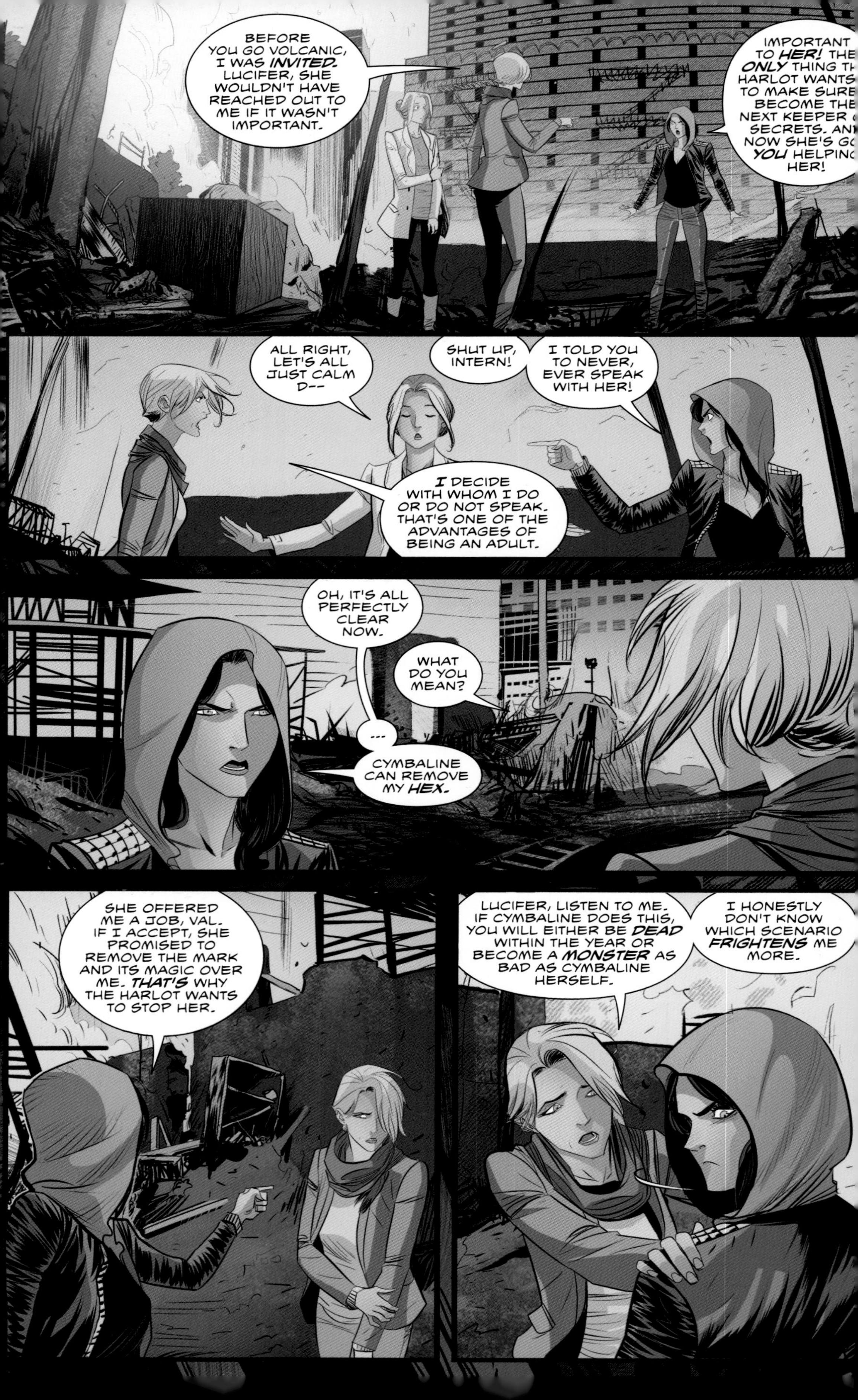
BEFORE YOU GO VOLCANIC, I WAS INVITED. LUCIFER, SHE WOULDN'T HAVE REACHED OUT TO ME IF IT WASN'T IMPORTANT.
IMPORTANT TO HER! THE ONLY THING TH HARLOT WANTS TO MAKE SURE BECOME THE NEXT KEEPER SECRETS. AN NOW SHE'S G YOU HELPING HER!
ALL RIGHT, LET'S ALL JUST CALM D--
SHUT UP, INTERN!
I TOLD YOU TO NEVER, EVER SPEAK WITH HER!
I DECIDE WITH WHOM I DO OR DO NOT SPEAK. THAT'S ONE OF THE ADVANTAGES OF BEING AN ADULT.
OH, IT'S ALL PERFECTLY CLEAR NOW.
WHAT DO YOU MEAN?
...
CYMBALINE CAN REMOVE MY HEX.
SHE OFFERED ME A JOB, VAL. IF I ACCEPT, SHE PROMISED TO REMOVE THE MARK AND ITS MAGIC OVER ME. THAT'S WHY THE HARLOT WANTS TO STOP HER.
LUCIFER, LISTEN TO ME. IF CYMBALINE DOES THIS, YOU WILL EITHER BE DEAD WITHIN THE YEAR OR BECOME A MONSTER AS BAD AS CYMBALINE HERSELF.
I HONESTLY DON'T KNOW WHICH SCENARIO FRIGHTENS ME MORE.

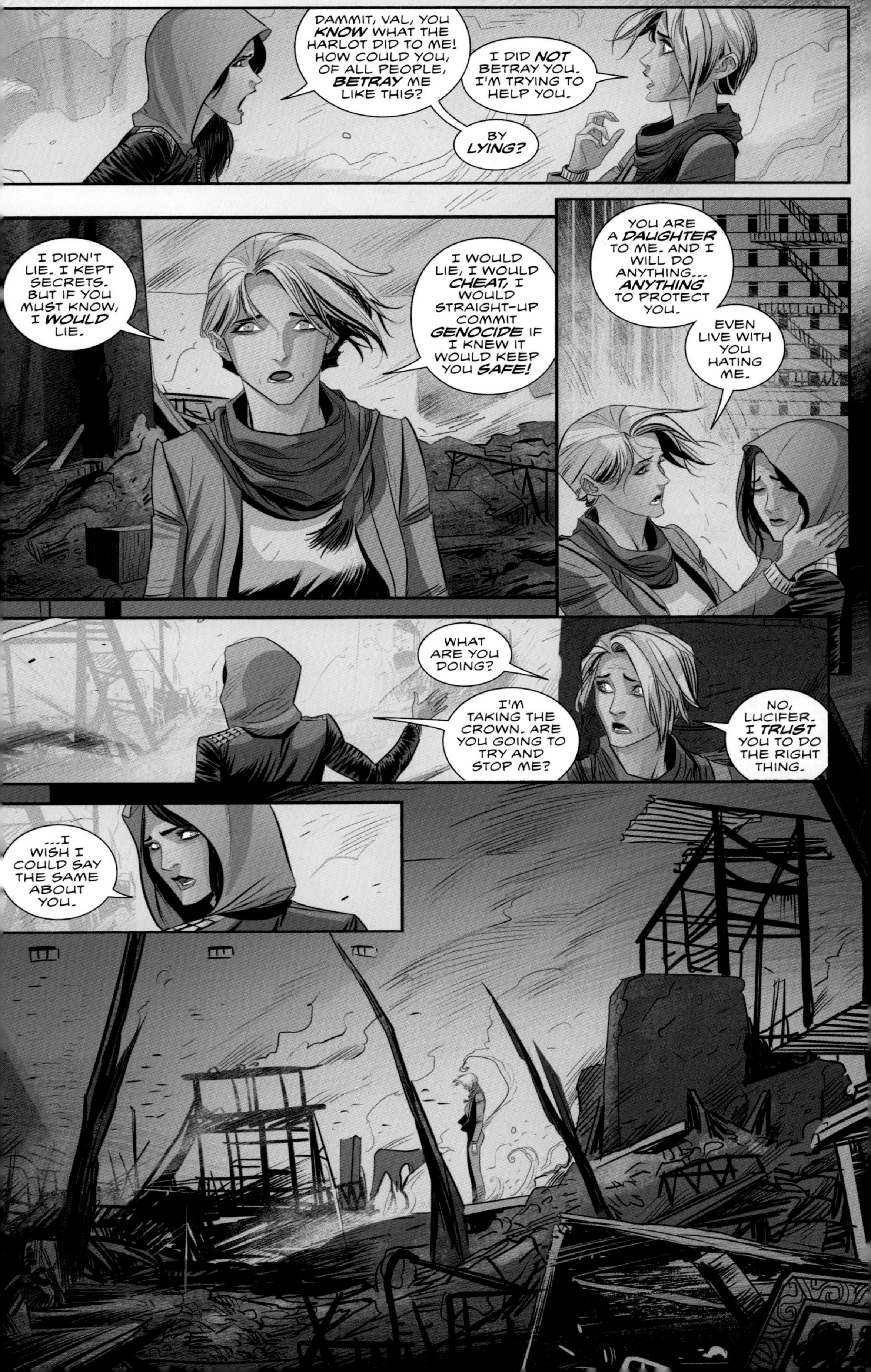
DAMMIT, VAL, YOU KNOW WHAT THE HARLOT DID TO ME! HOW COULD YOU, OF ALL PEOPLE, BETRAY ME LIKE THIS?
I DID NOT BETRAY YOU. I'M TRYING TO HELP YOU.
BY LYING?
I DIDN'T LIE. I KEPT SECRETS. BUT IF YOU MUST KNOW, I WOULD LIE.
I WOULD LIE, I WOULD CHEAT, I WOULD STRAIGHT-UP COMMIT GENOCIDE IF I KNEW IT WOULD KEEP YOU SAFE!
YOU ARE A DAUGHTER TO ME. AND I WILL DO ANYTHING... ANYTHING TO PROTECT YOU.
EVEN LIVE WITH YOU HATING ME.
WHAT ARE YOU DOING?
I'M TAKING THE CROWN. ARE YOU GOING TO TRY AND STOP ME?
NO, LUCIFER. I TRUST YOU TO DO THE RIGHT THING.
...I WISH I COULD SAY THE SAME ABOUT YOU.

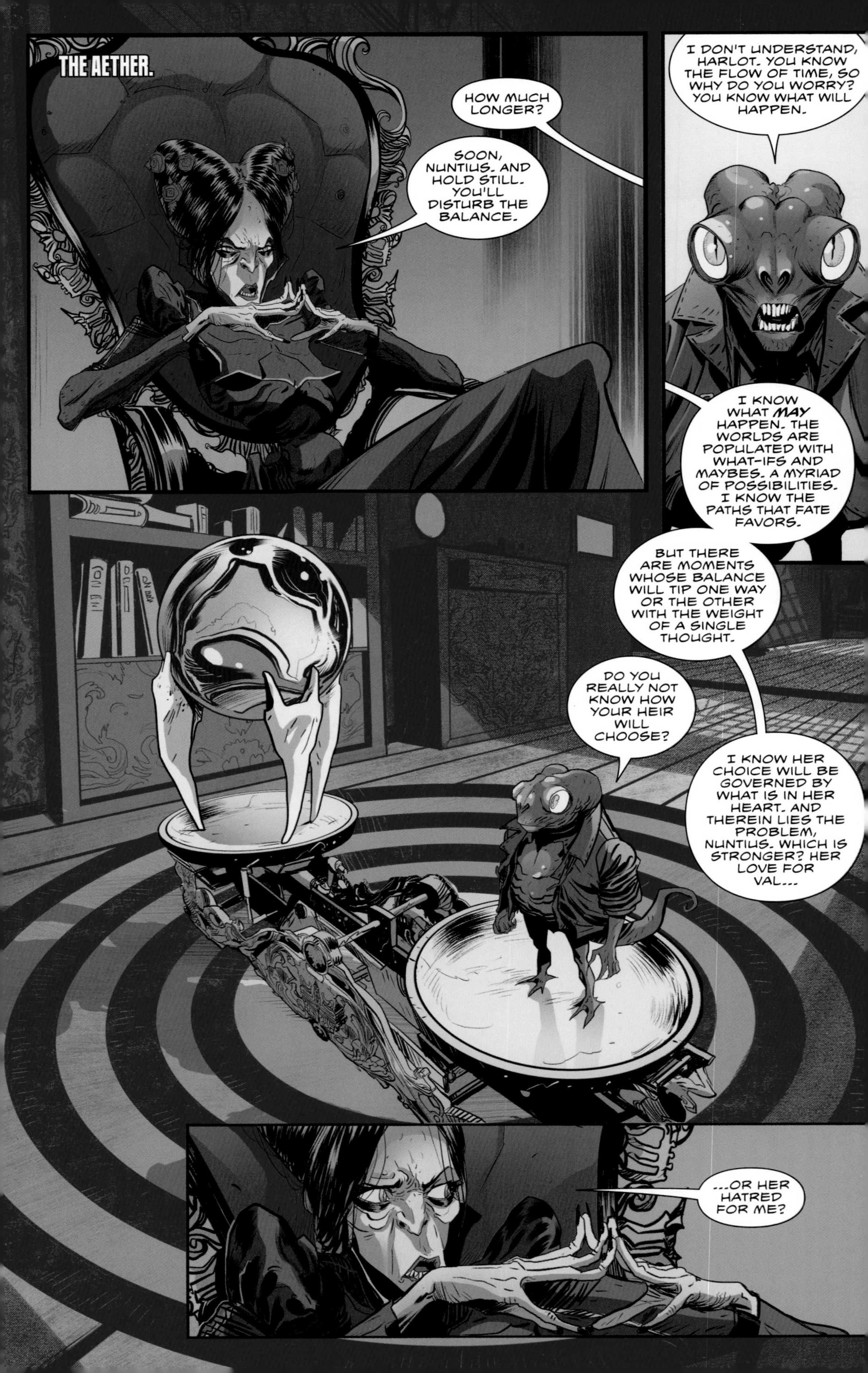
THE AETHER.
HOW MUCH LONGER?
SOON, NUNTIUS. AND HOLD STILL. YOU'LL DISTURB THE BALANCE.
I DON'T UNDERSTAND, HARLOT. YOU KNOW THE FLOW OF TIME, SO WHY DO YOU WORRY? YOU KNOW WHAT WILL HAPPEN.
I KNOW WHAT MAY HAPPEN. THE WORLDS ARE POPULATED WITH WHAT-IFS AND MAYBES. A MYRIAD OF POSSIBILITIES. I KNOW THE PATHS THAT FATE FAVORS.
BUT THERE ARE MOMENTS WHOSE BALANCE WILL TIP ONE WAY OR THE OTHER WITH THE WEIGHT OF A SINGLE THOUGHT.
DO YOU REALLY NOT KNOW HOW YOUR HEIR WILL CHOOSE?
I KNOW HER CHOICE WILL BE GOVERNED BY WHAT IS IN HER HEART. AND THEREIN LIES THE PROBLEM, NUNTIUS. WHICH IS STRONGER? HER LOVE FOR VAL...
...OR HER HATRED FOR ME?

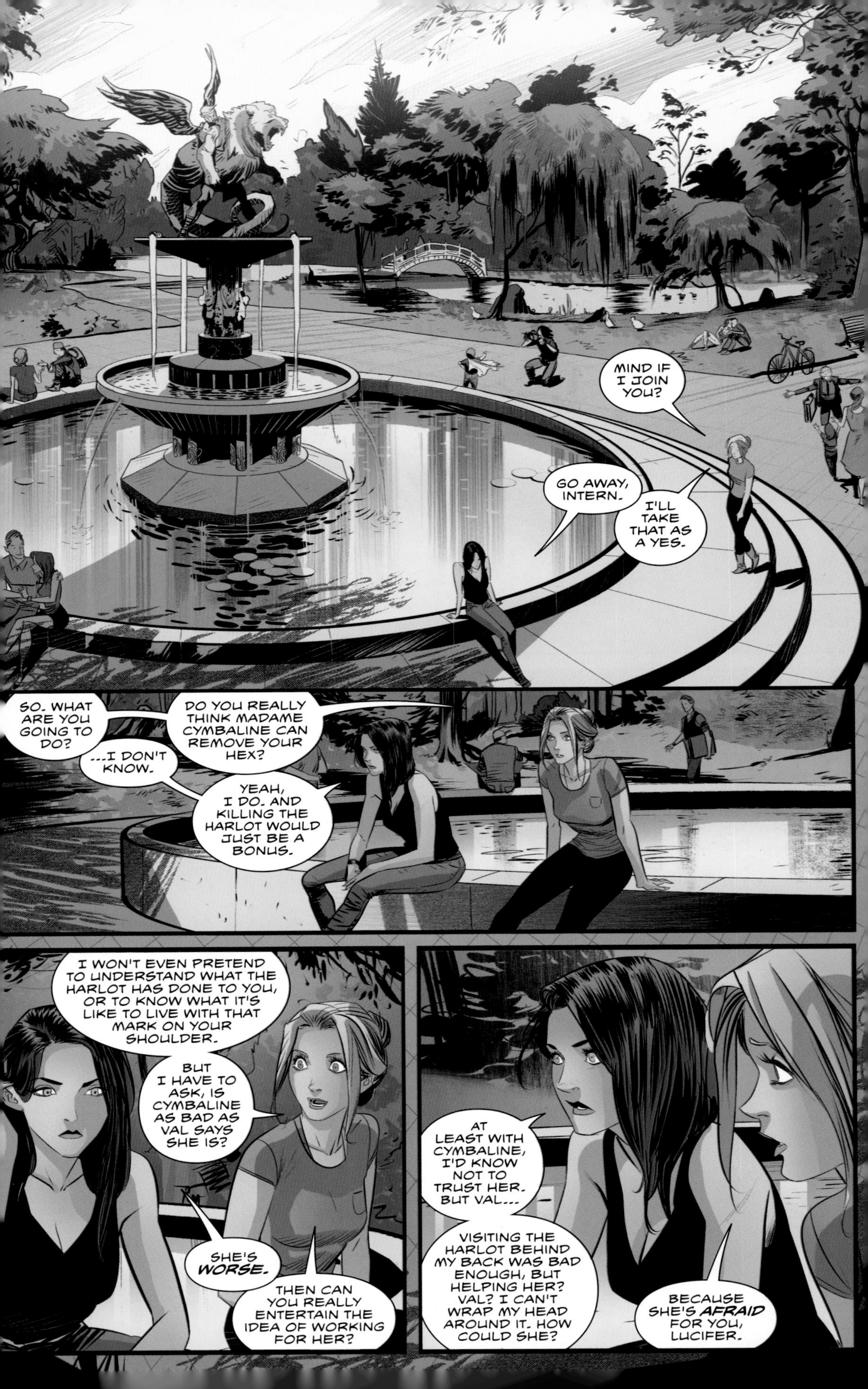
MIND IF I JOIN YOU?
GO AWAY, INTERN.
I'LL TAKE THAT AS A YES.
SO. WHAT ARE YOU GOING TO DO?
...I DON'T KNOW.
DO YOU REALLY THINK MADAME CYMBALINE CAN REMOVE YOUR HEX?
YEAH, I DO. AND KILLING THE HARLOT WOULD JUST BE A BONUS.
I WON'T EVEN PRETEND TO UNDERSTAND WHAT THE HARLOT HAS DONE TO YOU, OR TO KNOW WHAT IT'S LIKE TO LIVE WITH THAT MARK ON YOUR SHOULDER.
BUT I HAVE TO ASK, IS CYMBALINE AS BAD AS VAL SAYS SHE IS?
SHE'S *WORSE.*
THEN CAN YOU REALLY ENTERTAIN THE IDEA OF WORKING FOR HER?
AT LEAST WITH CYMBALINE, I'D KNOW NOT TO TRUST HER. BUT VAL...
VISITING THE HARLOT BEHIND MY BACK WAS BAD ENOUGH, BUT HELPING HER? VAL? I CAN'T WRAP MY HEAD AROUND IT. HOW COULD SHE?
BECAUSE SHE'S *AFRAID* FOR YOU, LUCIFER.

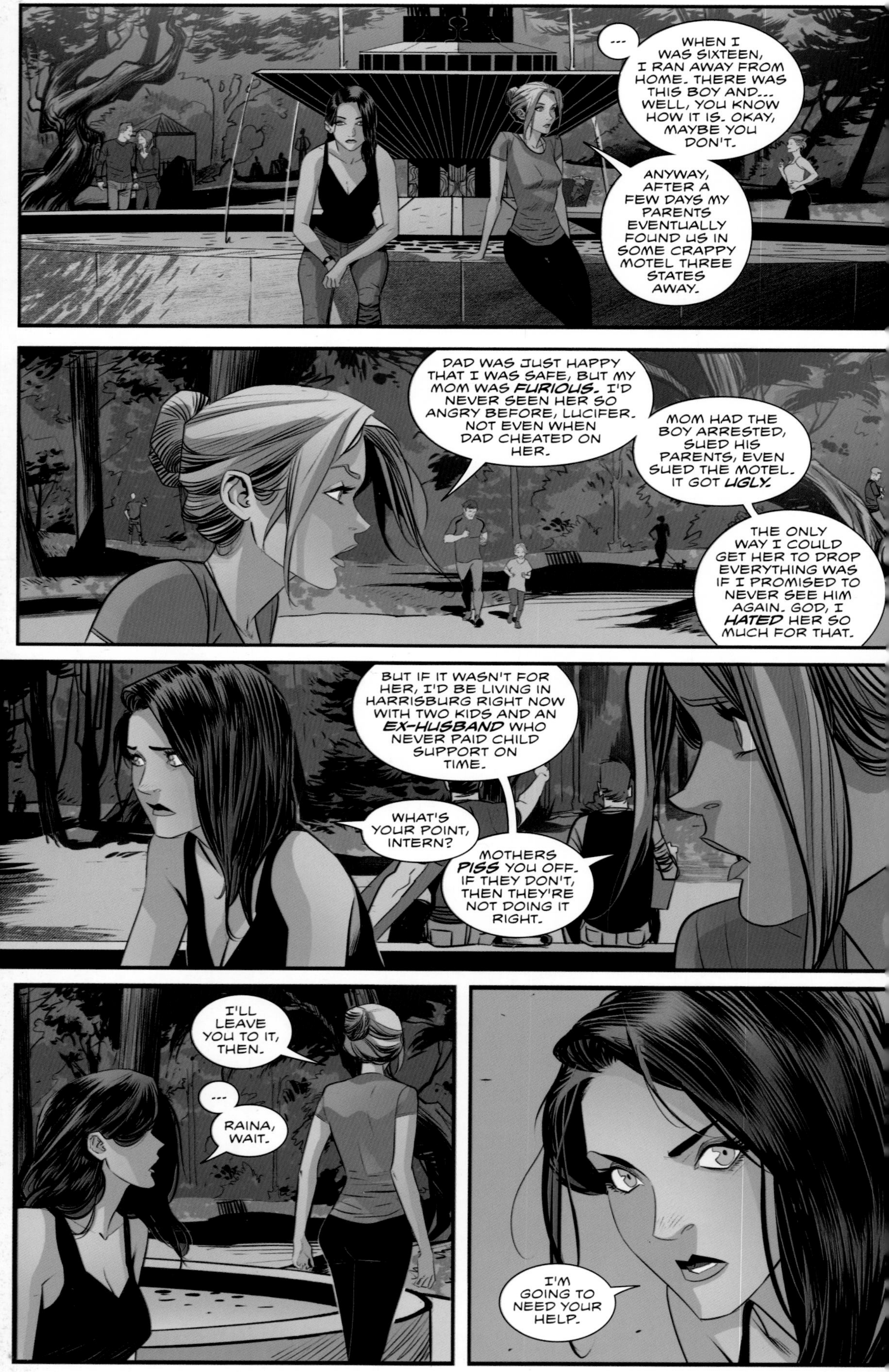
...
WHEN I WAS SIXTEEN, I RAN AWAY FROM HOME. THERE WAS THIS BOY AND... WELL, YOU KNOW HOW IT IS. OKAY, MAYBE YOU DON'T.
ANYWAY, AFTER A FEW DAYS MY PARENTS EVENTUALLY FOUND US IN SOME CRAPPY MOTEL THREE STATES AWAY.
DAD WAS JUST HAPPY THAT I WAS SAFE, BUT MY MOM WAS FURIOUS. I'D NEVER SEEN HER SO ANGRY BEFORE, LUCIFER. NOT EVEN WHEN DAD CHEATED ON HER.
MOM HAD THE BOY ARRESTED, SUED HIS PARENTS, EVEN SUED THE MOTEL. IT GOT UGLY.
THE ONLY WAY I COULD GET HER TO DROP EVERYTHING WAS IF I PROMISED TO NEVER SEE HIM AGAIN. GOD, I HATED HER SO MUCH FOR THAT.
BUT IF IT WASN'T FOR HER, I'D BE LIVING IN HARRISBURG RIGHT NOW WITH TWO KIDS AND AN EX-HUSBAND WHO NEVER PAID CHILD SUPPORT ON TIME.
WHAT'S YOUR POINT, INTERN?
MOTHERS PISS YOU OFF. IF THEY DON'T, THEN THEY'RE NOT DOING IT RIGHT.
I'LL LEAVE YOU TO IT, THEN.
...
RAINA, WAIT.
I'M GOING TO NEED YOUR HELP.

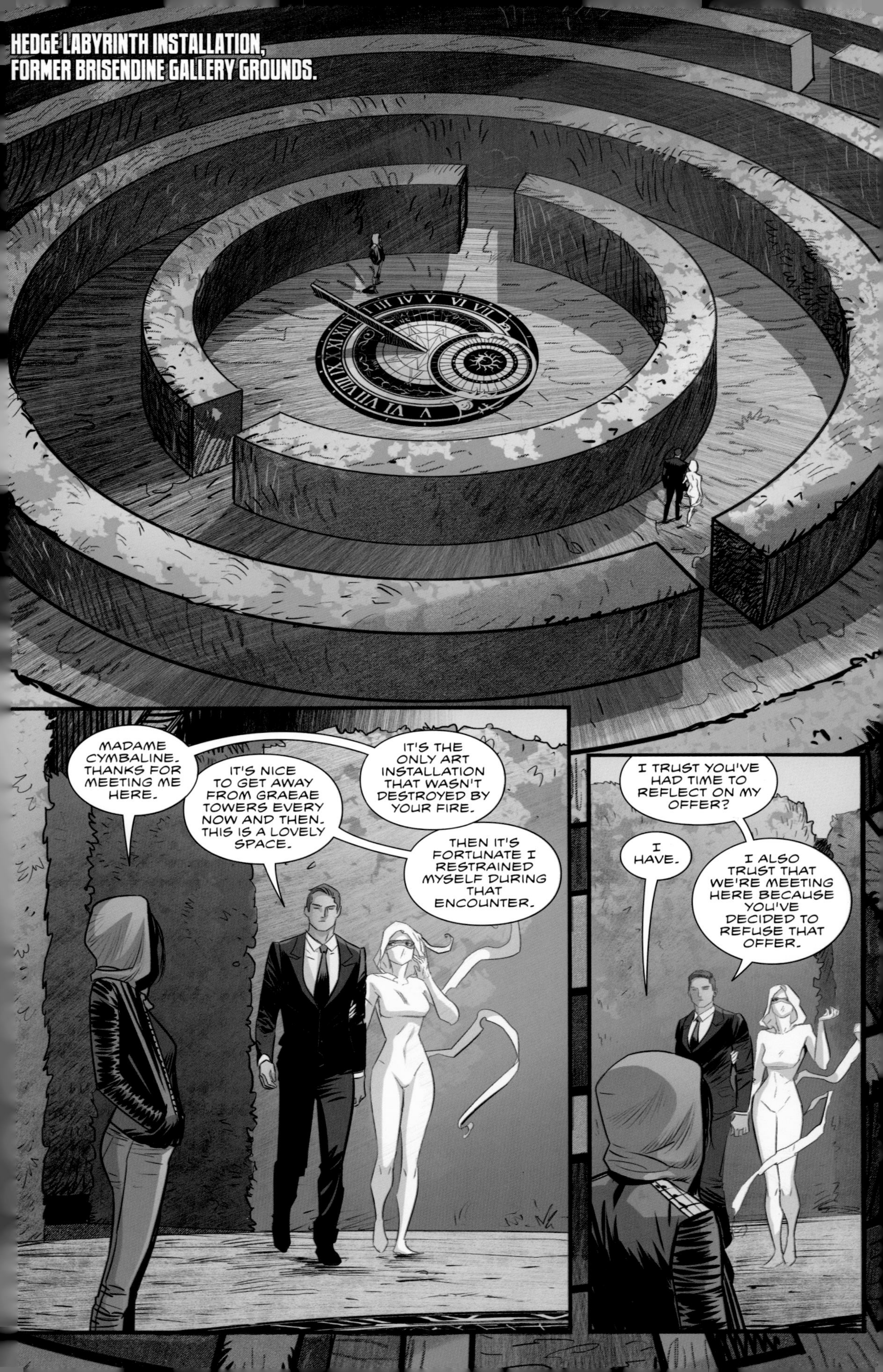
HEDGE LABYRINTH INSTALLATION, FORMER BRISENDINE GALLERY GROUNDS.
MADAME CYMBALINE. THANKS FOR MEETING ME HERE.
IT'S NICE TO GET AWAY FROM GRAEAE TOWERS EVERY NOW AND THEN. THIS IS A LOVELY SPACE.
IT'S THE ONLY ART INSTALLATION THAT WASN'T DESTROYED BY YOUR FIRE.
THEN IT'S FORTUNATE I RESTRAINED MYSELF DURING THAT ENCOUNTER.
I TRUST YOU'VE HAD TIME TO REFLECT ON MY OFFER?
I HAVE.
I ALSO TRUST THAT WE'RE MEETING HERE BECAUSE YOU'VE DECIDED TO REFUSE THAT OFFER.

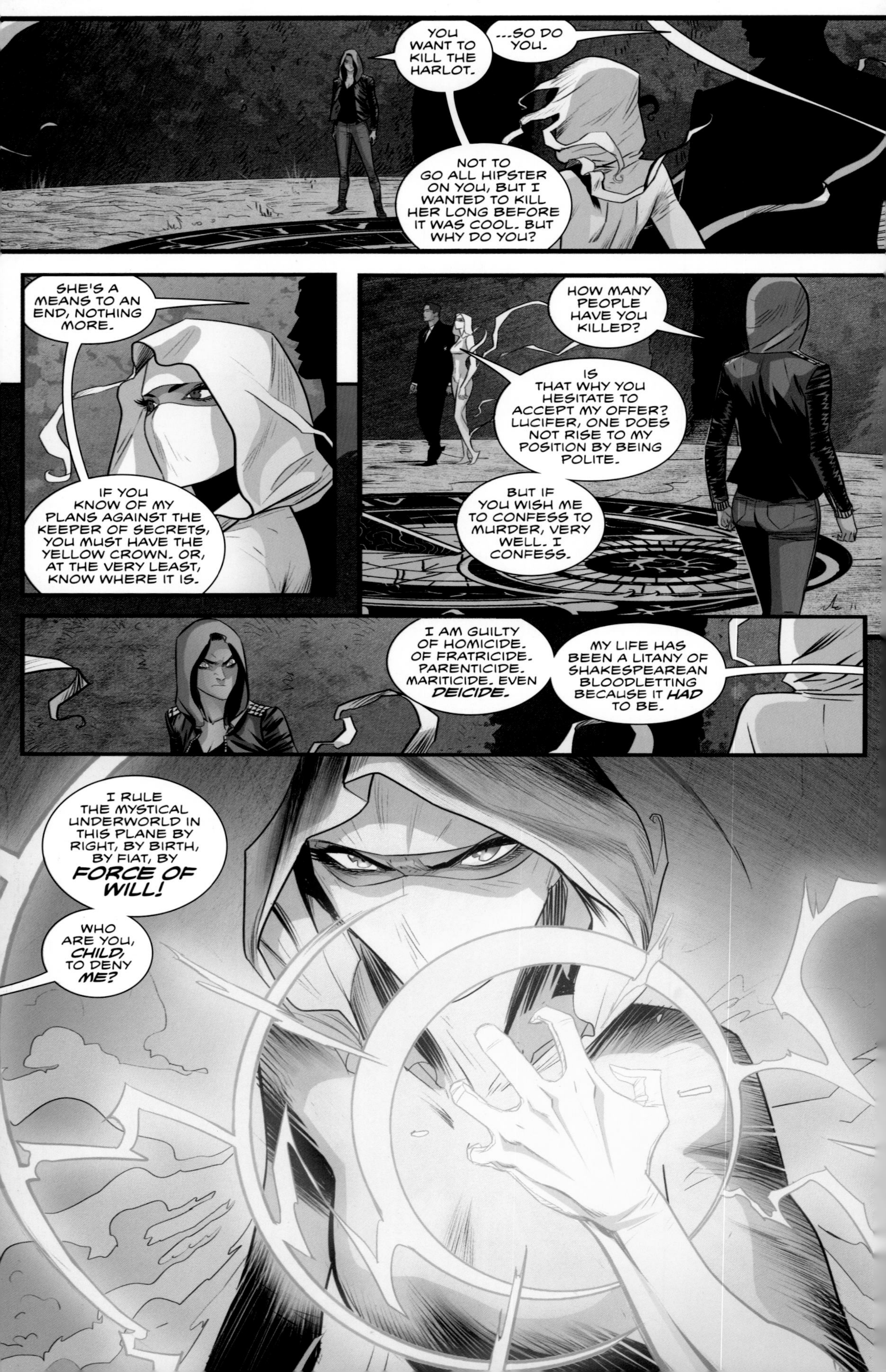
YOU WANT TO KILL THE HARLOT.
...SO DO YOU.
NOT TO GO ALL HIPSTER ON YOU, BUT I WANTED TO KILL HER LONG BEFORE IT WAS COOL. BUT WHY DO YOU?
SHE'S A MEANS TO AN END, NOTHING MORE.
IF YOU KNOW OF MY PLANS AGAINST THE KEEPER OF SECRETS, YOU MUST HAVE THE YELLOW CROWN. OR, AT THE VERY LEAST, KNOW WHERE IT IS.
HOW MANY PEOPLE HAVE YOU KILLED?
IS THAT WHY YOU HESITATE TO ACCEPT MY OFFER? LUCIFER, ONE DOES NOT RISE TO MY POSITION BY BEING POLITE.
BUT IF YOU WISH ME TO CONFESS TO MURDER, VERY WELL. I CONFESS.
I AM GUILTY OF HOMICIDE. OF FRATRICIDE. PARENTICIDE. MARITICIDE. EVEN DEICIDE.
MY LIFE HAS BEEN A LITANY OF SHAKESPEAREAN BLOODLETTING BECAUSE IT HAD TO BE.
I RULE THE MYSTICAL UNDERWORLD IN THIS PLANE BY RIGHT, BY BIRTH, BY FIAT, BY FORCE OF WILL!
WHO ARE YOU, CHILD, TO DENY ME?

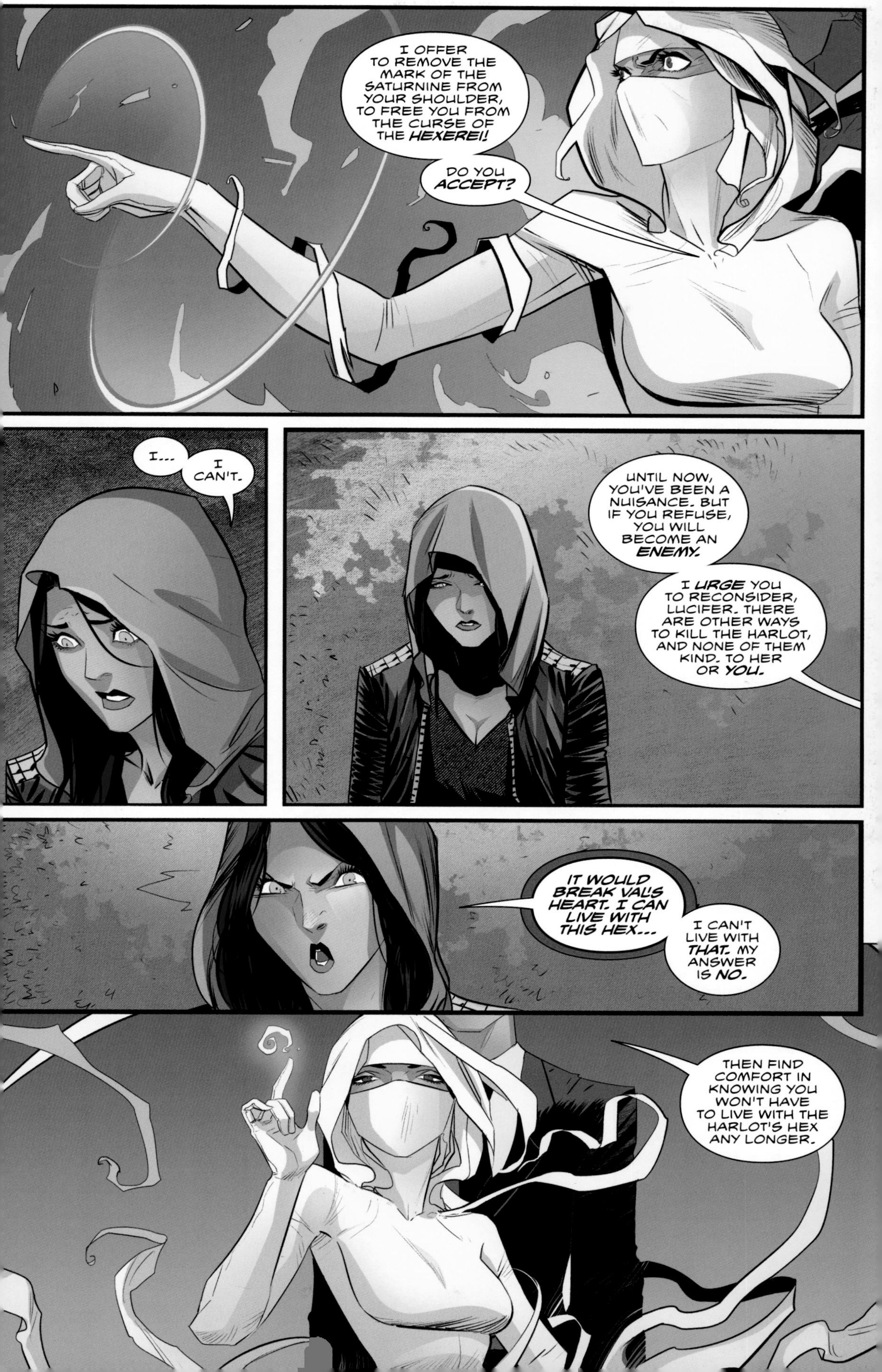
I OFFER TO REMOVE THE MARK OF THE SATURNINE FROM YOUR SHOULDER, TO FREE YOU FROM THE CURSE OF THE HEXEREI!
DO YOU ACCEPT?
I... I CAN'T.
UNTIL NOW, YOU'VE BEEN A NUISANCE. BUT IF YOU REFUSE, YOU WILL BECOME AN ENEMY.
I URGE YOU TO RECONSIDER, LUCIFER. THERE ARE OTHER WAYS TO KILL THE HARLOT, AND NONE OF THEM KIND. TO HER OR YOU.
IT WOULD BREAK VAL'S HEART. I CAN LIVE WITH THIS HEX...
I CAN'T LIVE WITH THAT. MY ANSWER IS NO.
THEN FIND COMFORT IN KNOWING YOU WON'T HAVE TO LIVE WITH THE HARLOT'S HEX ANY LONGER.

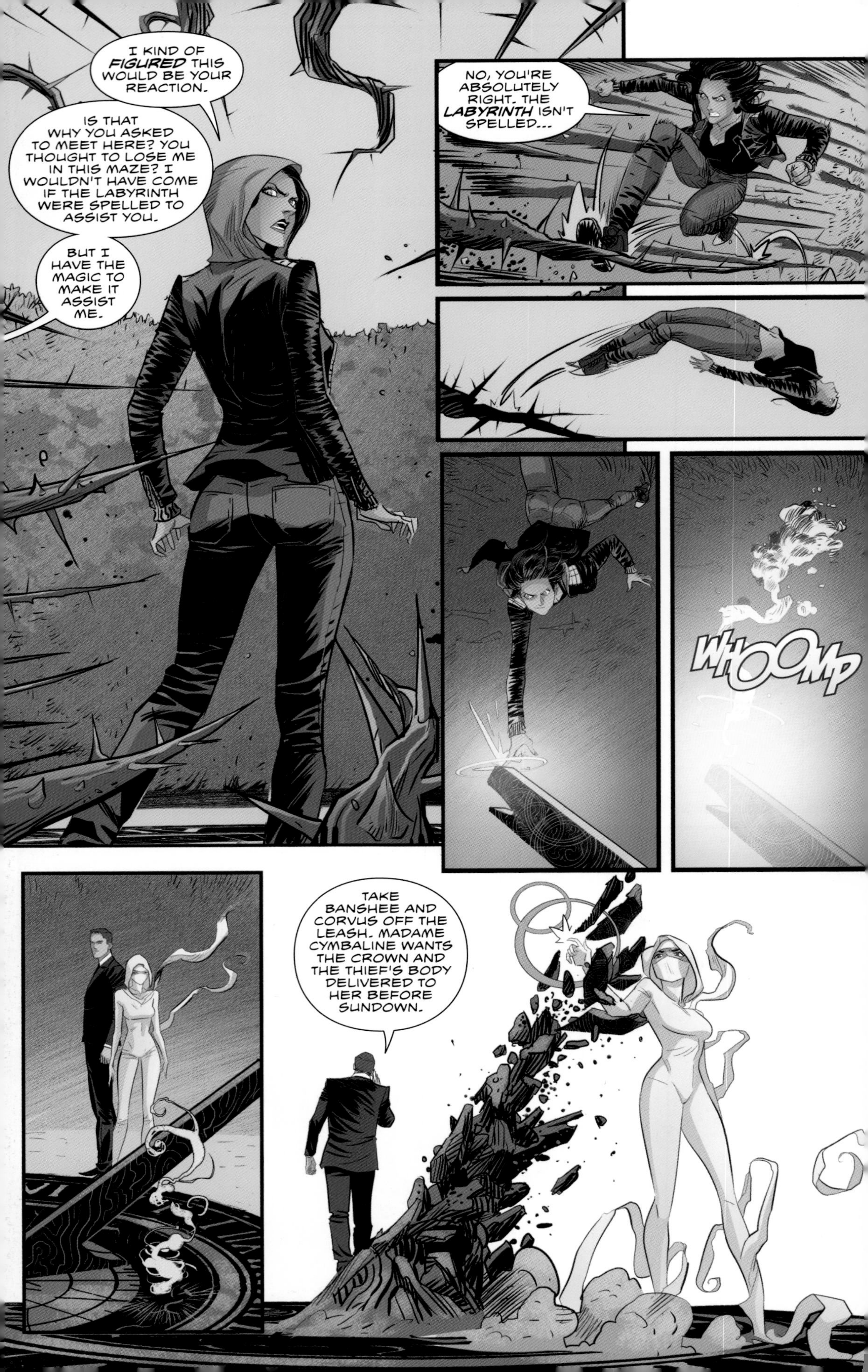
I KIND OF FIGURED THIS WOULD BE YOUR REACTION.
IS THAT WHY YOU ASKED TO MEET HERE? YOU THOUGHT TO LOSE ME IN THIS MAZE? I WOULDN'T HAVE COME IF THE LABYRINTH WERE SPELLED TO ASSIST YOU.
BUT I HAVE THE MAGIC TO MAKE IT ASSIST ME.
NO, YOU'RE ABSOLUTELY RIGHT. THE LABYRINTH ISN'T SPELLED...
WHOOMP
TAKE BANSHEE AND CORVUS OFF THE LEASH. MADAME CYMBALINE WANTS THE CROWN AND THE THIEF'S BODY DELIVERED TO HER BEFORE SUNDOWN.

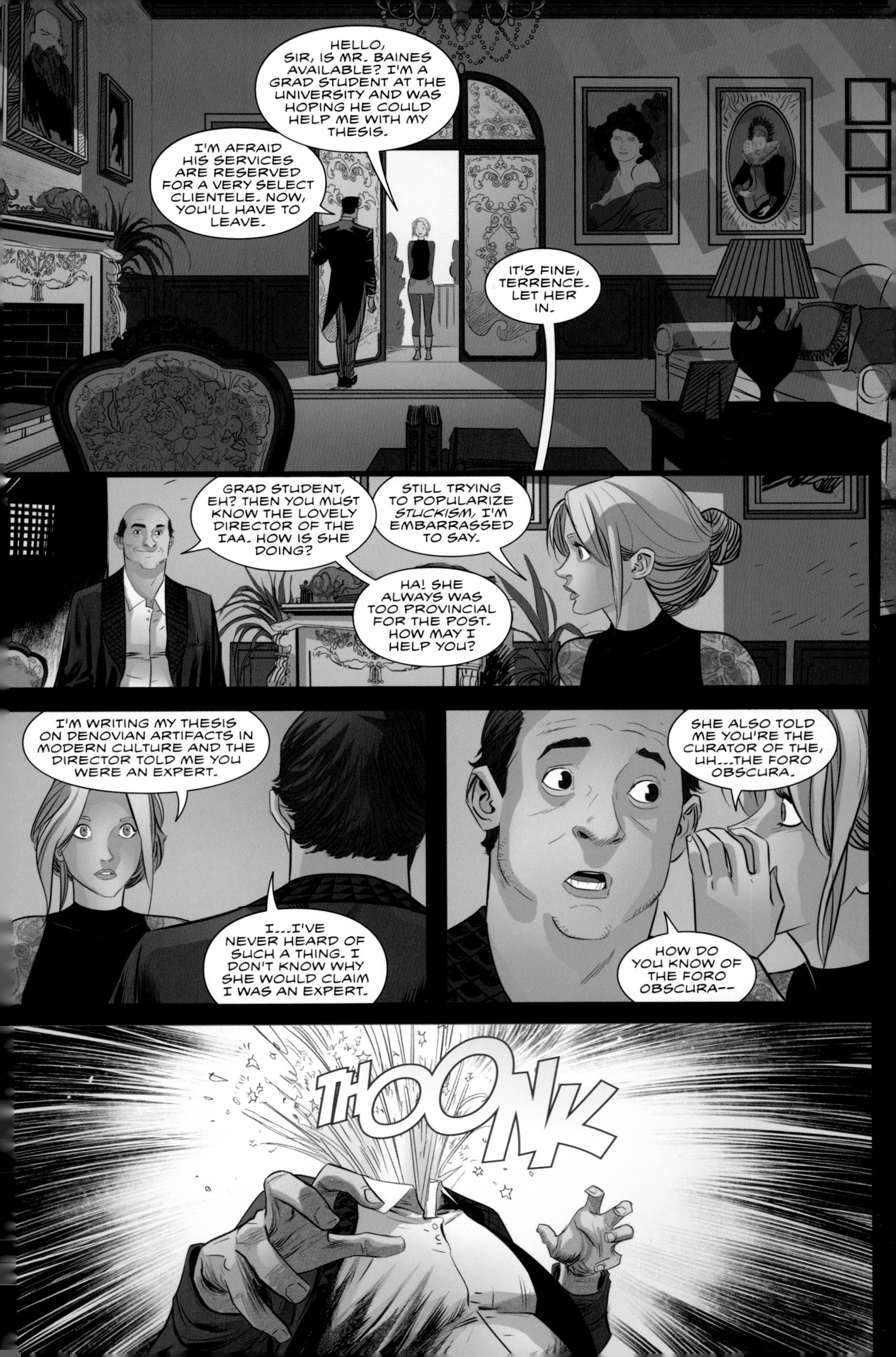
HELLO, SIR, IS MR. BAINES AVAILABLE? I'M A GRAD STUDENT AT THE UNIVERSITY AND WAS HOPING HE COULD HELP ME WITH MY THESIS.
I'M AFRAID HIS SERVICES ARE RESERVED FOR A VERY SELECT CLIENTELE. NOW, YOU'LL HAVE TO LEAVE.
IT'S FINE, TERRENCE. LET HER IN.
GRAD STUDENT, EH? THEN YOU MUST KNOW THE LOVELY DIRECTOR OF THE IAA. HOW IS SHE DOING?
STILL TRYING TO POPULARIZE *STUCKISM*, I'M EMBARRASSED TO SAY.
HA! SHE ALWAYS WAS TOO PROVINCIAL FOR THE POST. HOW MAY I HELP YOU?
I'M WRITING MY THESIS ON DENOVIAN ARTIFACTS IN MODERN CULTURE AND THE DIRECTOR TOLD ME YOU WERE AN EXPERT.
I...I'VE NEVER HEARD OF SUCH A THING. I DON'T KNOW WHY SHE WOULD CLAIM I WAS AN EXPERT.
SHE ALSO TOLD ME YOU'RE THE CURATOR OF THE, UH...THE FORO OBSCURA.
HOW DO YOU KNOW OF THE FORO OBSCURA--
THOONK

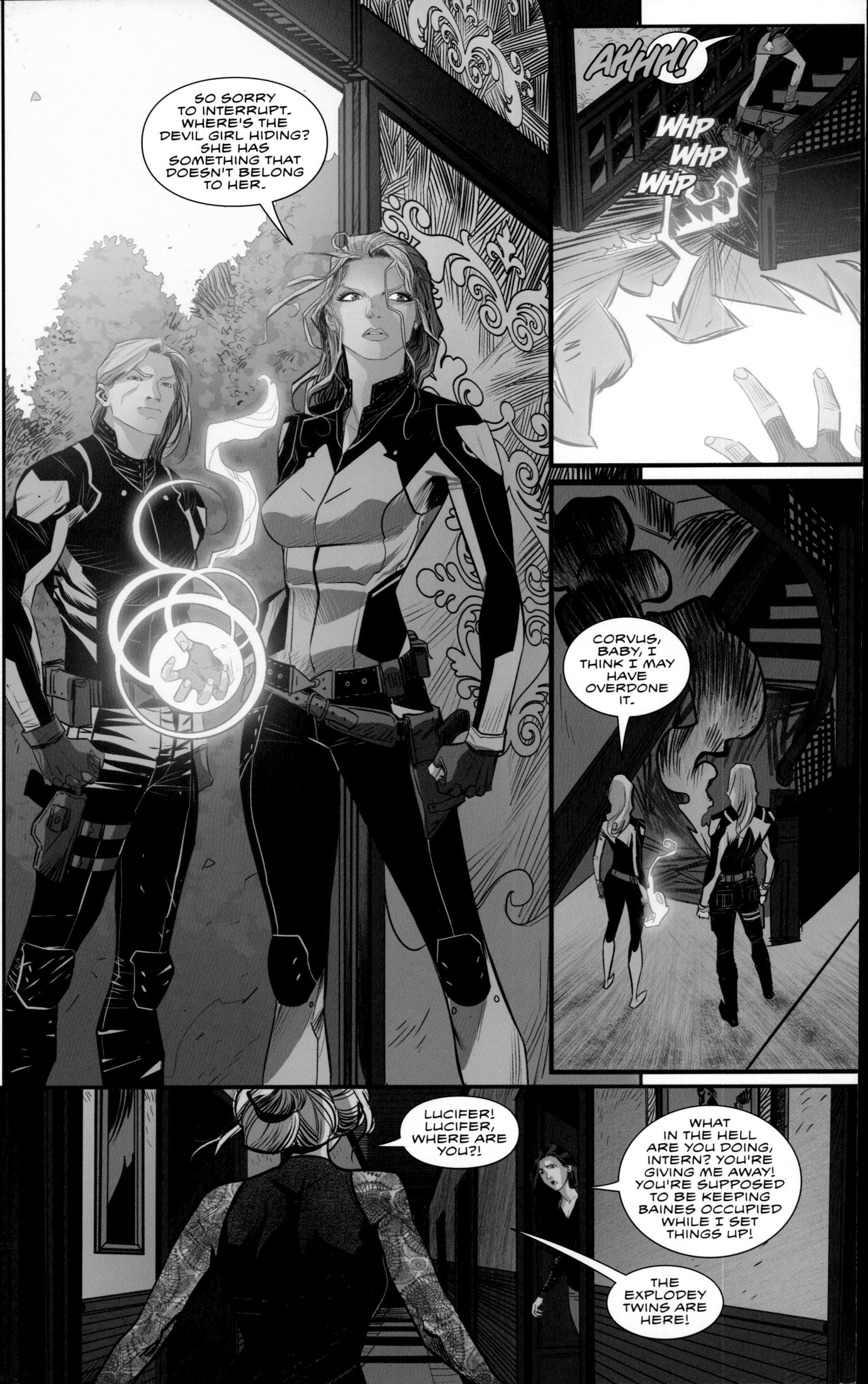

SO SORRY TO INTERRUPT. WHERE'S THE DEVIL GIRL HIDING? SHE HAS SOMETHING THAT DOESN'T BELONG TO HER.
AHHH!
WHP
WHP
WHP
CORVUS, BABY, I THINK I MAY HAVE OVERDONE IT.
LUCIFER! LUCIFER, WHERE ARE YOU?!
WHAT IN THE HELL ARE YOU DOING, INTERN? YOU'RE GIVING ME AWAY! YOU'RE SUPPOSED TO BE KEEPING BAINES OCCUPIED WHILE I SET THINGS UP!
THE EXPLODEY TWINS ARE HERE!

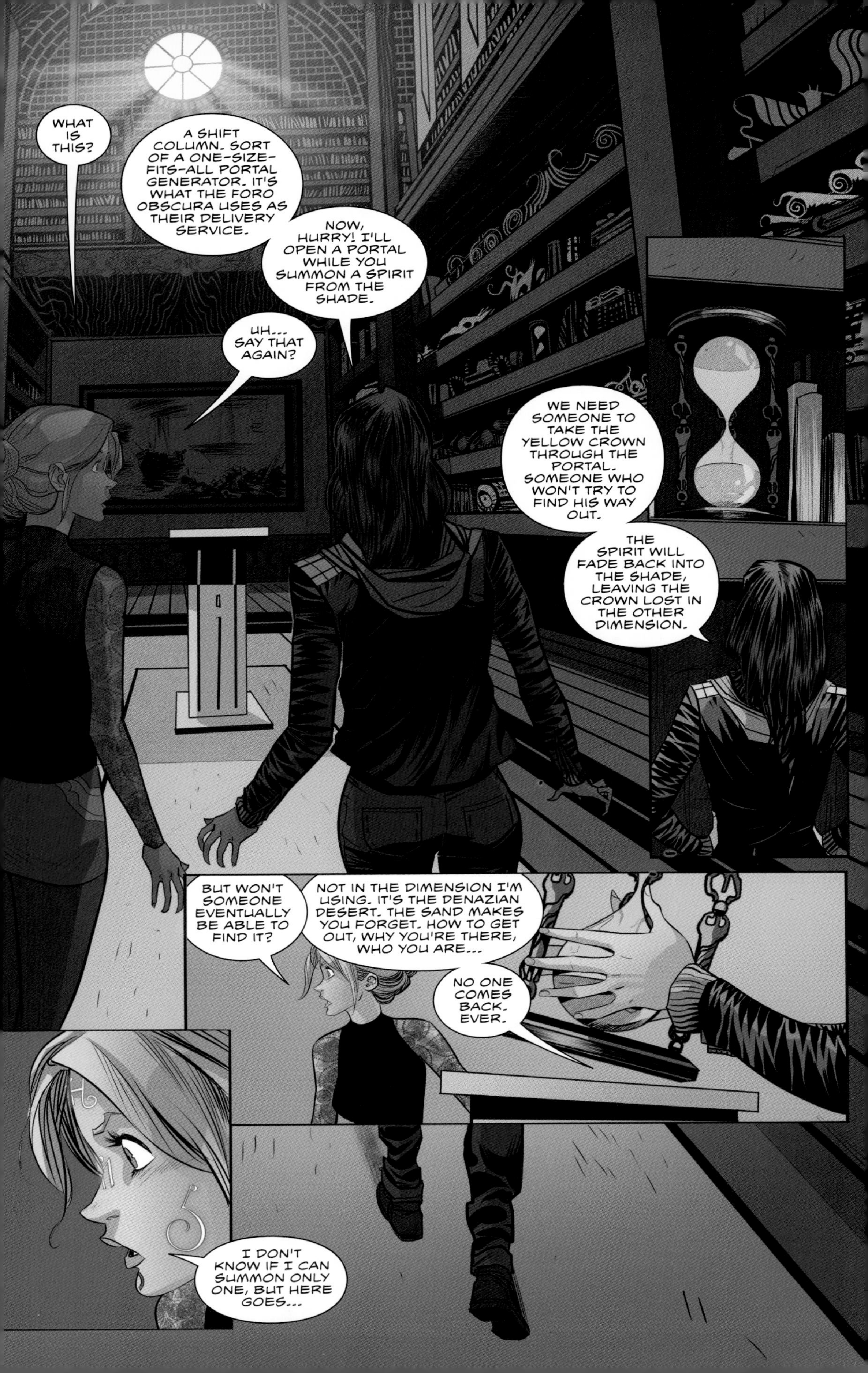
WHAT IS THIS?
A SHIFT COLUMN. SORT OF A ONE-SIZE-FITS-ALL PORTAL GENERATOR. IT'S WHAT THE FORO OBSCURA USES AS THEIR DELIVERY SERVICE.
NOW, HURRY! I'LL OPEN A PORTAL WHILE YOU SUMMON A SPIRIT FROM THE SHADE.
UH... SAY THAT AGAIN?
WE NEED SOMEONE TO TAKE THE YELLOW CROWN THROUGH THE PORTAL. SOMEONE WHO WON'T TRY TO FIND HIS WAY OUT.
THE SPIRIT WILL FADE BACK INTO THE SHADE, LEAVING THE CROWN LOST IN THE OTHER DIMENSION.
BUT WON'T SOMEONE EVENTUALLY BE ABLE TO FIND IT?
NOT IN THE DIMENSION I'M USING. IT'S THE DENAZIAN DESERT. THE SAND MAKES YOU FORGET. HOW TO GET OUT, WHY YOU'RE THERE, WHO YOU ARE...
NO ONE COMES BACK. EVER.
I DON'T KNOW IF I CAN SUMMON ONLY ONE, BUT HERE GOES...

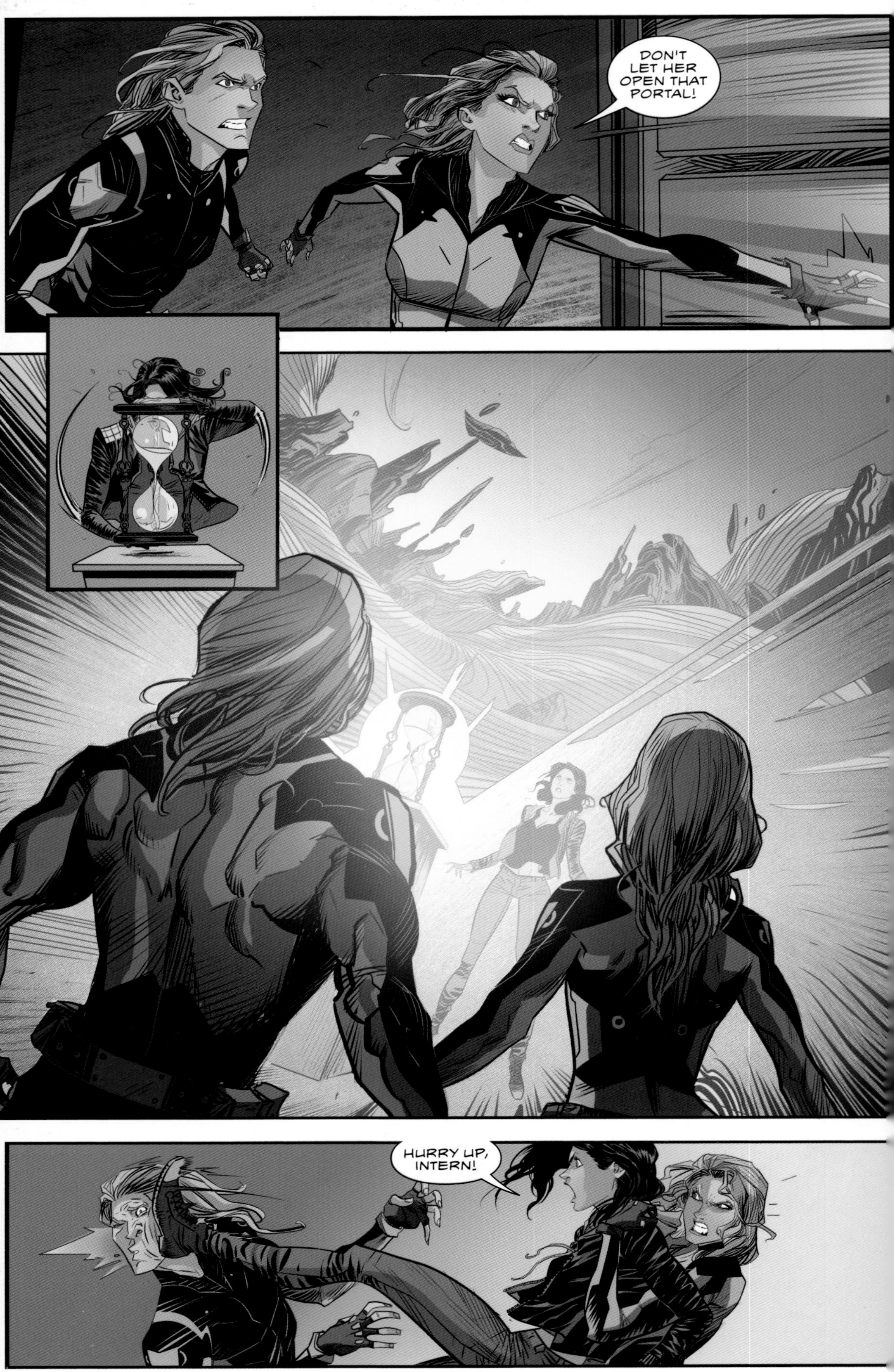
DON'T LET HER OPEN THAT PORTAL!
HURRY UP, INTERN!

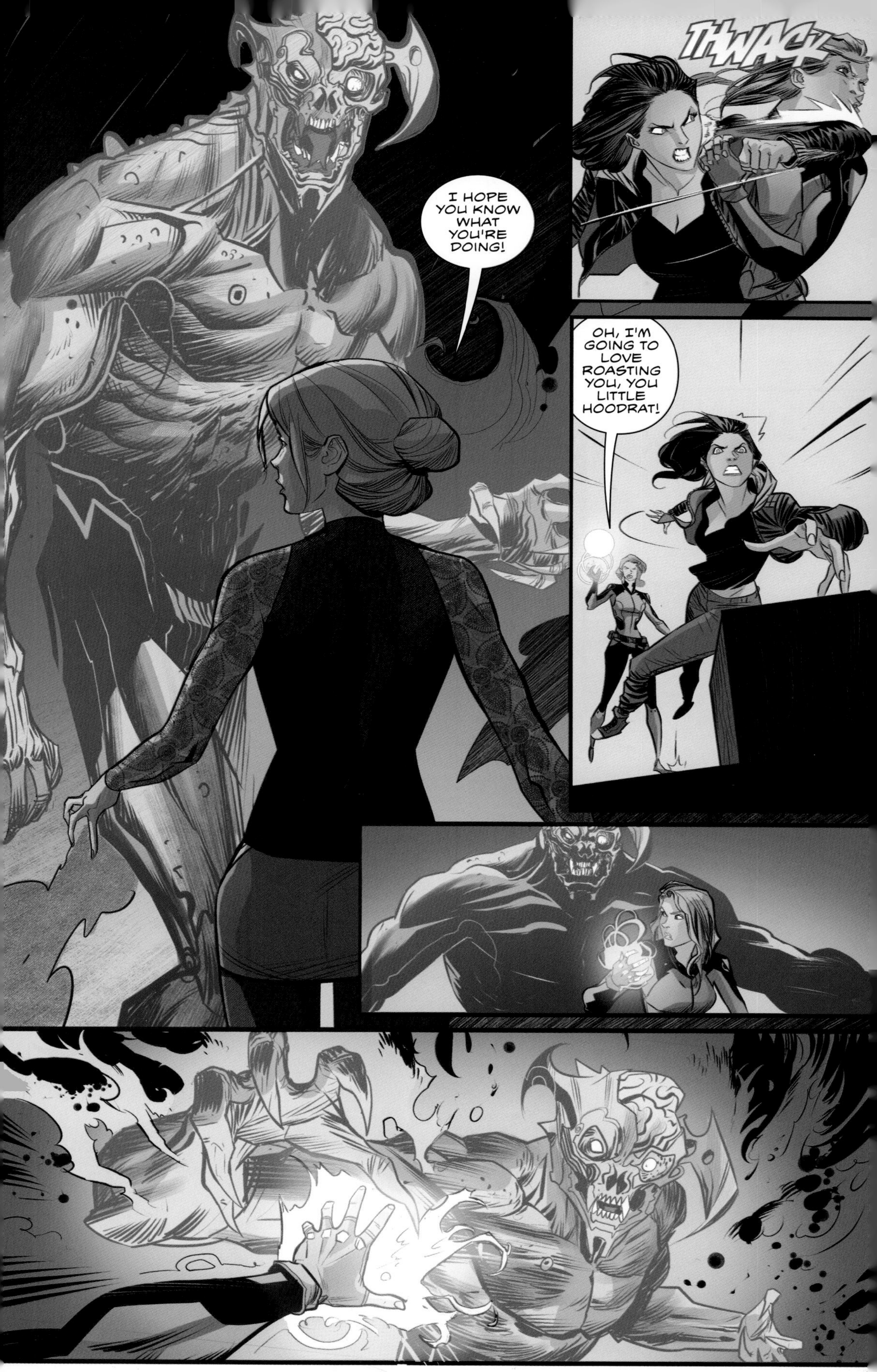
I HOPE YOU KNOW WHAT YOU'RE DOING!
THWACK
OH, I'M GOING TO LOVE ROASTING YOU, YOU LITTLE HOODRAT!

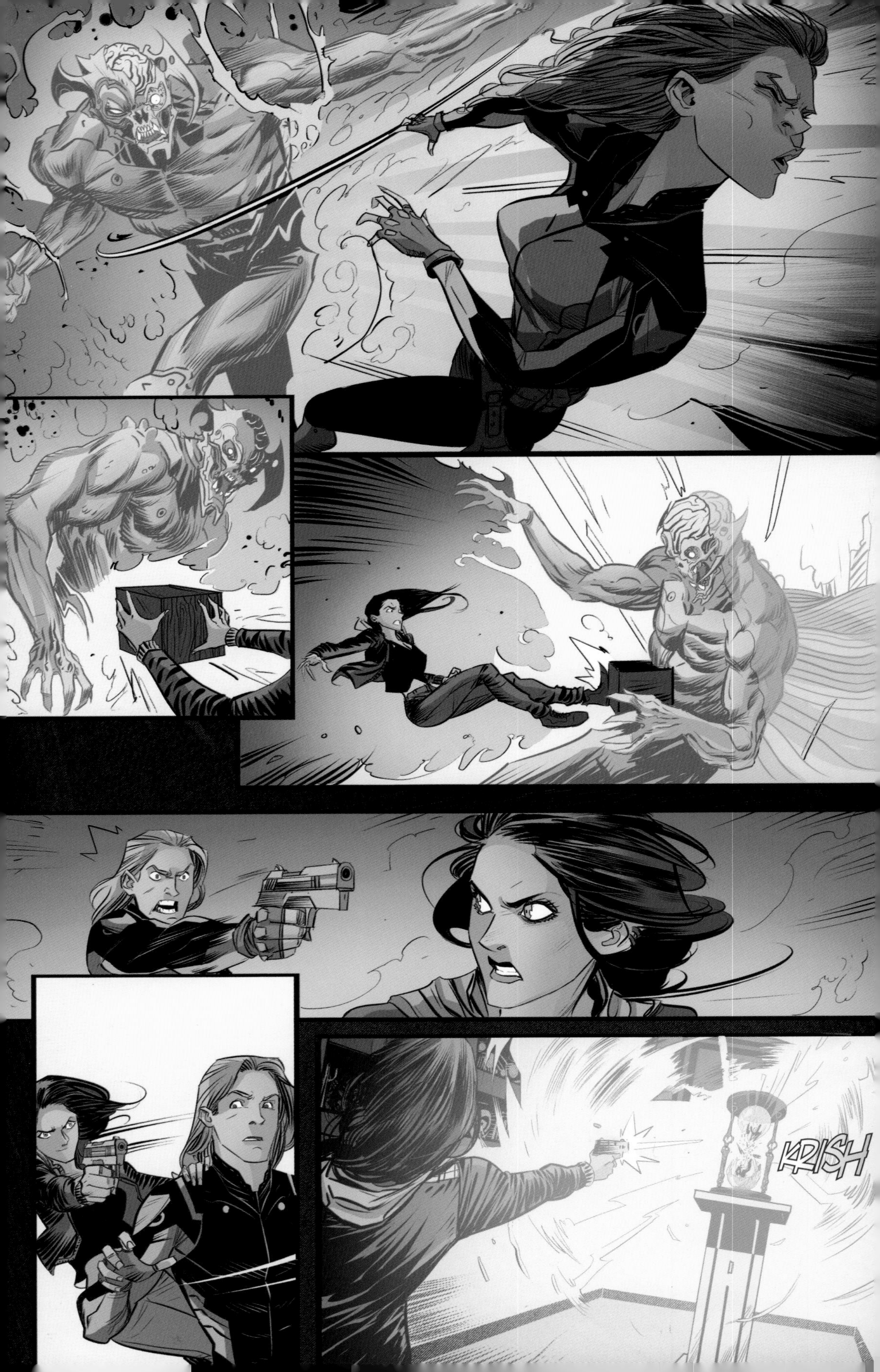
KRISH

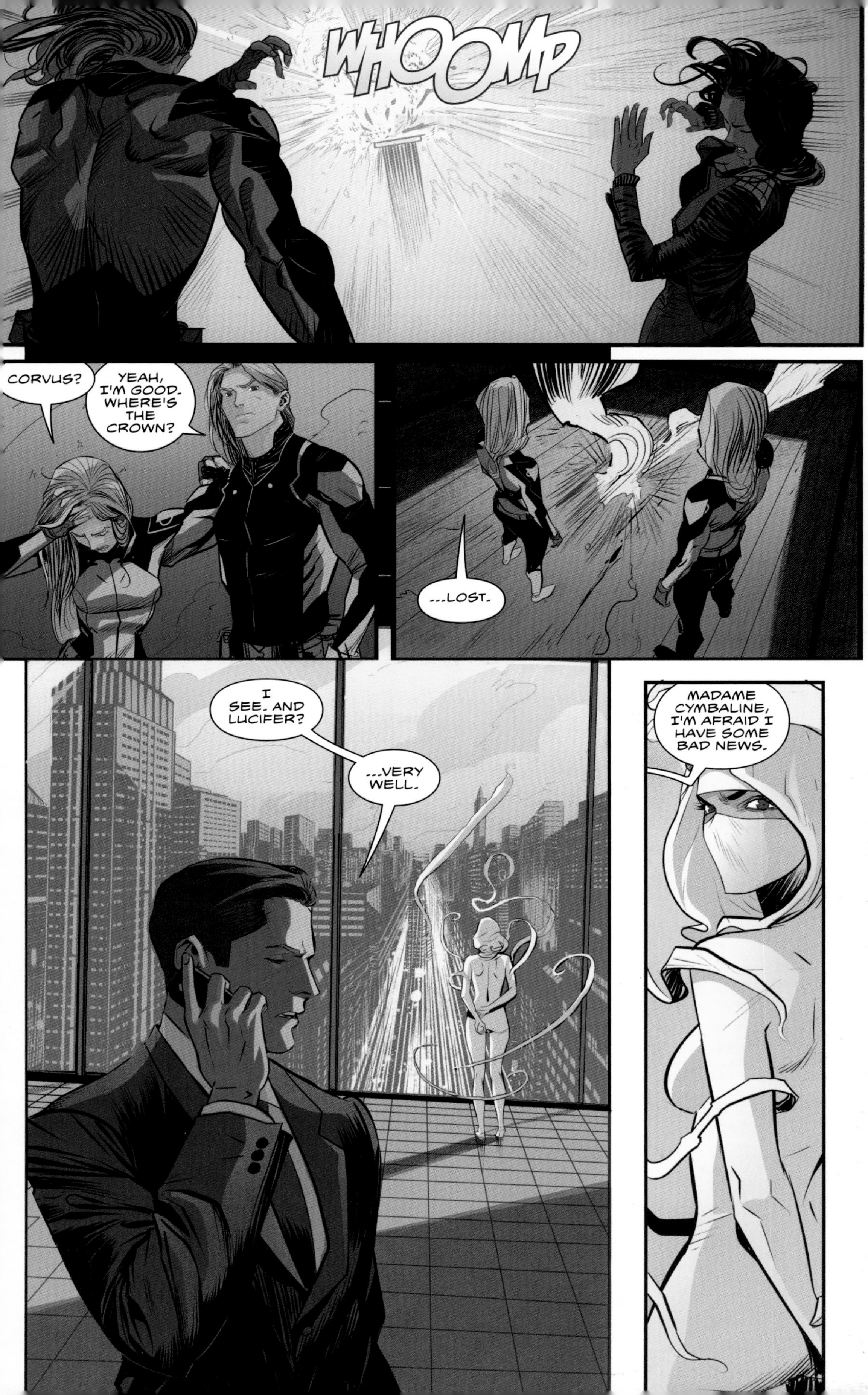
WHOOOMP
CORVUS?
YEAH, I'M GOOD. WHERE'S THE CROWN?
...LOST.
I SEE. AND LUCIFER?
...VERY WELL.
MADAME CYMBALINE, I'M AFRAID I HAVE SOME BAD NEWS.

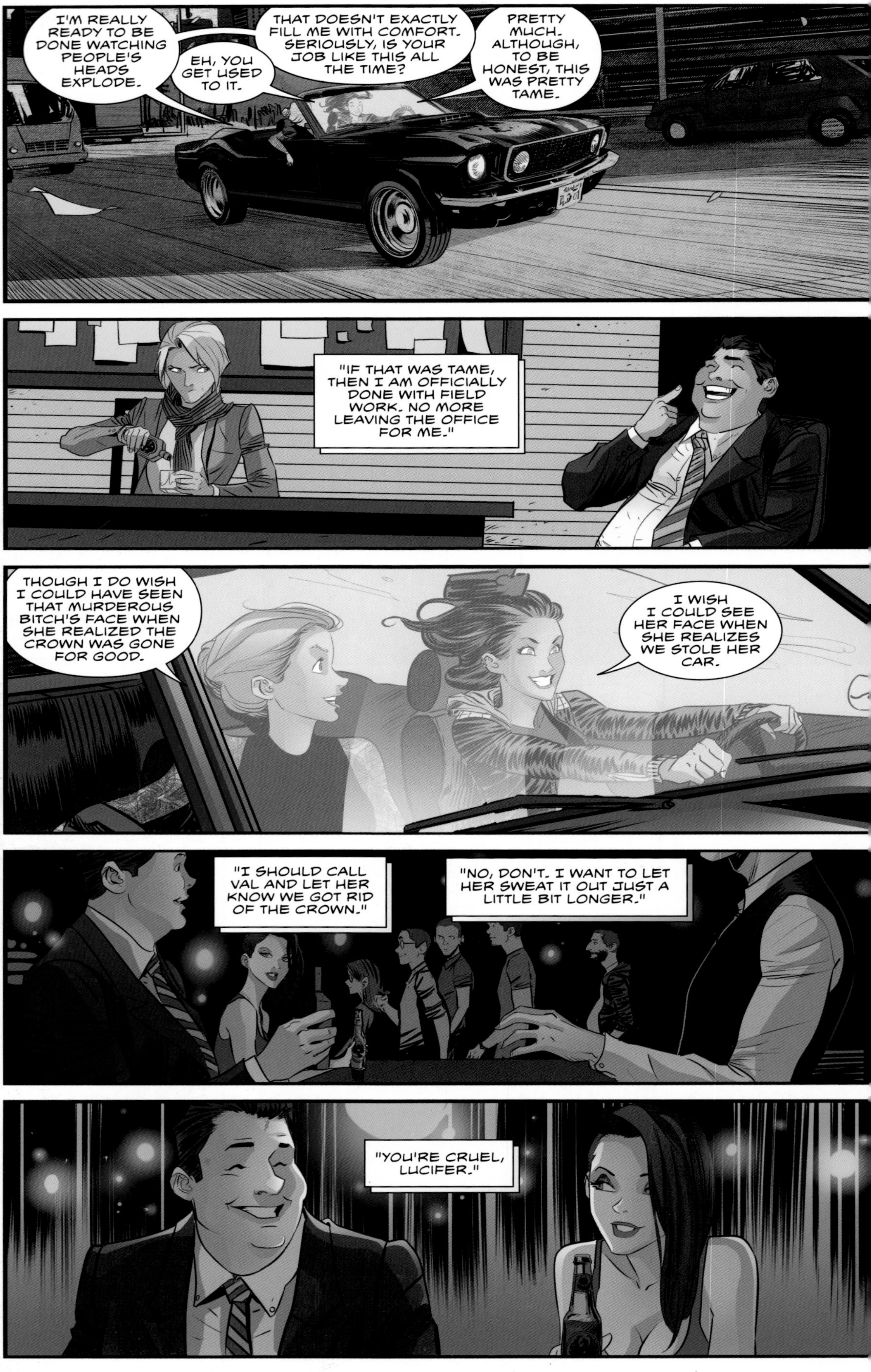
I'M REALLY READY TO BE DONE WATCHING PEOPLE'S HEADS EXPLODE.
EH, YOU GET USED TO IT.
THAT DOESN'T EXACTLY FILL ME WITH COMFORT. SERIOUSLY, IS YOUR JOB LIKE THIS ALL THE TIME?
PRETTY MUCH. ALTHOUGH, TO BE HONEST, THIS WAS PRETTY TAME.
"IF THAT WAS TAME, THEN I AM OFFICIALLY DONE WITH FIELD WORK. NO MORE LEAVING THE OFFICE FOR ME."
THOUGH I DO WISH I COULD HAVE SEEN THAT MURDEROUS BITCH'S FACE WHEN SHE REALIZED THE CROWN WAS GONE FOR GOOD.
I WISH I COULD SEE HER FACE WHEN SHE REALIZES WE STOLE HER CAR.
"I SHOULD CALL VAL AND LET HER KNOW WE GOT RID OF THE CROWN."
"NO, DON'T. I WANT TO LET HER SWEAT IT OUT JUST A LITTLE BIT LONGER."
"YOU'RE CRUEL, LUCIFER."

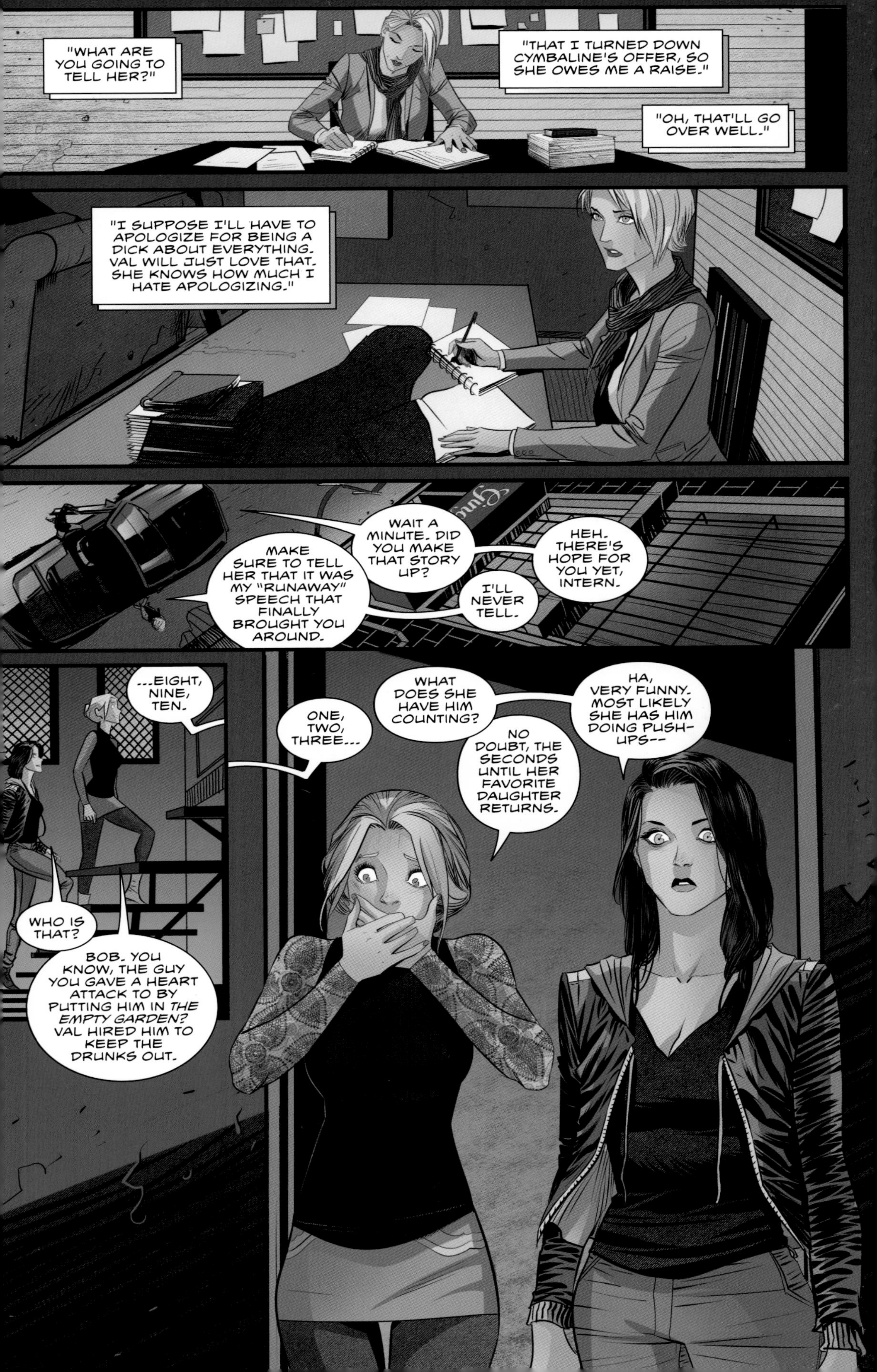
"WHAT ARE YOU GOING TO TELL HER?"
"THAT I TURNED DOWN CYMBALINE'S OFFER, SO SHE OWES ME A RAISE."
"OH, THAT'LL GO OVER WELL."
"I SUPPOSE I'LL HAVE TO APOLOGIZE FOR BEING A DICK ABOUT EVERYTHING. VAL WILL JUST LOVE THAT. SHE KNOWS HOW MUCH I HATE APOLOGIZING."
MAKE SURE TO TELL HER THAT IT WAS MY "RUNAWAY" SPEECH THAT FINALLY BROUGHT YOU AROUND.
WAIT A MINUTE. DID YOU MAKE THAT STORY UP?
I'LL NEVER TELL.
HEH. THERE'S HOPE FOR YOU YET, INTERN.
...EIGHT, NINE, TEN.
ONE, TWO, THREE...
WHAT DOES SHE HAVE HIM COUNTING?
HA, VERY FUNNY. MOST LIKELY SHE HAS HIM DOING PUSH-UPS--
NO DOUBT, THE SECONDS UNTIL HER FAVORITE DAUGHTER RETURNS.
WHO IS THAT?
BOB. YOU KNOW, THE GUY YOU GAVE A HEART ATTACK TO BY PUTTING HIM IN *THE EMPTY GARDEN*? VAL HIRED HIM TO KEEP THE DRUNKS OUT.

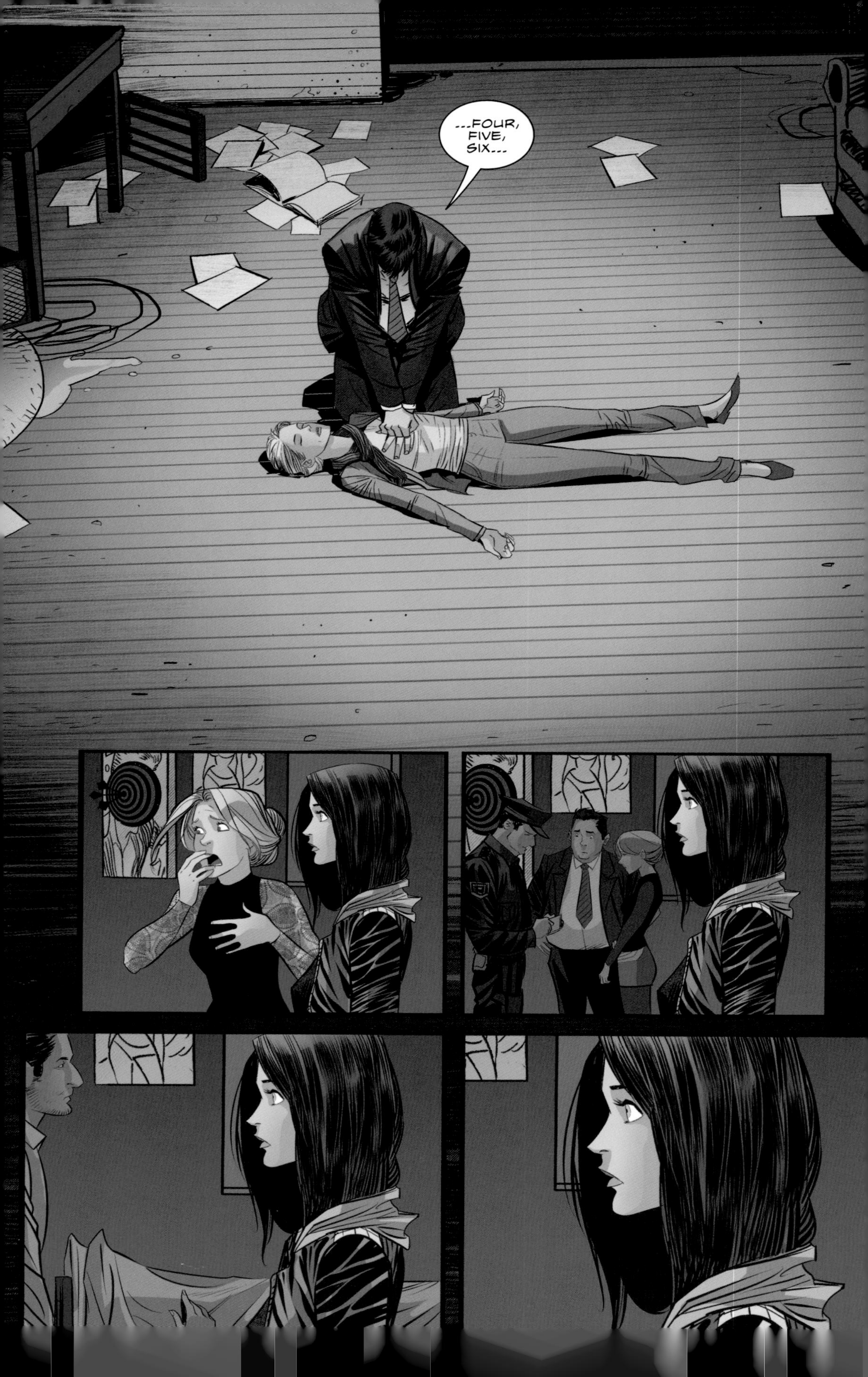
...FOUR, FIVE, SIX...

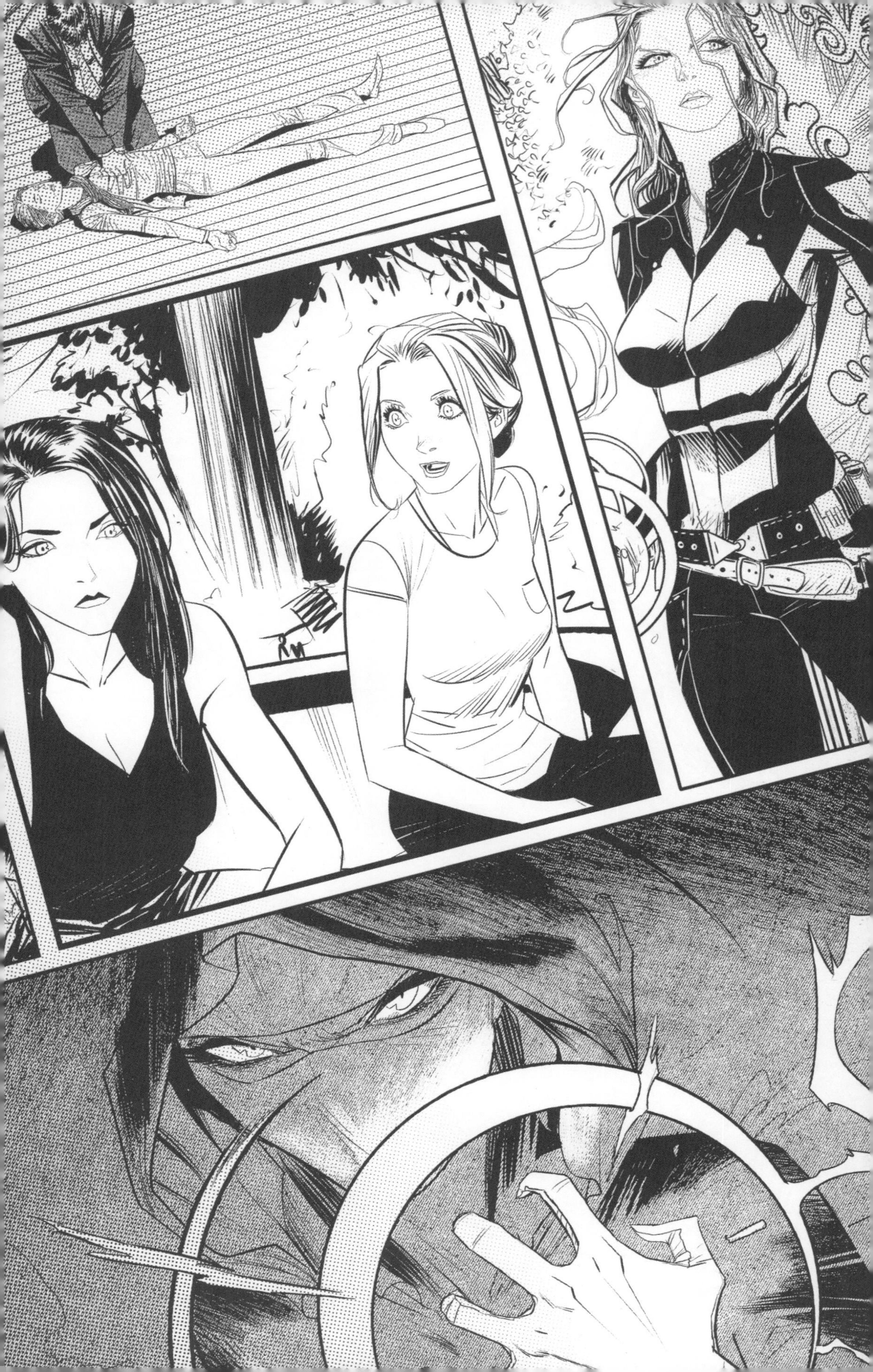

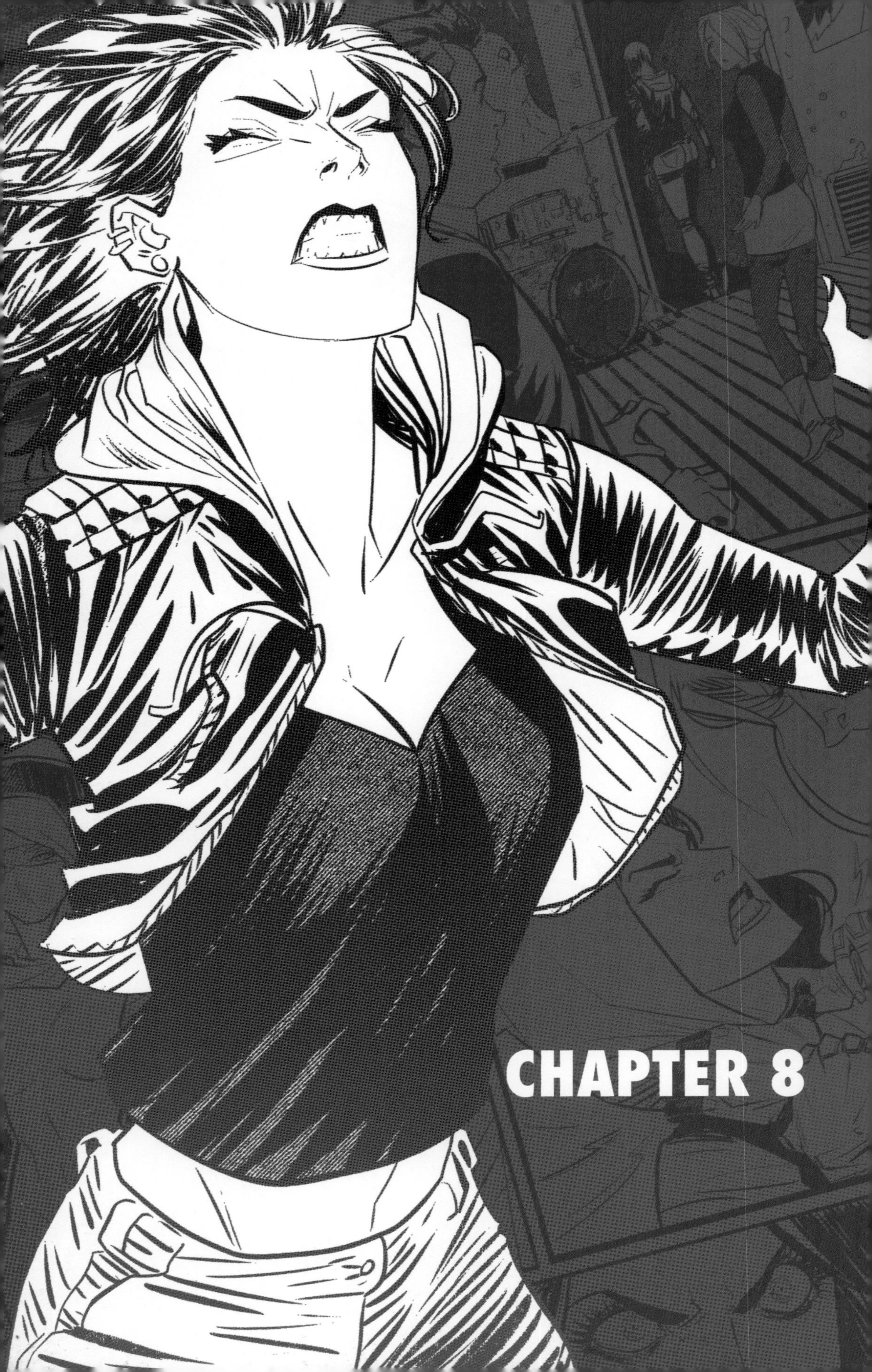

CHAPTER 8

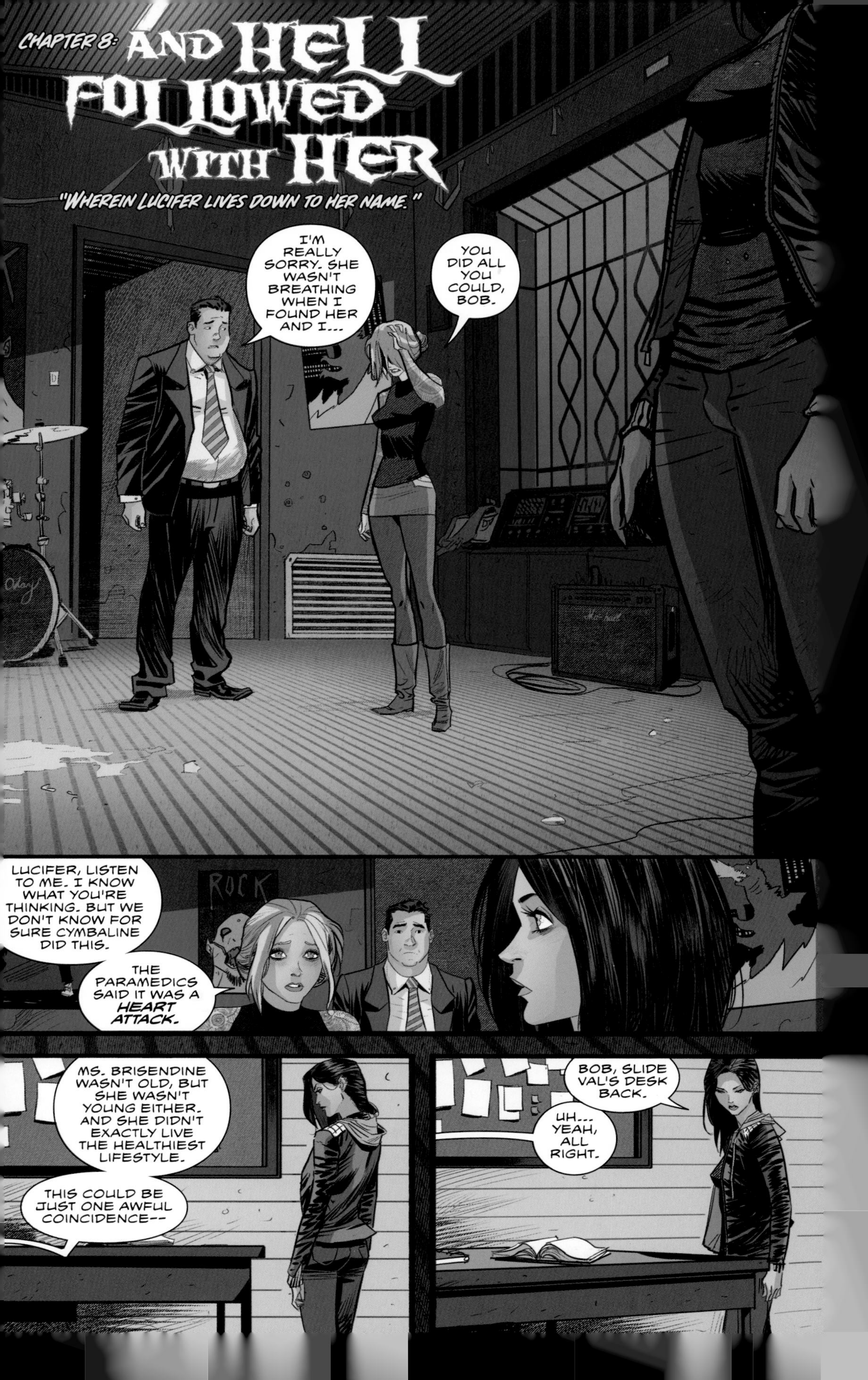
CHAPTER 8: AND HELL FOLLOWED WITH HER
"WHEREIN LUCIFER LIVES DOWN TO HER NAME."
I'M REALLY SORRY. SHE WASN'T BREATHING WHEN I FOUND HER AND I...
YOU DID ALL YOU COULD, BOB.
LUCIFER, LISTEN TO ME. I KNOW WHAT YOU'RE THINKING. BUT WE DON'T KNOW FOR SURE CYMBALINE DID THIS.
THE PARAMEDICS SAID IT WAS A HEART ATTACK.
MS. BRISENDINE WASN'T OLD, BUT SHE WASN'T YOUNG EITHER. AND SHE DIDN'T EXACTLY LIVE THE HEALTHIEST LIFESTYLE.
THIS COULD BE JUST ONE AWFUL COINCIDENCE--
BOB, SLIDE VAL'S DESK BACK.
UH... YEAH, ALL RIGHT.

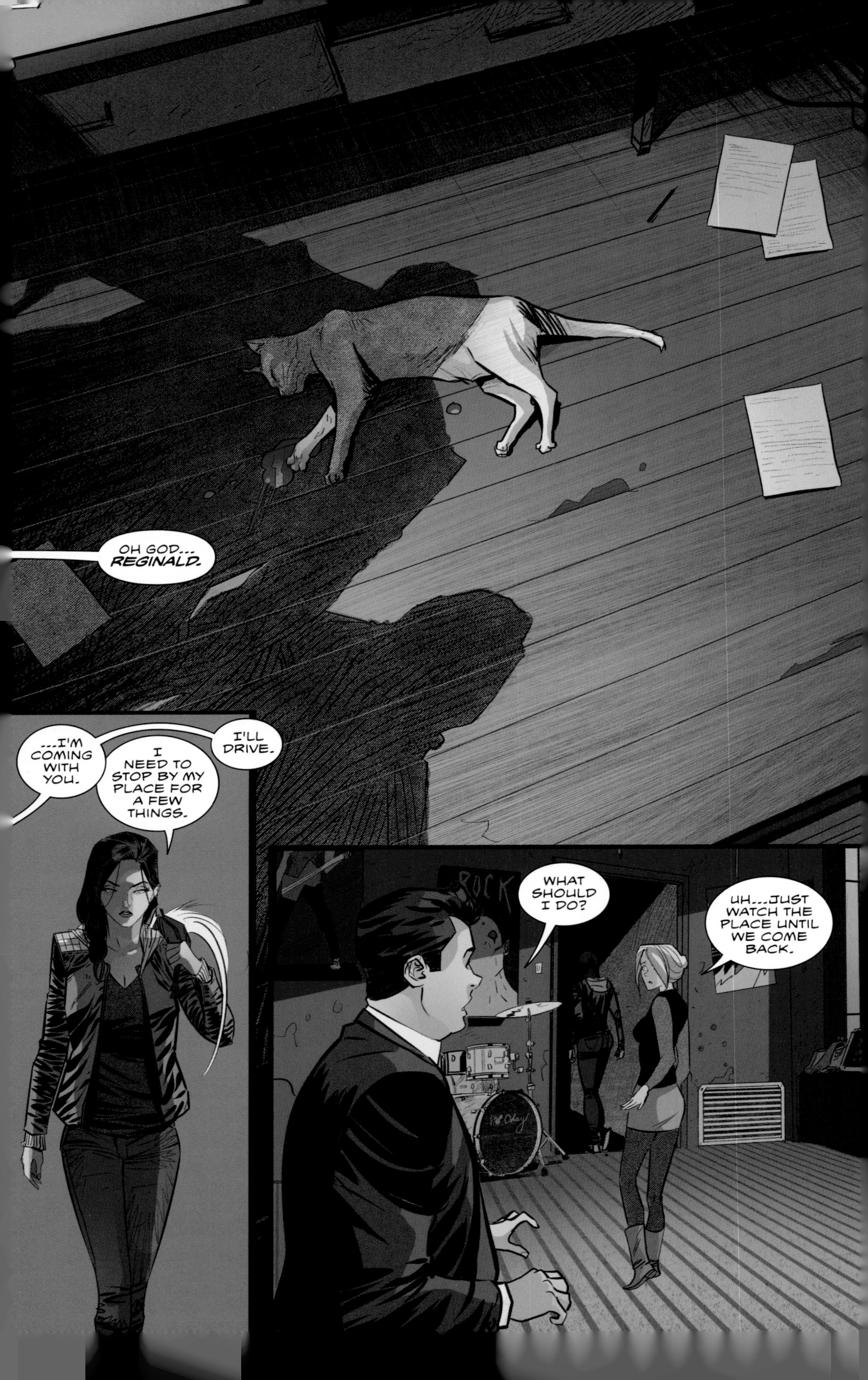

OH GOD... REGINALD.
...I'M COMING WITH YOU.
I NEED TO STOP BY MY PLACE FOR A FEW THINGS.
I'LL DRIVE.
ROCK
WHAT SHOULD I DO?
UH...JUST WATCH THE PLACE UNTIL WE COME BACK.

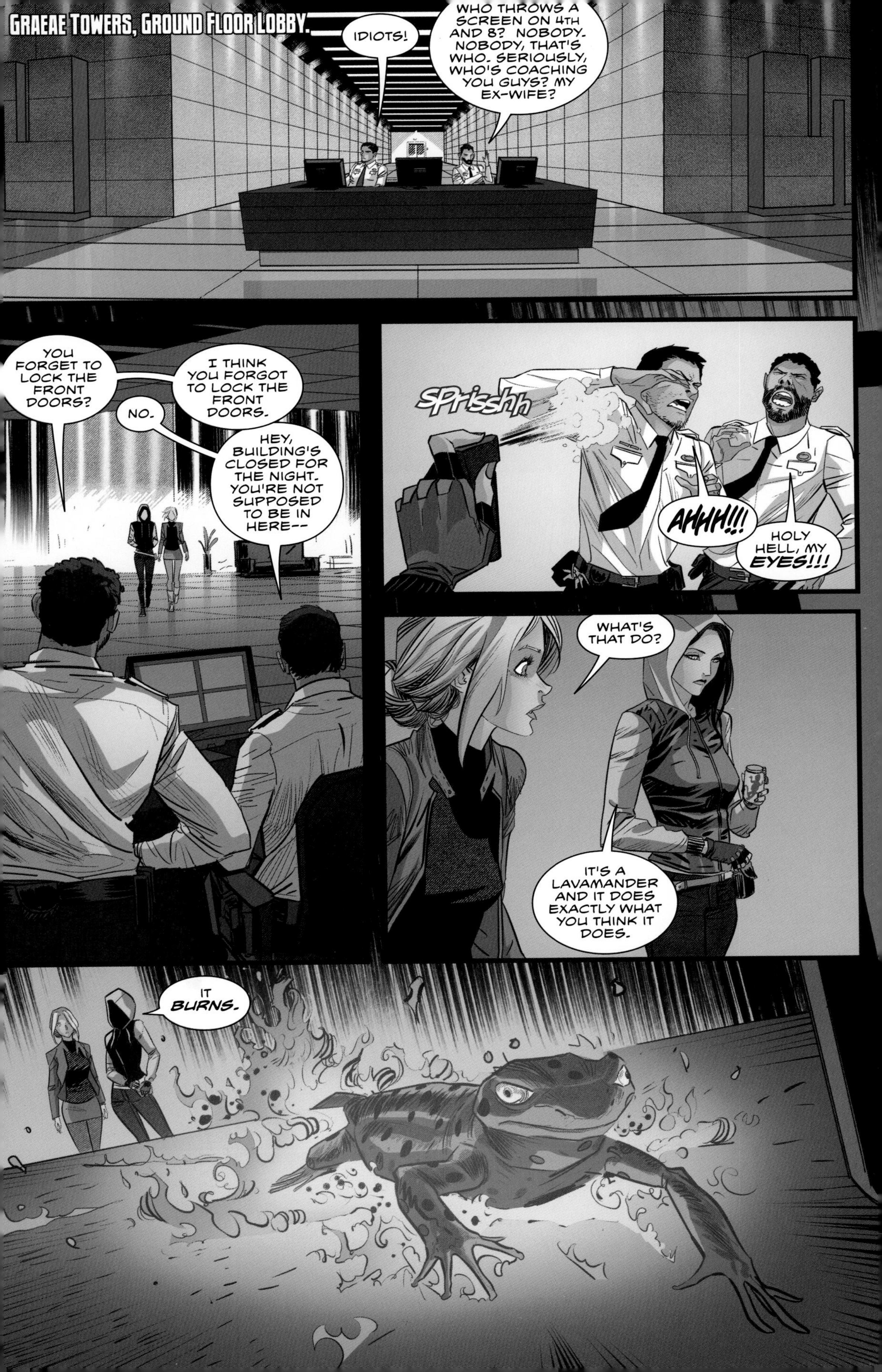
GRAEAE TOWERS, GROUND FLOOR LOBBY.
IDIOTS!
WHO THROWS A SCREEN ON 4TH AND 8? NOBODY. NOBODY, THAT'S WHO. SERIOUSLY, WHO'S COACHING YOU GUYS? MY EX-WIFE?
YOU FORGET TO LOCK THE FRONT DOORS?
I THINK YOU FORGOT TO LOCK THE FRONT DOORS.
NO.
HEY, BUILDING'S CLOSED FOR THE NIGHT. YOU'RE NOT SUPPOSED TO BE IN HERE--
SPRISSHH
AHHH!!!
HOLY HELL, MY EYES!!!
WHAT'S THAT DO?
IT'S A LAVAMANDER AND IT DOES EXACTLY WHAT YOU THINK IT DOES.
IT BURNS.

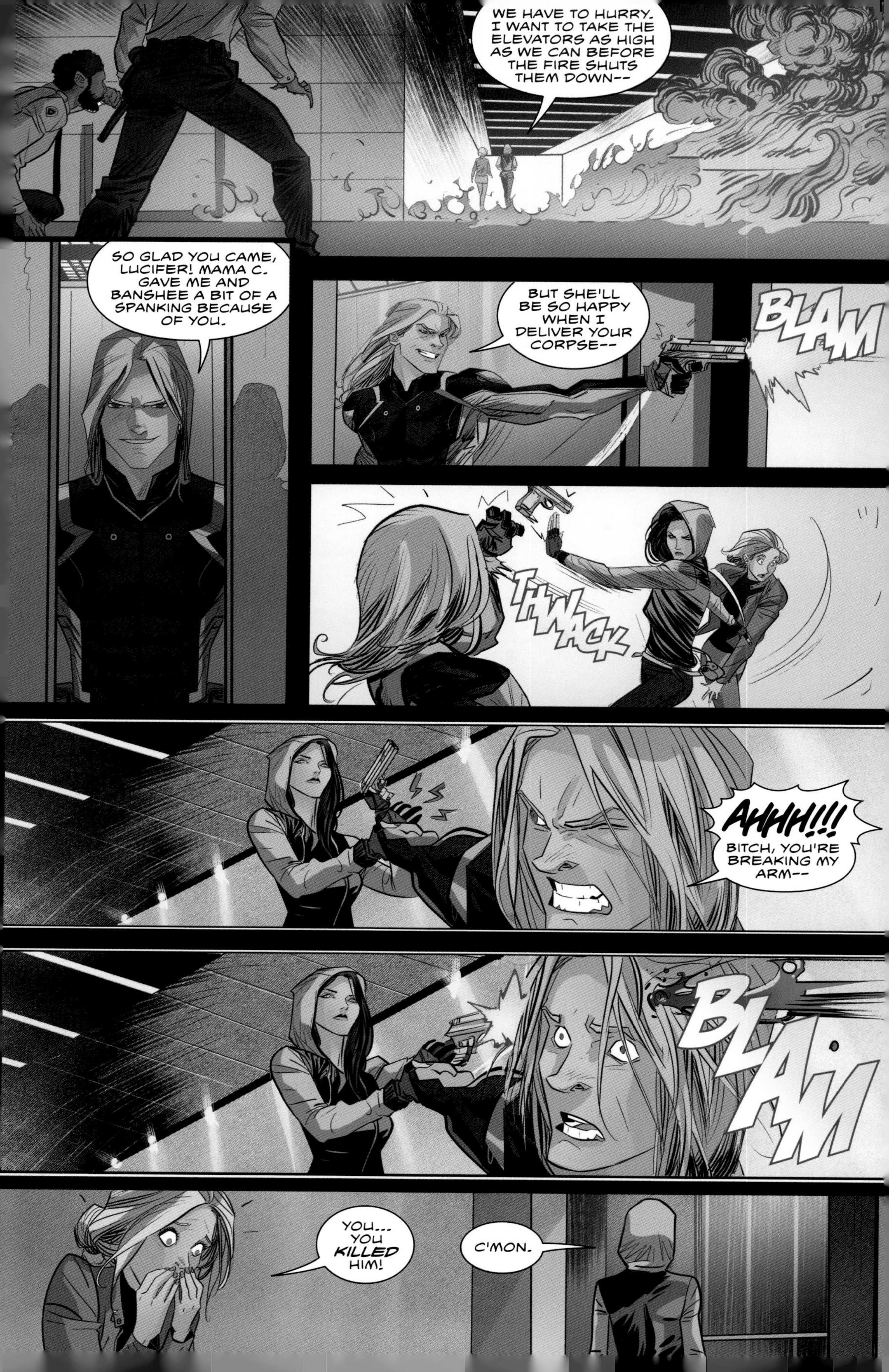

WE HAVE TO HURRY. I WANT TO TAKE THE ELEVATORS AS HIGH AS WE CAN BEFORE THE FIRE SHUTS THEM DOWN--
SO GLAD YOU CAME, LUCIFER! MAMA C. GAVE ME AND BANSHEE A BIT OF A SPANKING BECAUSE OF YOU.
BUT SHE'LL BE SO HAPPY WHEN I DELIVER YOUR CORPSE--
BLAM
THWACK
AHHH!!!
BITCH, YOU'RE BREAKING MY ARM--
BLAM
YOU... YOU KILLED HIM!
C'MON.

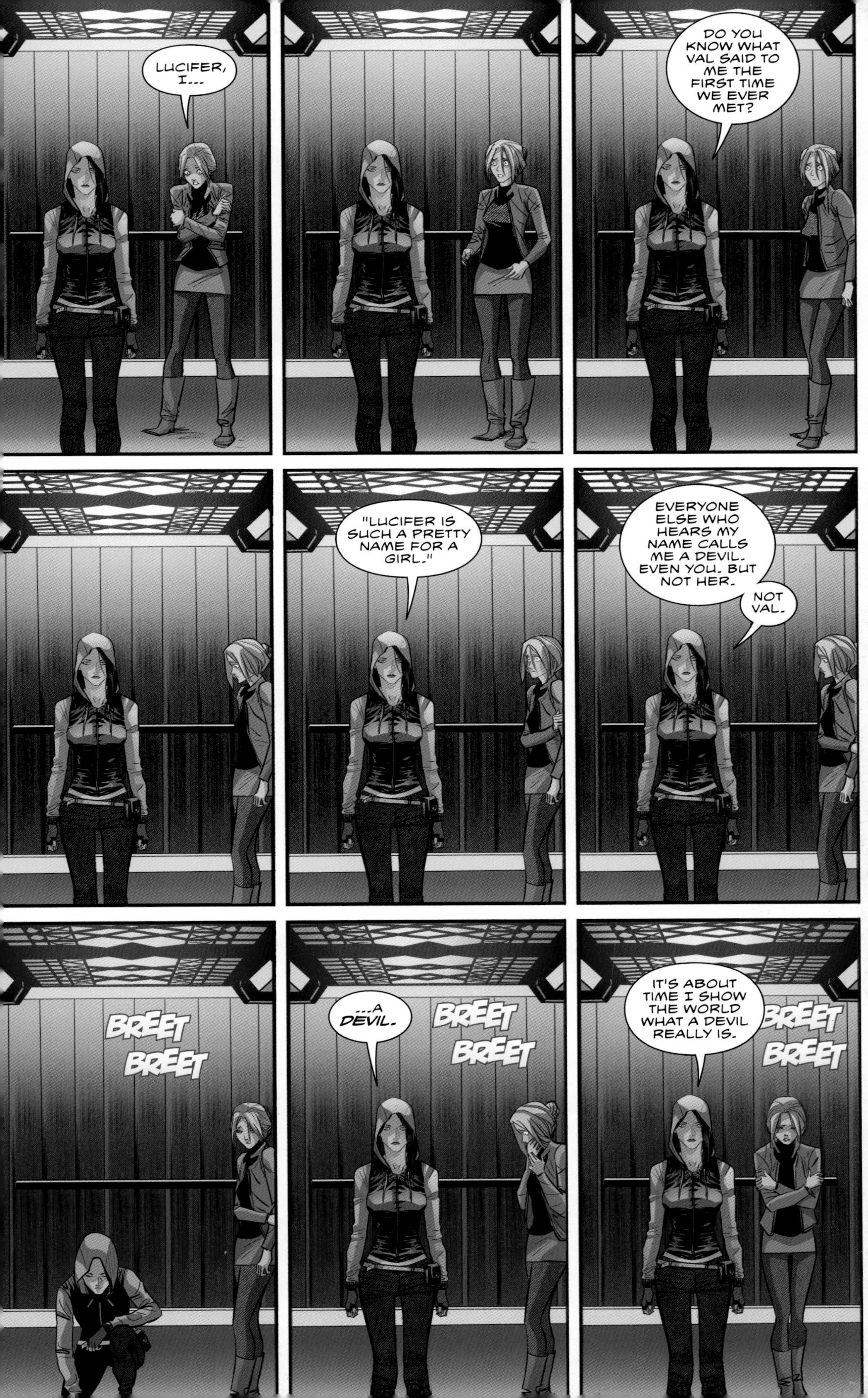
LUCIFER, I...
DO YOU KNOW WHAT VAL SAID TO ME THE FIRST TIME WE EVER MET?
"LUCIFER IS SUCH A PRETTY NAME FOR A GIRL."
EVERYONE ELSE WHO HEARS MY NAME CALLS ME A DEVIL. EVEN YOU. BUT NOT HER.
NOT VAL.
BREET BREET
...A DEVIL.
BREET BREET
IT'S ABOUT TIME I SHOW THE WORLD WHAT A DEVIL REALLY IS.
BREET BREET

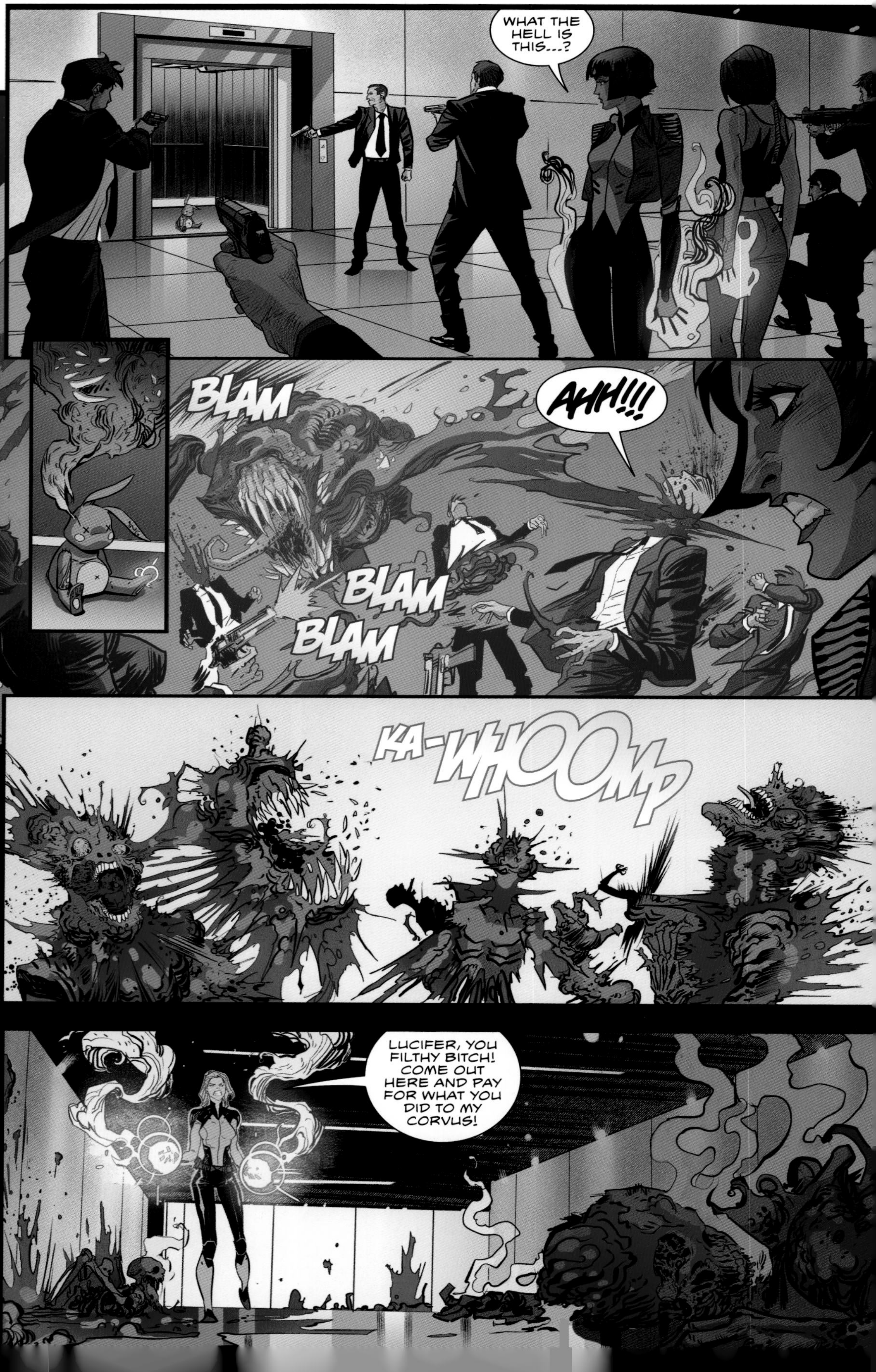
WHAT THE HELL IS THIS...?
BLAM
AHH!!!
BLAM
BLAM
KA-WHOOMP
LUCIFER, YOU FILTHY BITCH! COME OUT HERE AND PAY FOR WHAT YOU DID TO MY CORVUS!

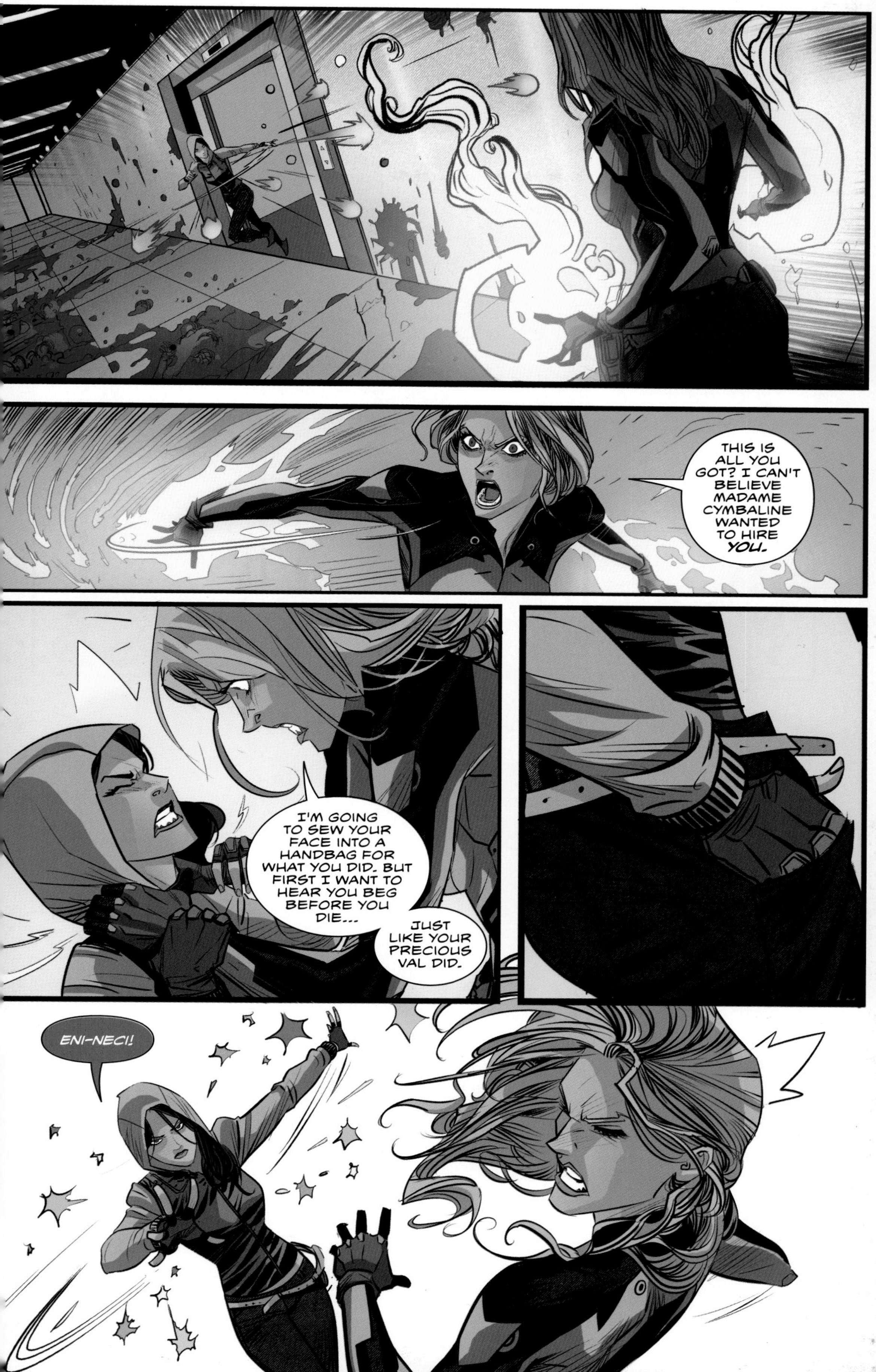
THIS IS ALL YOU GOT? I CAN'T BELIEVE MADAME CYMBALINE WANTED TO HIRE YOU.
I'M GOING TO SEW YOUR FACE INTO A HANDBAG FOR WHAT YOU DID. BUT FIRST I WANT TO HEAR YOU BEG BEFORE YOU DIE...
JUST LIKE YOUR PRECIOUS VAL DID.
ENI-NECI!

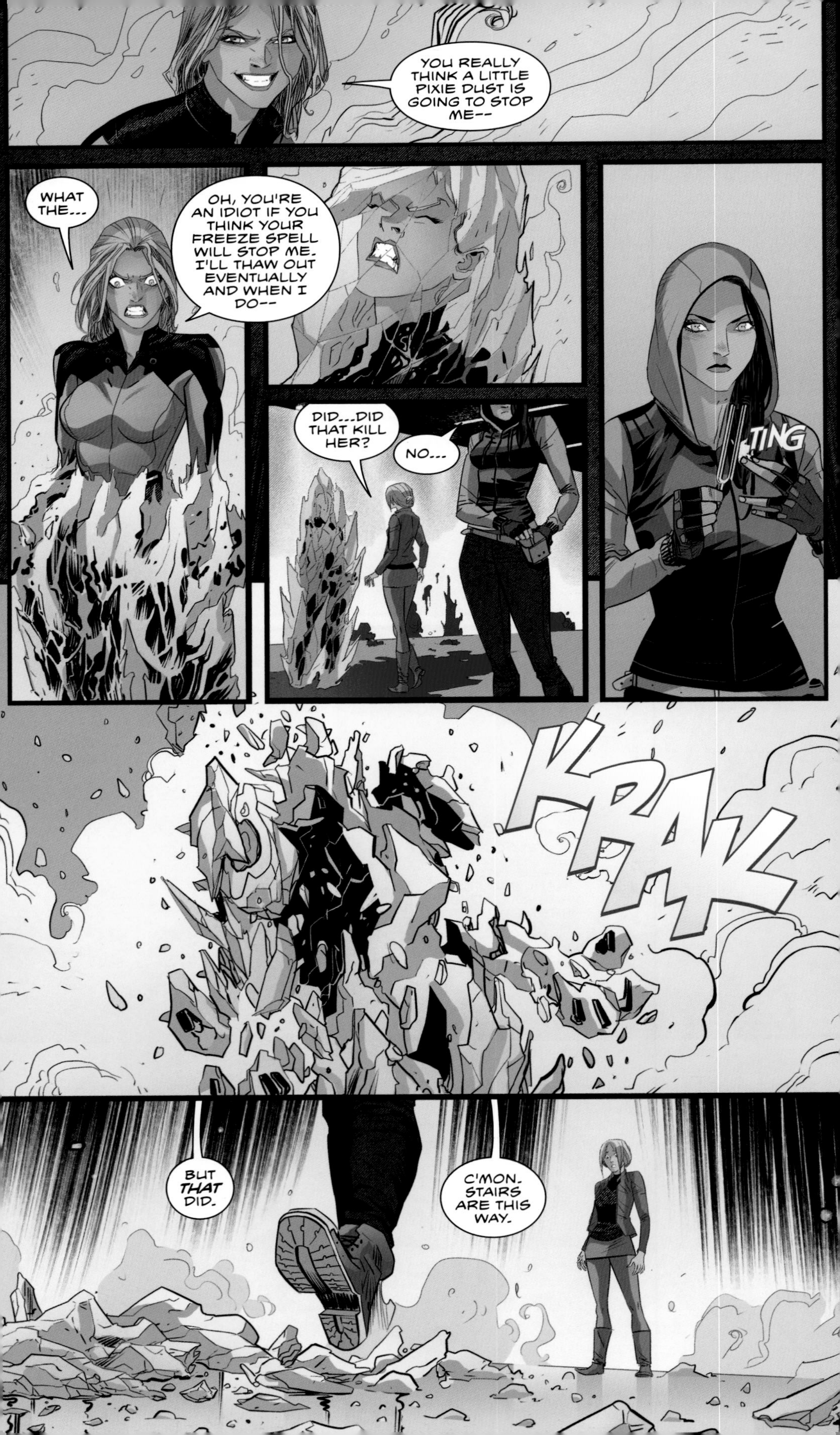
YOU REALLY THINK A LITTLE PIXIE DUST IS GOING TO STOP ME--
WHAT THE...
OH, YOU'RE AN IDIOT IF YOU THINK YOUR FREEZE SPELL WILL STOP ME. I'LL THAW OUT EVENTUALLY AND WHEN I DO--
DID...DID THAT KILL HER?
NO...
TING
KRAK
BUT *THAT* DID.
C'MON. STAIRS ARE THIS WAY.

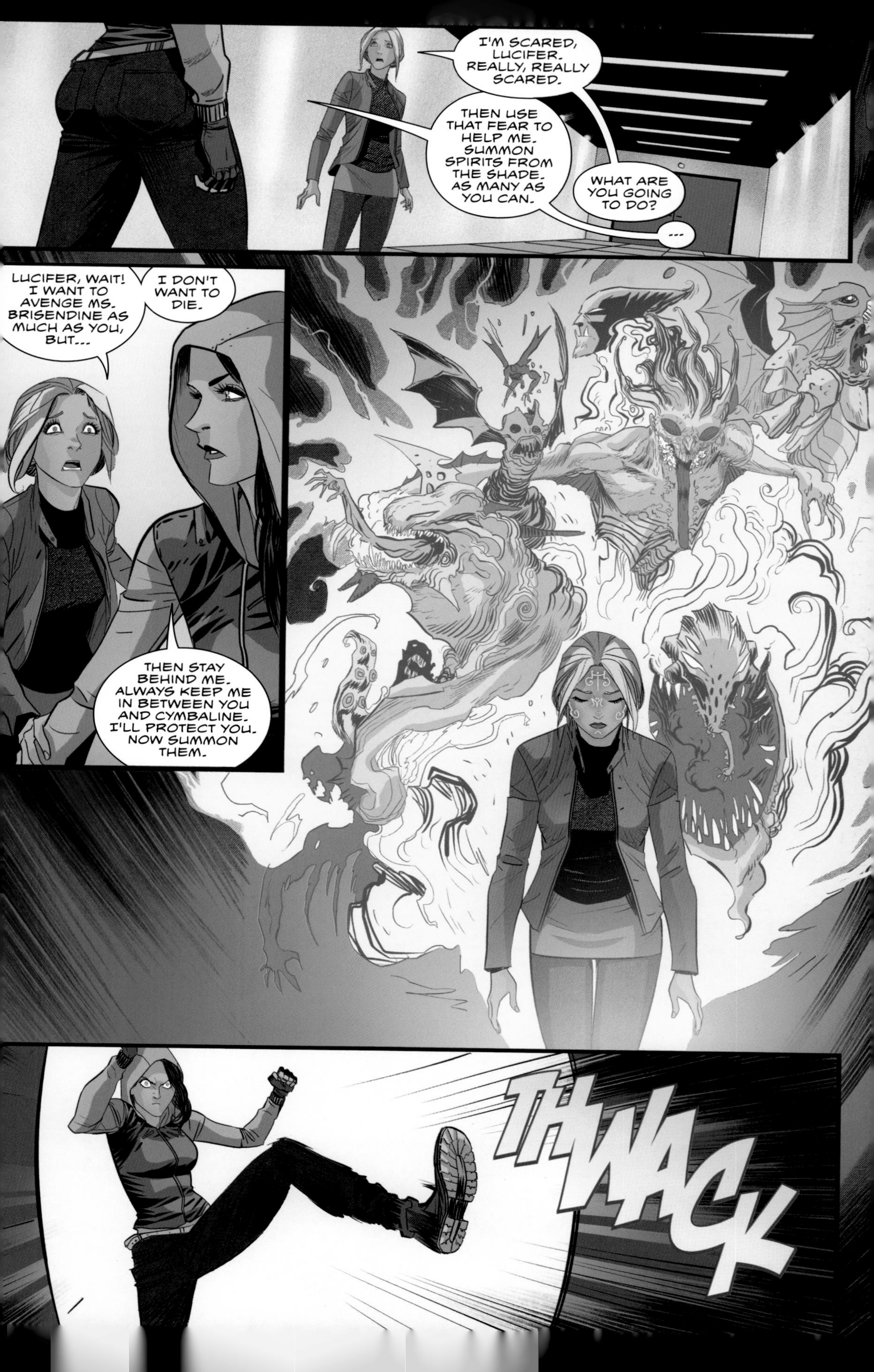
I'M SCARED, LUCIFER. REALLY, REALLY SCARED.
THEN USE THAT FEAR TO HELP ME. SUMMON SPIRITS FROM THE SHADE. AS MANY AS YOU CAN.
WHAT ARE YOU GOING TO DO?
...
LUCIFER, WAIT! I WANT TO AVENGE MS. BRISENDINE AS MUCH AS YOU, BUT...
I DON'T WANT TO DIE.
THEN STAY BEHIND ME. ALWAYS KEEP ME IN BETWEEN YOU AND CYMBALINE. I'LL PROTECT YOU. NOW SUMMON THEM.
THWACK

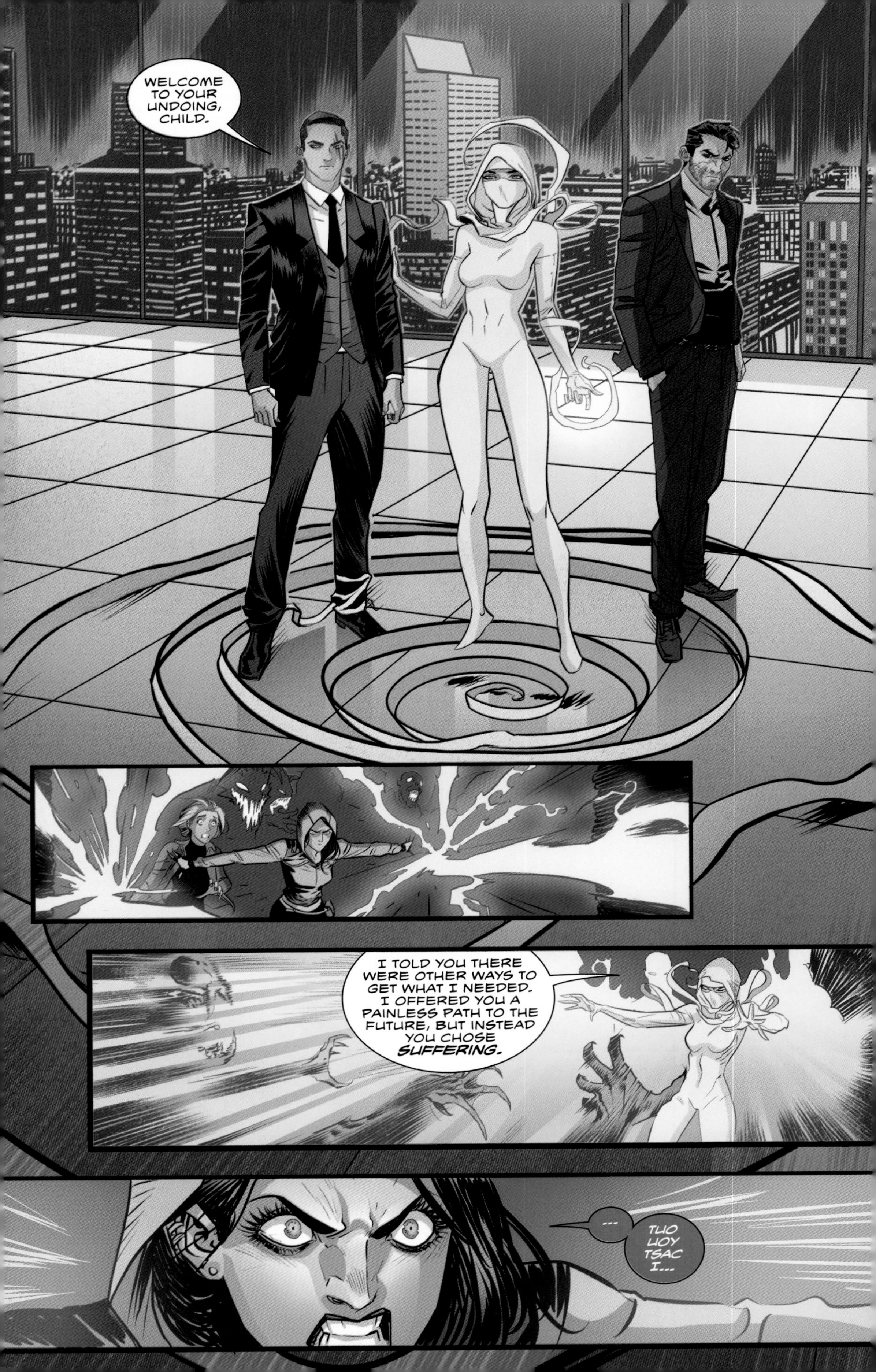
WELCOME TO YOUR UNDOING, CHILD.
I TOLD YOU THERE WERE OTHER WAYS TO GET WHAT I NEEDED. I OFFERED YOU A PAINLESS PATH TO THE FUTURE, BUT INSTEAD YOU CHOSE SUFFERING.
...
TUO UOY TSAC I...

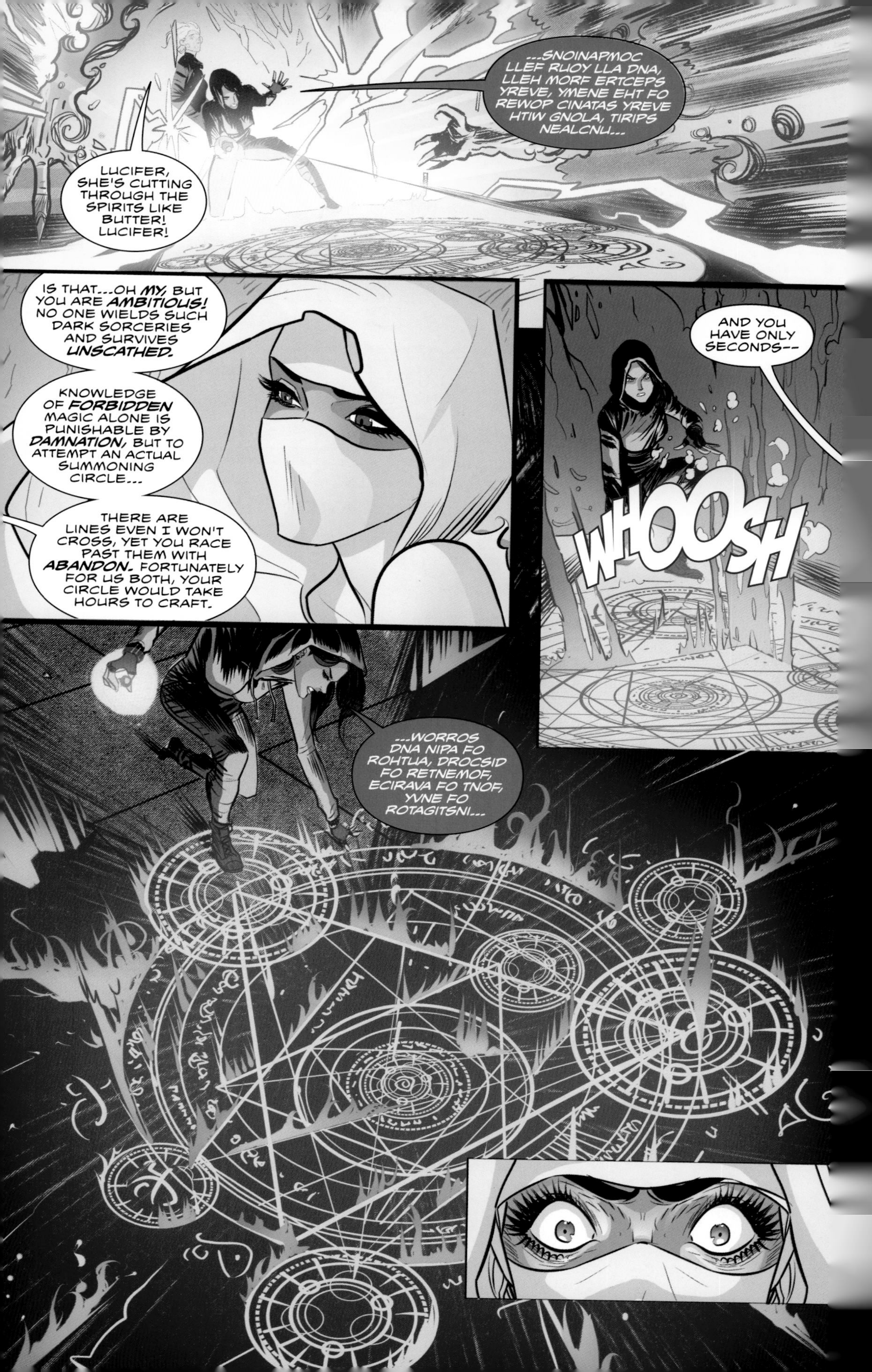

...SNOINAPMOC LLEF RUOY LLA DNA, LLEH MORF ERTCEPS YREVE, YMENE EHT FO REWOP CINATAS YREVE HTIW GNOLA, TIRIPS NEALCNU...
LUCIFER, SHE'S CUTTING THROUGH THE SPIRITS LIKE BUTTER! LUCIFER!
IS THAT...OH MY, BUT YOU ARE AMBITIOUS! NO ONE WIELDS SUCH DARK SORCERIES AND SURVIVES UNSCATHED.
KNOWLEDGE OF FORBIDDEN MAGIC ALONE IS PUNISHABLE BY DAMNATION, BUT TO ATTEMPT AN ACTUAL SUMMONING CIRCLE...
THERE ARE LINES EVEN I WON'T CROSS, YET YOU RACE PAST THEM WITH ABANDON. FORTUNATELY FOR US BOTH, YOUR CIRCLE WOULD TAKE HOURS TO CRAFT.
AND YOU HAVE ONLY SECONDS--
WHOOSH
...WORROS DNA NIPA FO ROHTUA, DROCSID FO RETNEMOF, ECIRAVA FO TNOF, YVNE FO ROTAGITSNI...

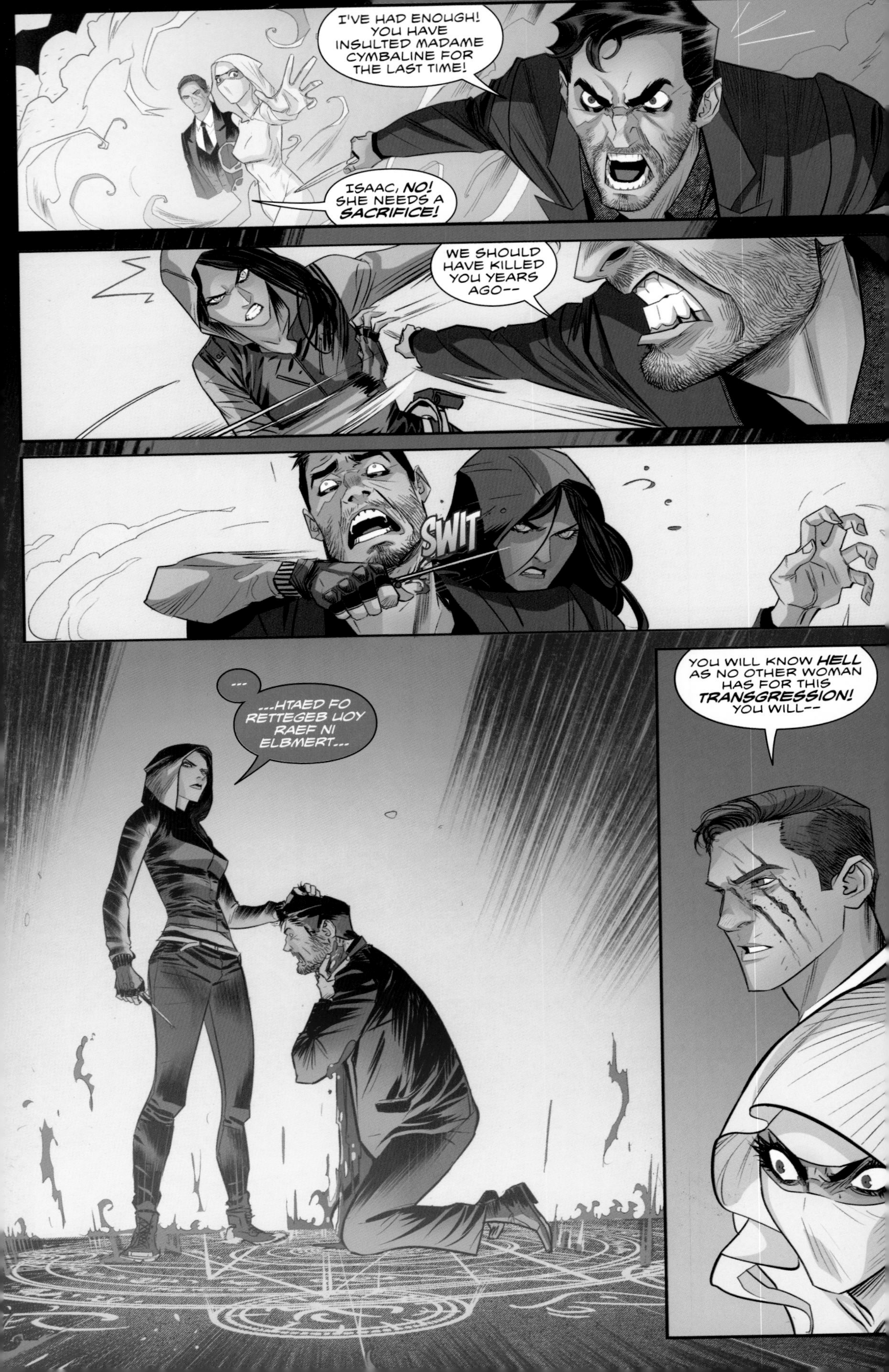

I'VE HAD ENOUGH! YOU HAVE INSULTED MADAME CYMBALINE FOR THE LAST TIME!
ISAAC, NO! SHE NEEDS A SACRIFICE!
WE SHOULD HAVE KILLED YOU YEARS AGO--
SWIT
...
...HTAED FO RETTEGEB UOY RAEF NI ELBMERT...
YOU WILL KNOW HELL AS NO OTHER WOMAN HAS FOR THIS TRANSGRESSION! YOU WILL--

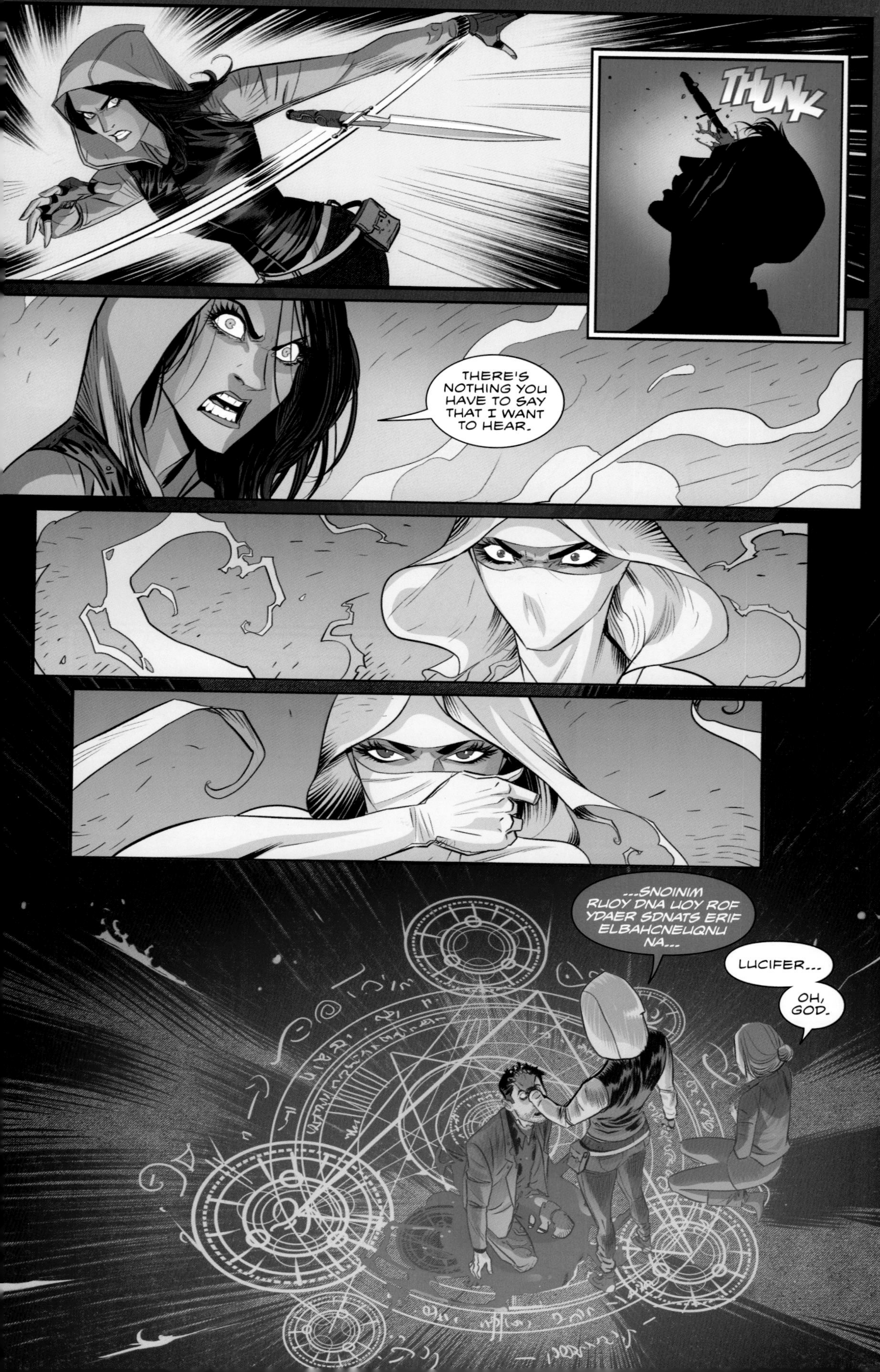
THUNK
THERE'S NOTHING YOU HAVE TO SAY THAT I WANT TO HEAR.
...SNOINIM RUOY DNA UOY ROF YDAER SDNATS ERIF ELBAHCNEUQNU NA...
LUCIFER...
OH, GOD.

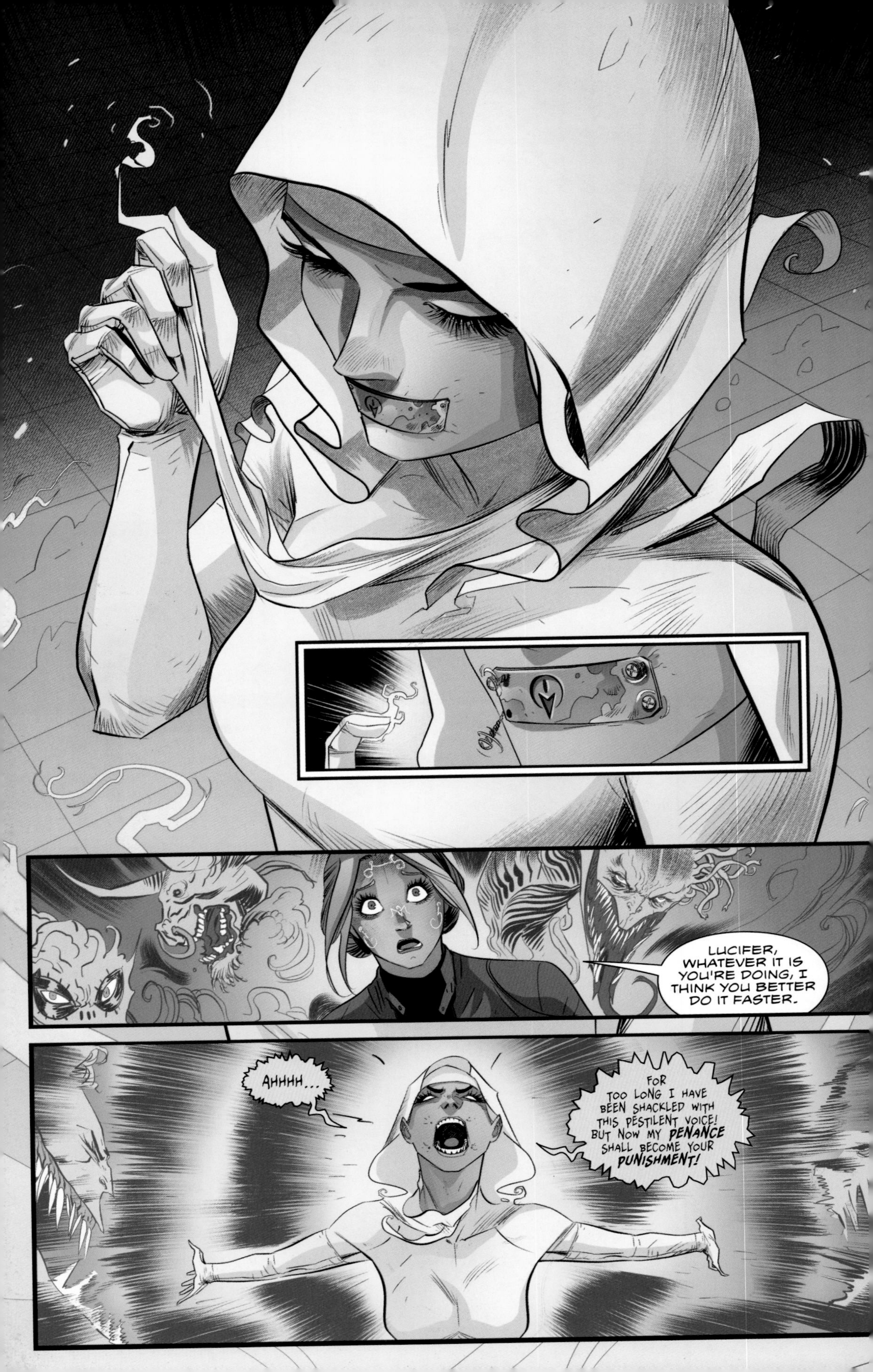
LUCIFER, WHATEVER IT IS YOU'RE DOING, I THINK YOU BETTER DO IT FASTER.
AHHHH...
FOR TOO LONG I HAVE BEEN SHACKLED WITH THIS PESTILENT VOICE! BUT NOW MY PENANCE SHALL BECOME YOUR PUNISHMENT!

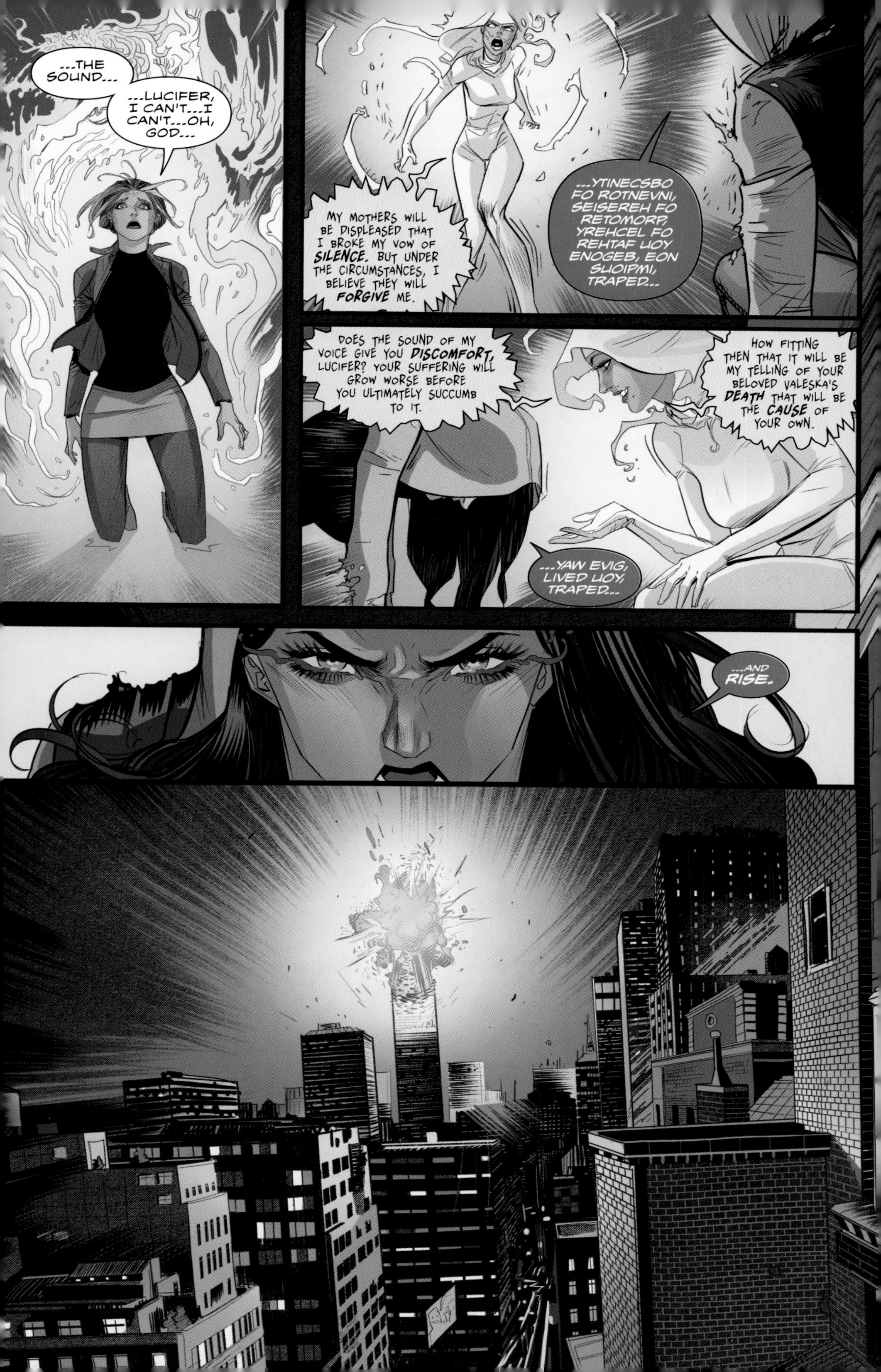

...THE SOUND...
...LUCIFER, I CAN'T...I CAN'T...OH, GOD...
MY MOTHERS WILL BE DISPLEASED THAT I BROKE MY VOW OF SILENCE. BUT UNDER THE CIRCUMSTANCES, I BELIEVE THEY WILL FORGIVE ME.
...YTINECSBO FO ROTNEVNI, SEISEREH FO RETOMORP, YREHCEL FO REHTAF UOY ENOGEB, EON SUOIPMI, TRAPED...
DOES THE SOUND OF MY VOICE GIVE YOU DISCOMFORT, LUCIFER? YOUR SUFFERING WILL GROW WORSE BEFORE YOU ULTIMATELY SUCCUMB TO IT.
HOW FITTING THEN THAT IT WILL BE MY TELLING OF YOUR BELOVED VALESKA'S DEATH THAT WILL BE THE CAUSE OF YOUR OWN.
...YAW EVIG, LIVED UOY, TRAPED...
...AND RISE.

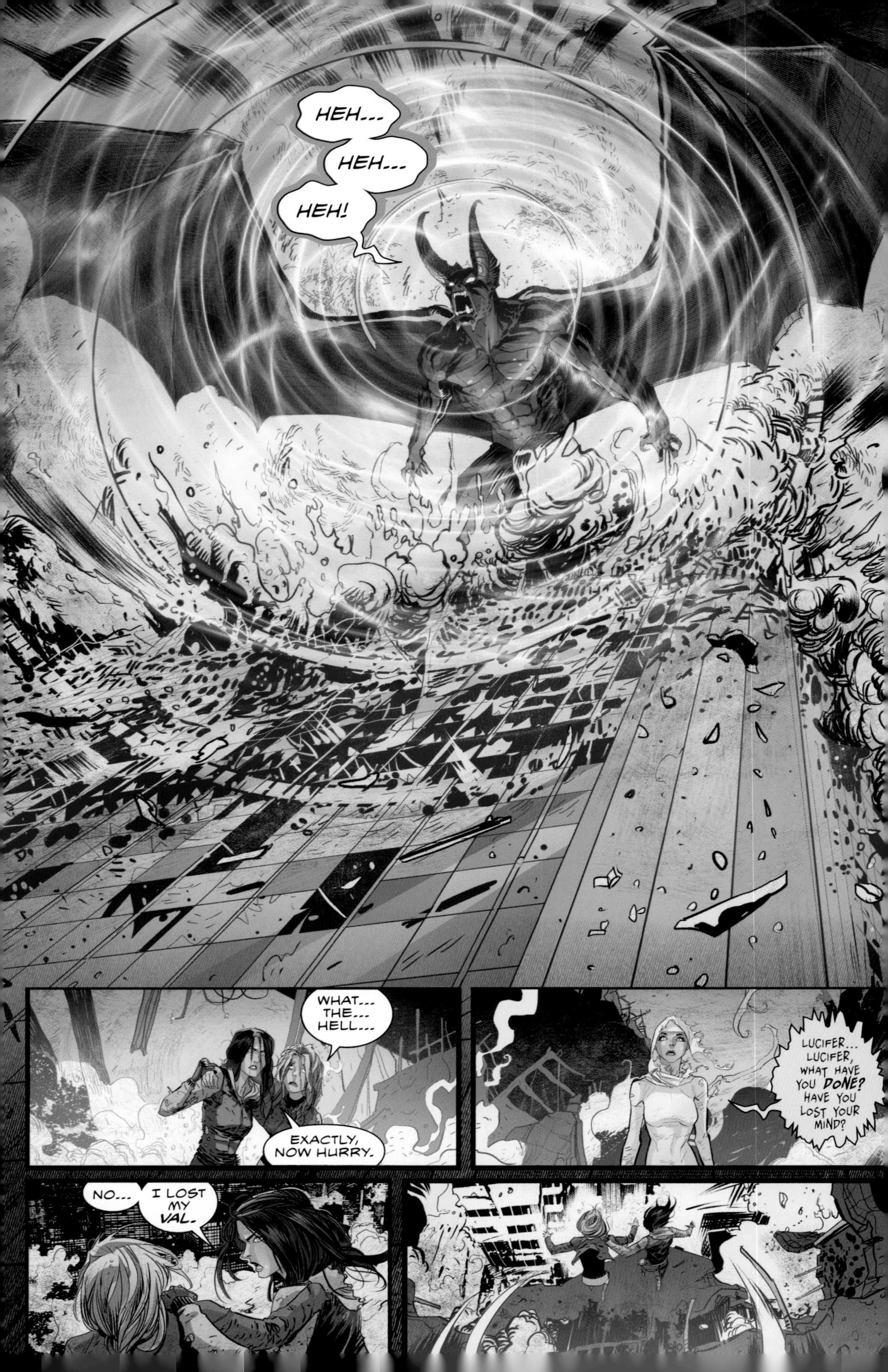
HEH...
HEH...
HEH!
WHAT... THE... HELL...
EXACTLY, NOW HURRY.
LUCIFER... LUCIFER, WHAT HAVE YOU DONE? HAVE YOU LOST YOUR MIND?
NO...
I LOST MY VAL.

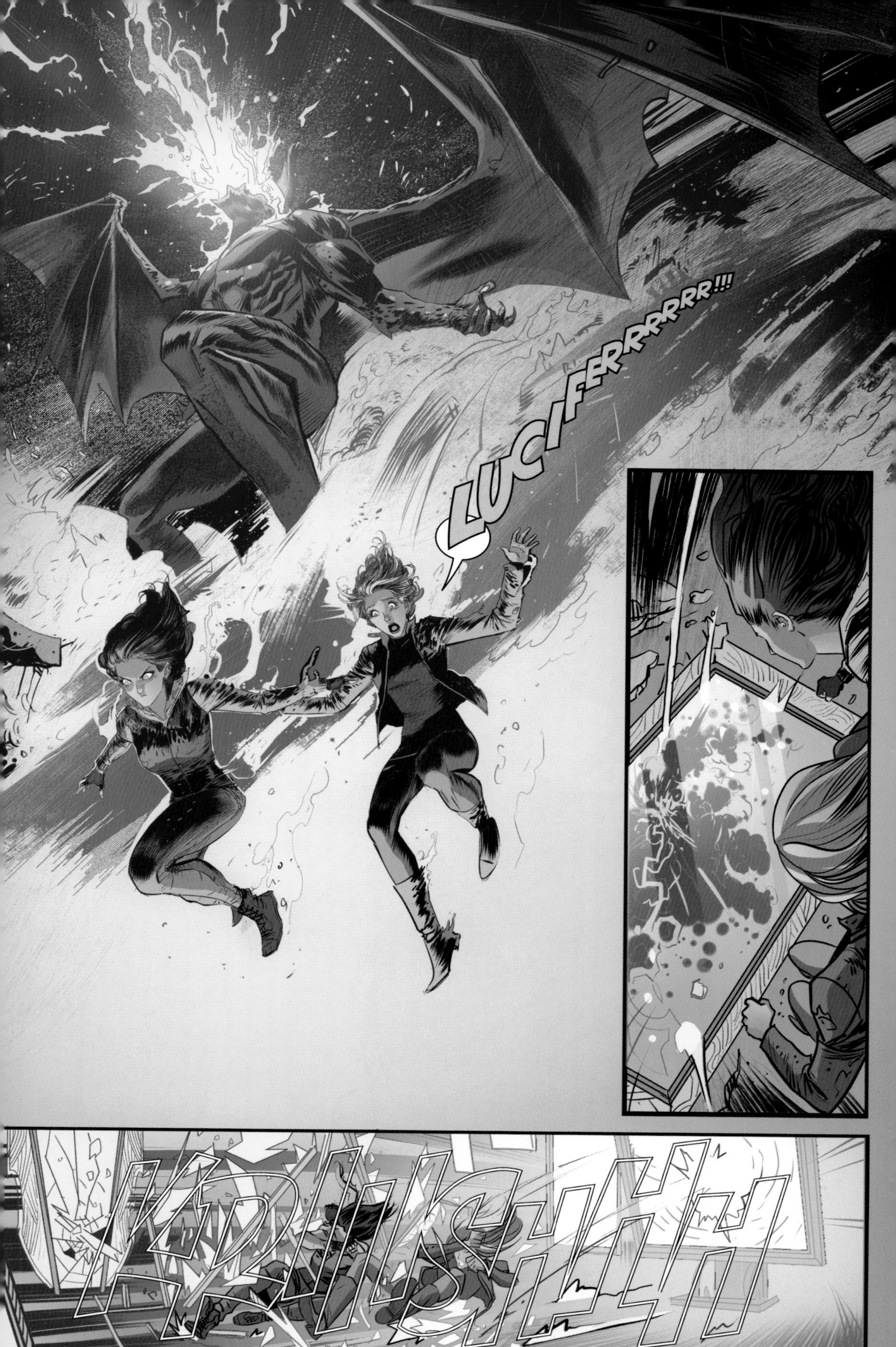
LUCIFERRRRRR!!!

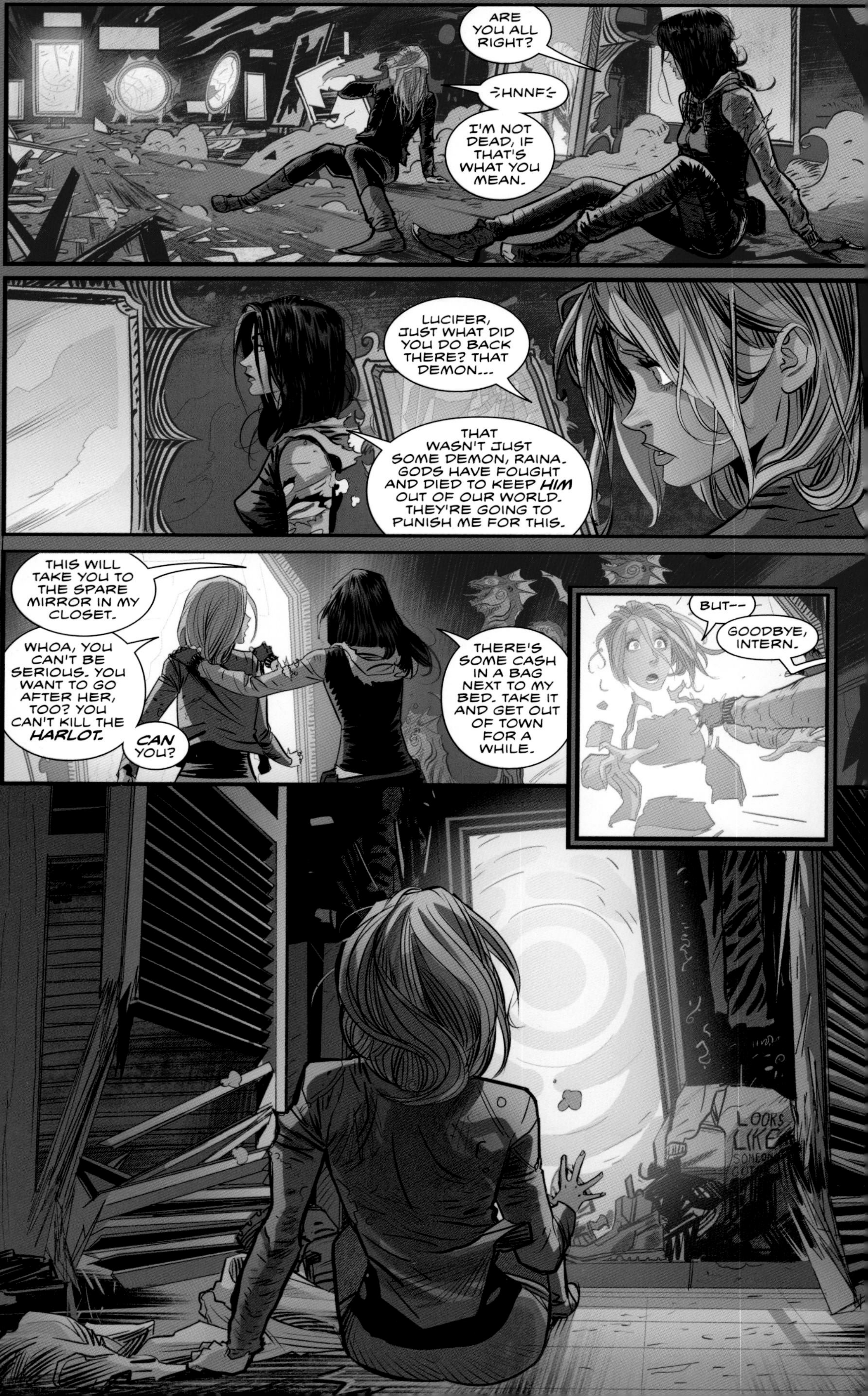
ARE YOU ALL RIGHT?
HNNF
I'M NOT DEAD, IF THAT'S WHAT YOU MEAN.
LUCIFER, JUST WHAT DID YOU DO BACK THERE? THAT DEMON...
THAT WASN'T JUST SOME DEMON, RAINA. GODS HAVE FOUGHT AND DIED TO KEEP HIM OUT OF OUR WORLD. THEY'RE GOING TO PUNISH ME FOR THIS.
THIS WILL TAKE YOU TO THE SPARE MIRROR IN MY CLOSET.
WHOA, YOU CAN'T BE SERIOUS. YOU WANT TO GO AFTER HER, TOO? YOU CAN'T KILL THE HARLOT.
CAN YOU?
THERE'S SOME CASH IN A BAG NEXT TO MY BED. TAKE IT AND GET OUT OF TOWN FOR A WHILE.
BUT--
GOODBYE, INTERN.
LOOKS LIKE

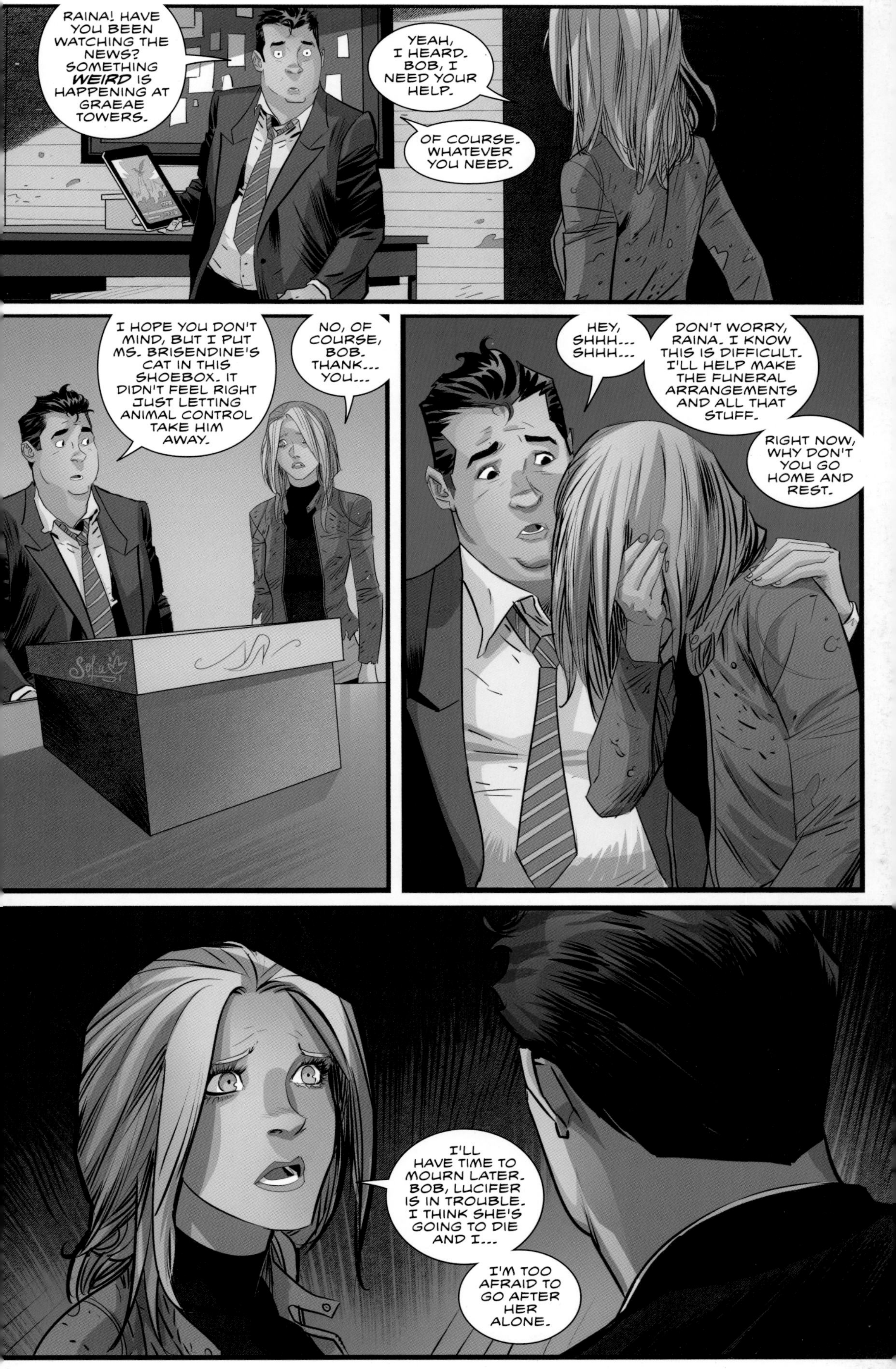
RAINA! HAVE YOU BEEN WATCHING THE NEWS? SOMETHING *WEIRD* IS HAPPENING AT GRAEAE TOWERS.
YEAH, I HEARD. BOB, I NEED YOUR HELP.
OF COURSE. WHATEVER YOU NEED.
I HOPE YOU DON'T MIND, BUT I PUT MS. BRISENDINE'S CAT IN THIS SHOEBOX. IT DIDN'T FEEL RIGHT JUST LETTING ANIMAL CONTROL TAKE HIM AWAY.
NO, OF COURSE, BOB. THANK... YOU...
HEY, SHHH... SHHH...
DON'T WORRY, RAINA. I KNOW THIS IS DIFFICULT. I'LL HELP MAKE THE FUNERAL ARRANGEMENTS AND ALL THAT STUFF.
RIGHT NOW, WHY DON'T YOU GO HOME AND REST.
I'LL HAVE TIME TO MOURN LATER. BOB, LUCIFER IS IN TROUBLE. I THINK SHE'S GOING TO DIE AND I...
I'M TOO AFRAID TO GO AFTER HER ALONE.

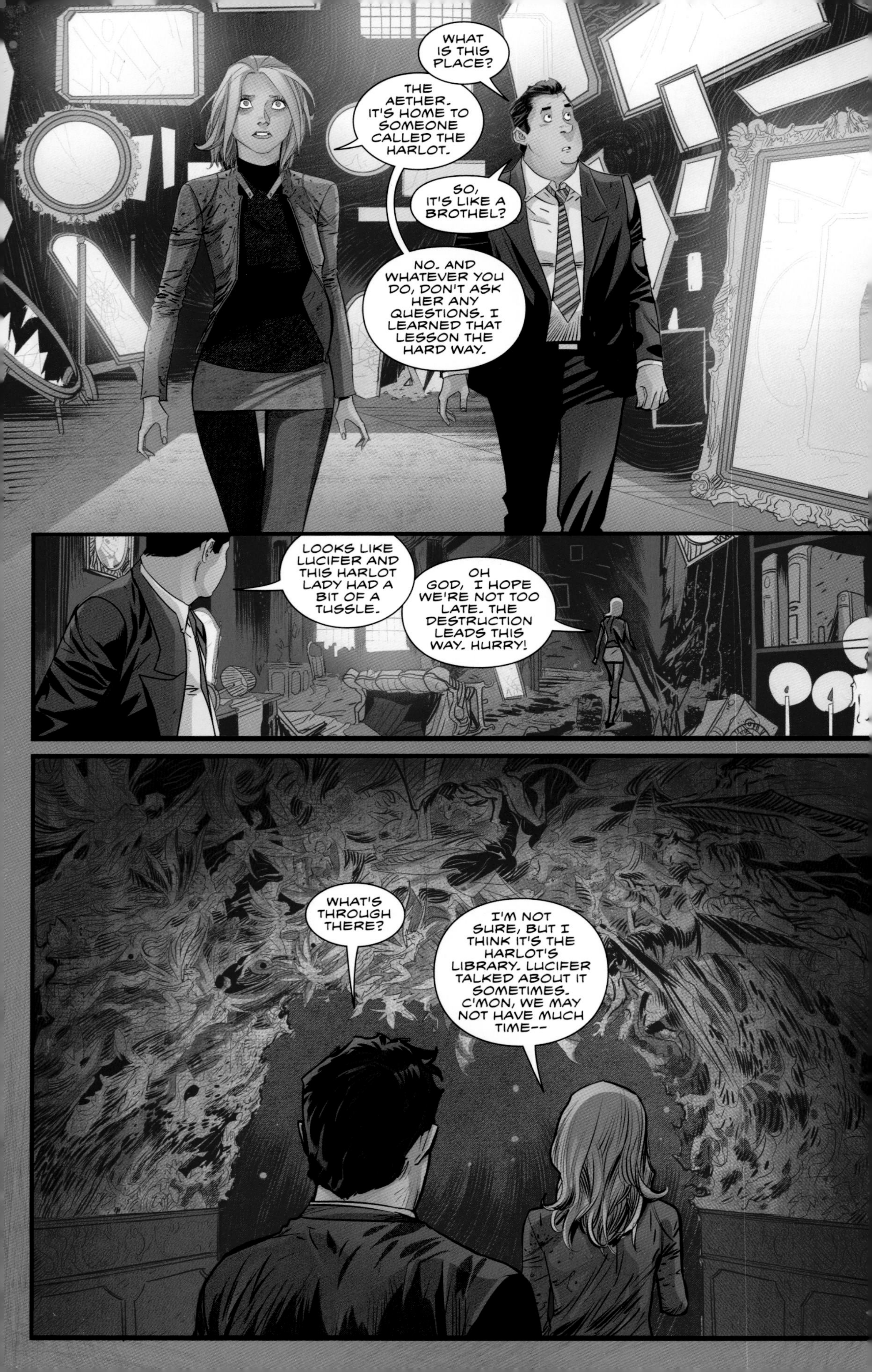
WHAT IS THIS PLACE?
THE AETHER. IT'S HOME TO SOMEONE CALLED THE HARLOT.
SO, IT'S LIKE A BROTHEL?
NO. AND WHATEVER YOU DO, DON'T ASK HER ANY QUESTIONS. I LEARNED THAT LESSON THE HARD WAY.
LOOKS LIKE LUCIFER AND THIS HARLOT LADY HAD A BIT OF A TUSSLE.
OH GOD, I HOPE WE'RE NOT TOO LATE. THE DESTRUCTION LEADS THIS WAY. HURRY!
WHAT'S THROUGH THERE?
I'M NOT SURE, BUT I THINK IT'S THE HARLOT'S LIBRARY. LUCIFER TALKED ABOUT IT SOMETIMES. C'MON, WE MAY NOT HAVE MUCH TIME--

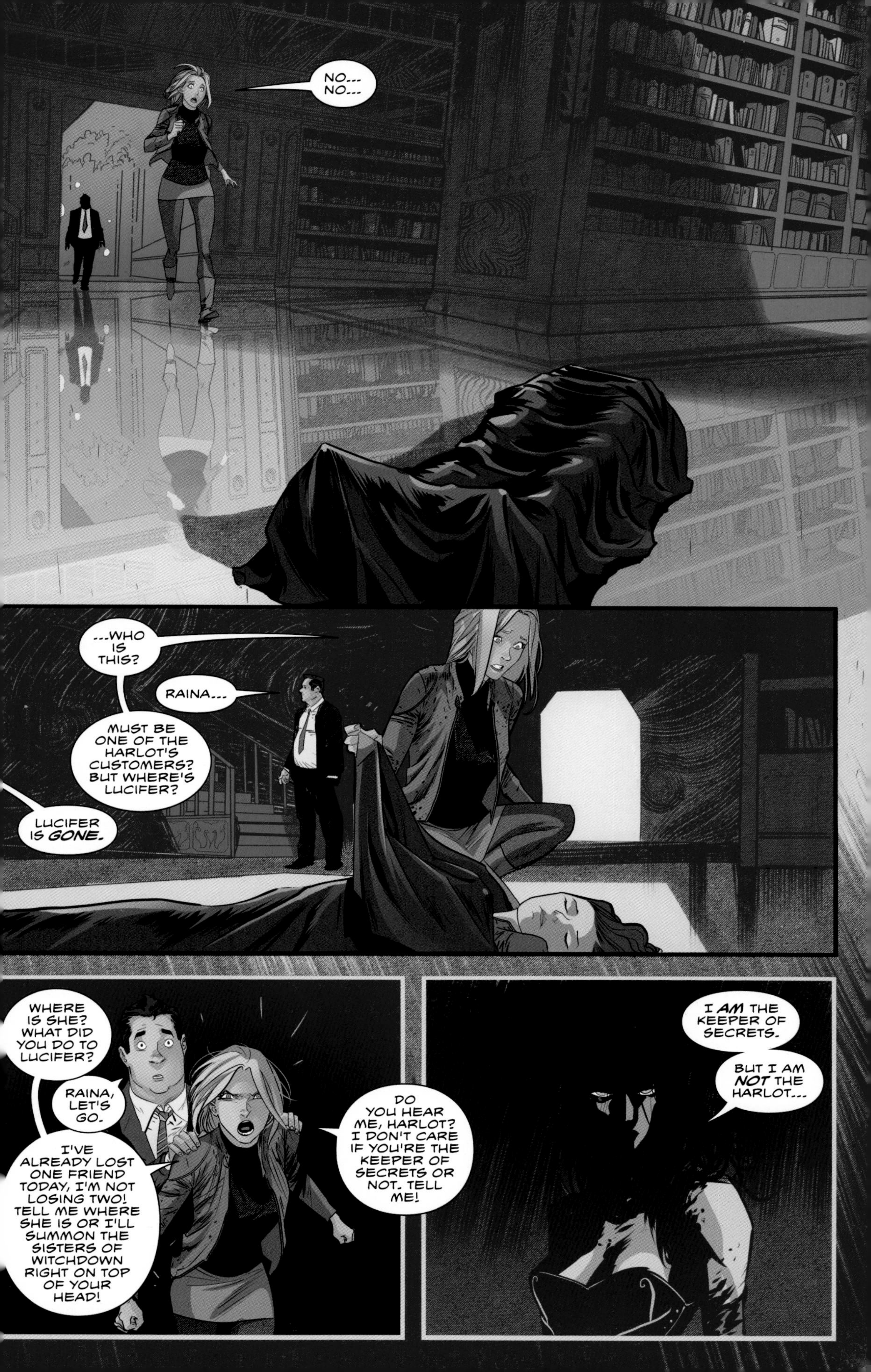
NO... NO...
...WHO IS THIS?
RAINA...
MUST BE ONE OF THE HARLOT'S CUSTOMERS? BUT WHERE'S LUCIFER?
LUCIFER IS *GONE.*
WHERE IS SHE? WHAT DID YOU DO TO LUCIFER?
RAINA, LET'S GO.
I'VE ALREADY LOST ONE FRIEND TODAY, I'M NOT LOSING TWO! TELL ME WHERE SHE IS OR I'LL SUMMON THE SISTERS OF WITCHDOWN RIGHT ON TOP OF YOUR HEAD!
DO YOU HEAR ME, HARLOT? I DON'T CARE IF YOU'RE THE KEEPER OF SECRETS OR NOT. TELL ME!
I *AM* THE KEEPER OF SECRETS.
BUT I AM *NOT* THE HARLOT...

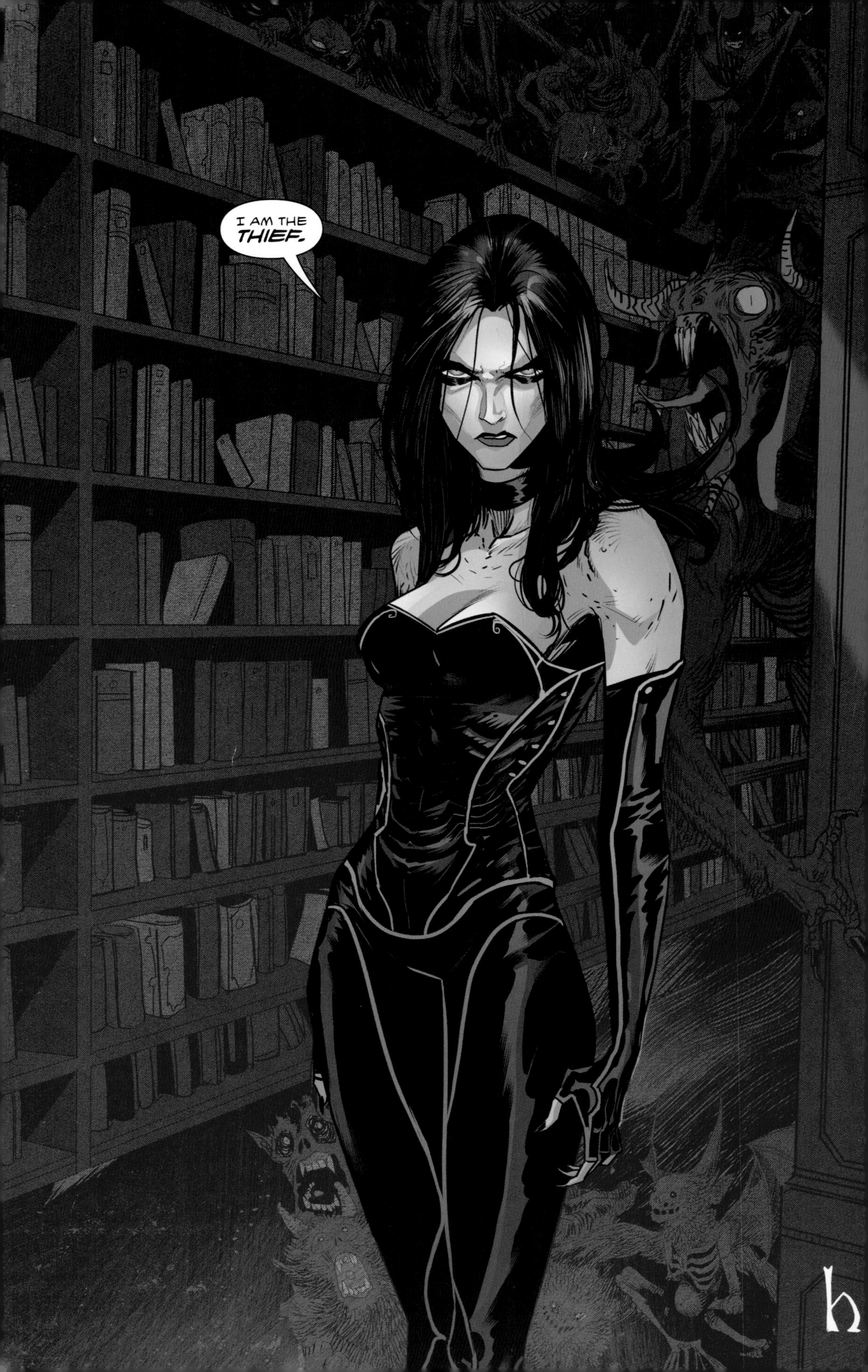
I AM THE *THIEF.*

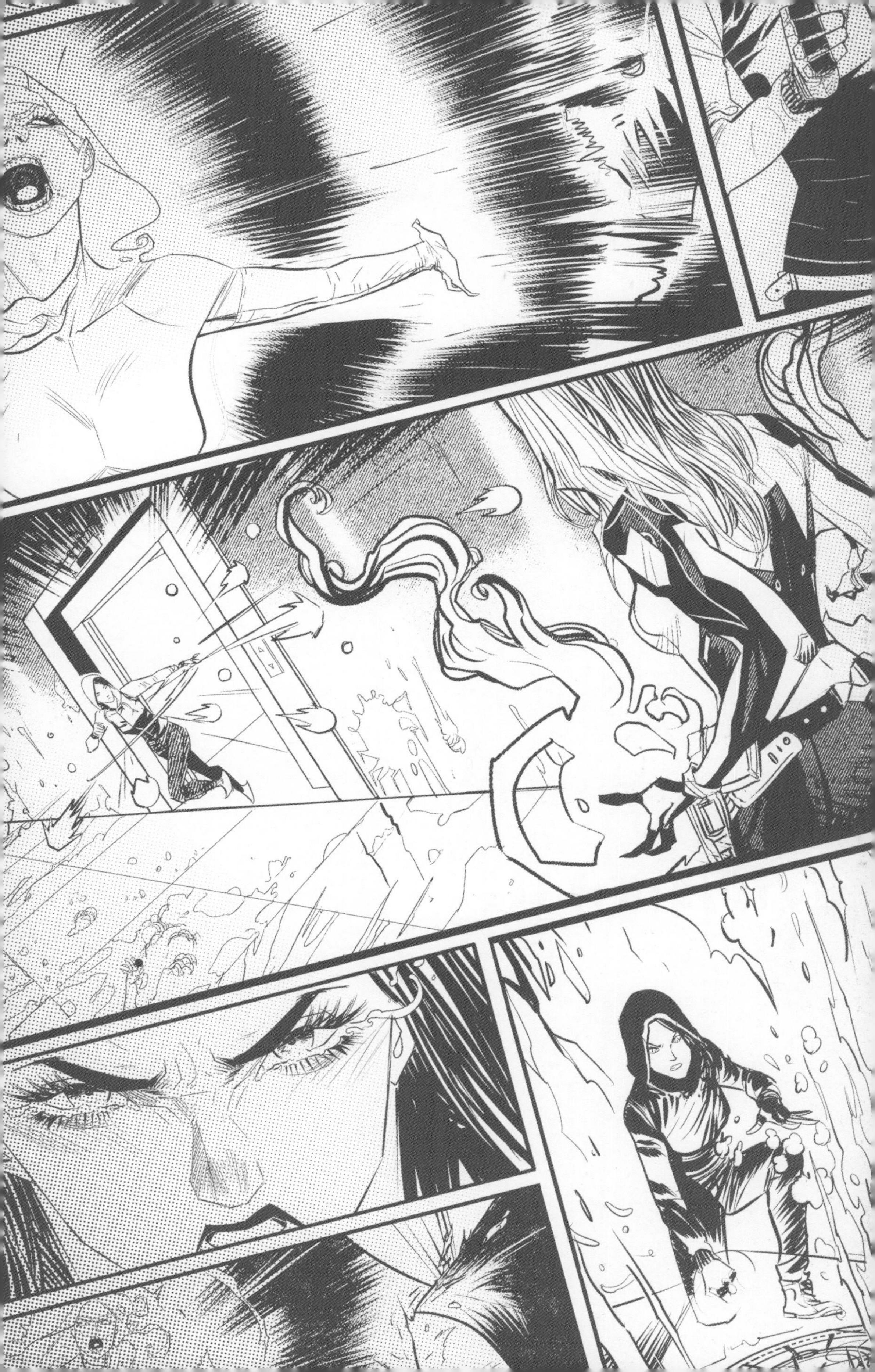

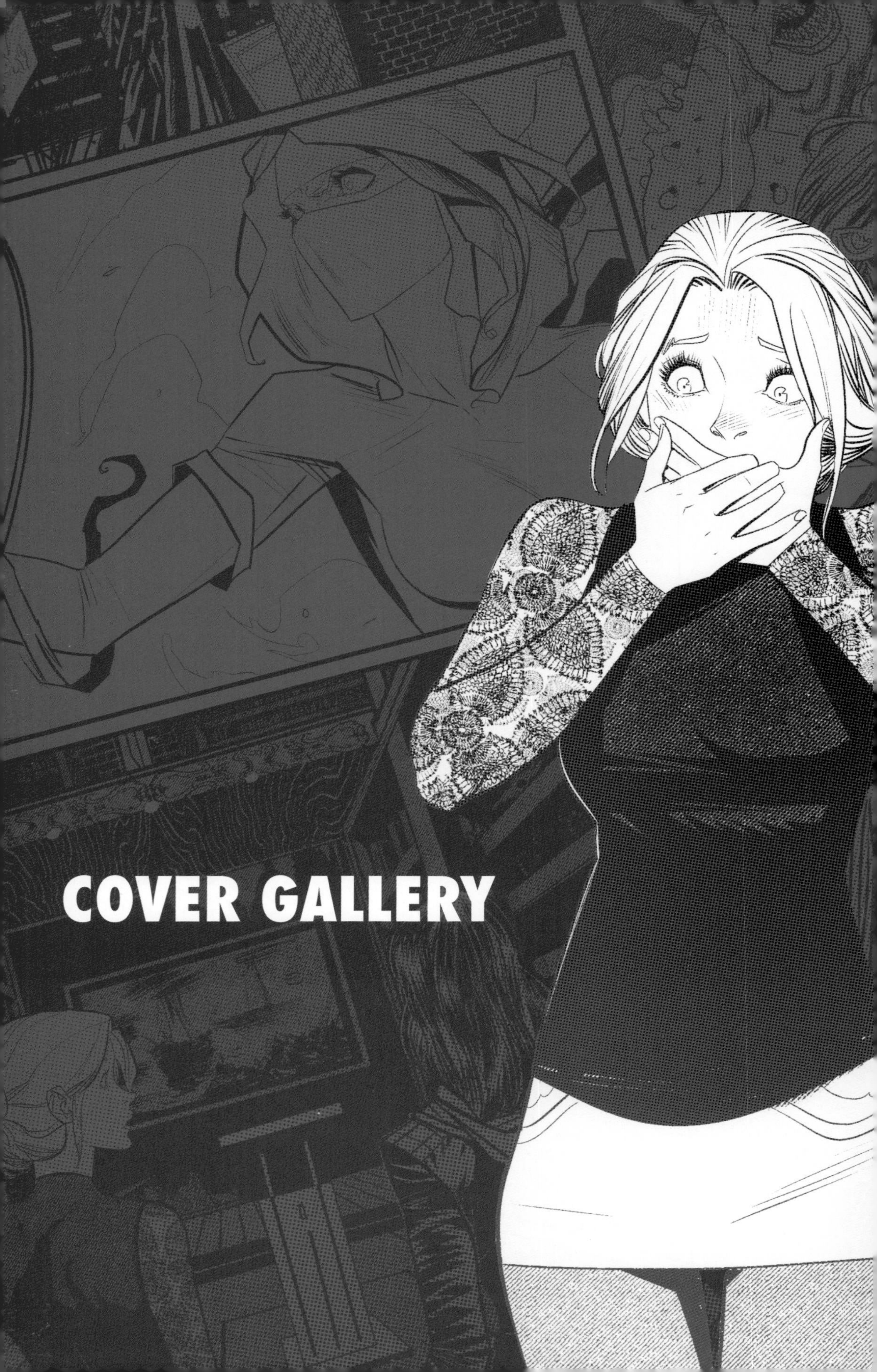

COVER GALLERY

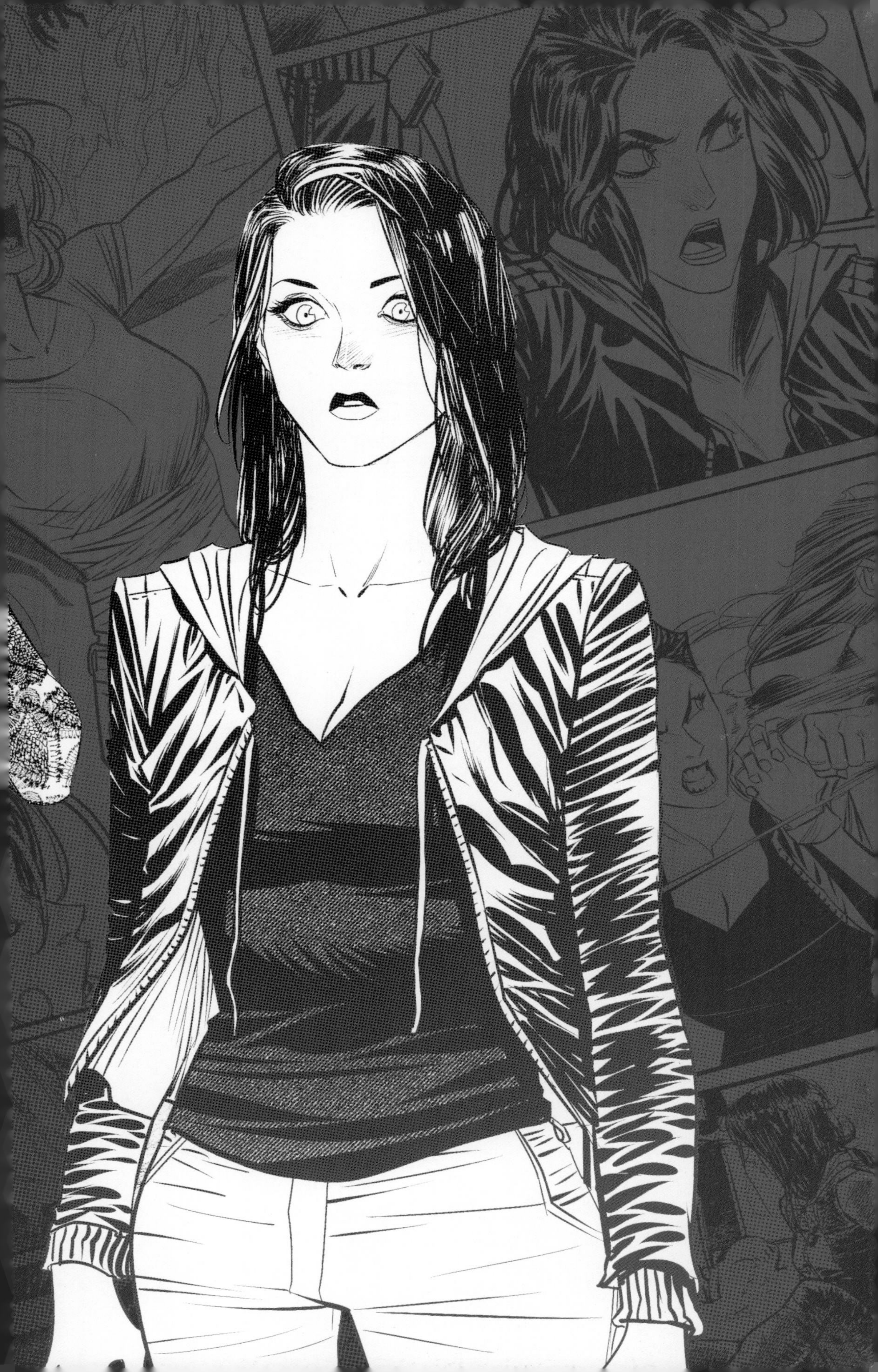

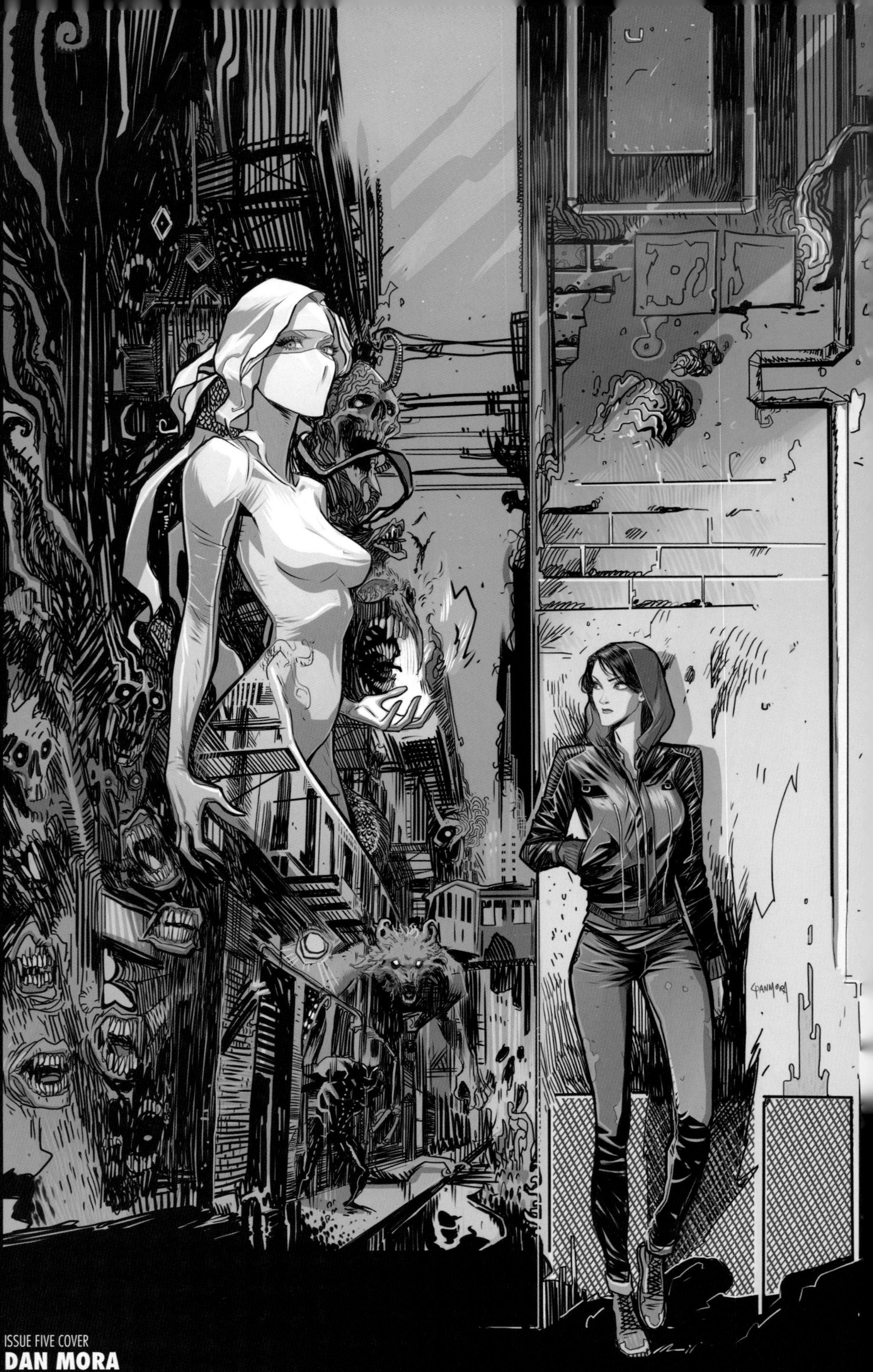
DANMORA

ISSUE FIVE COVER
DAN MORA

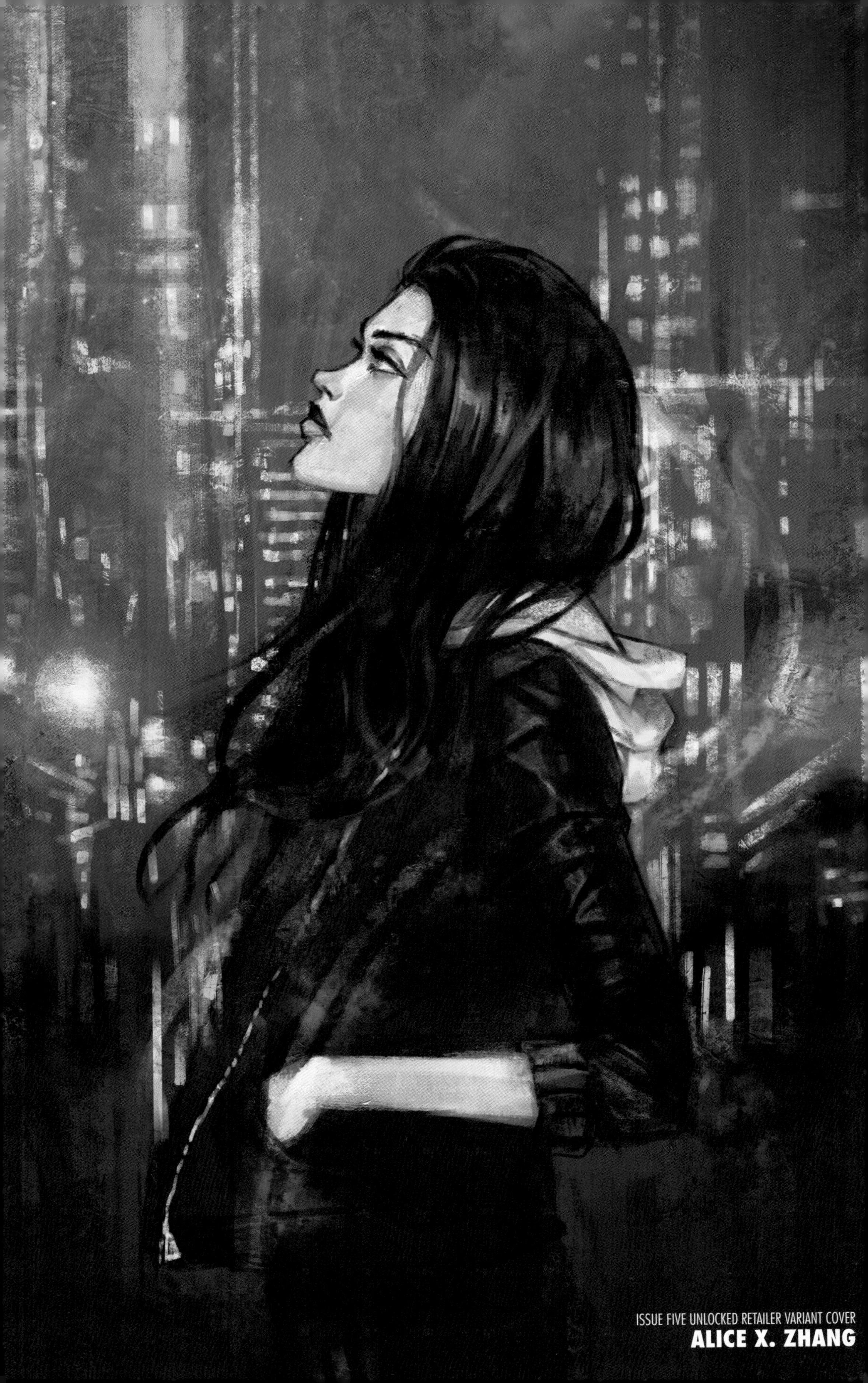

ISSUE FIVE UNLOCKED RETAILER VARIANT COVER
ALICE X. ZHANG

ISSUE SIX COVER
DAN MORA

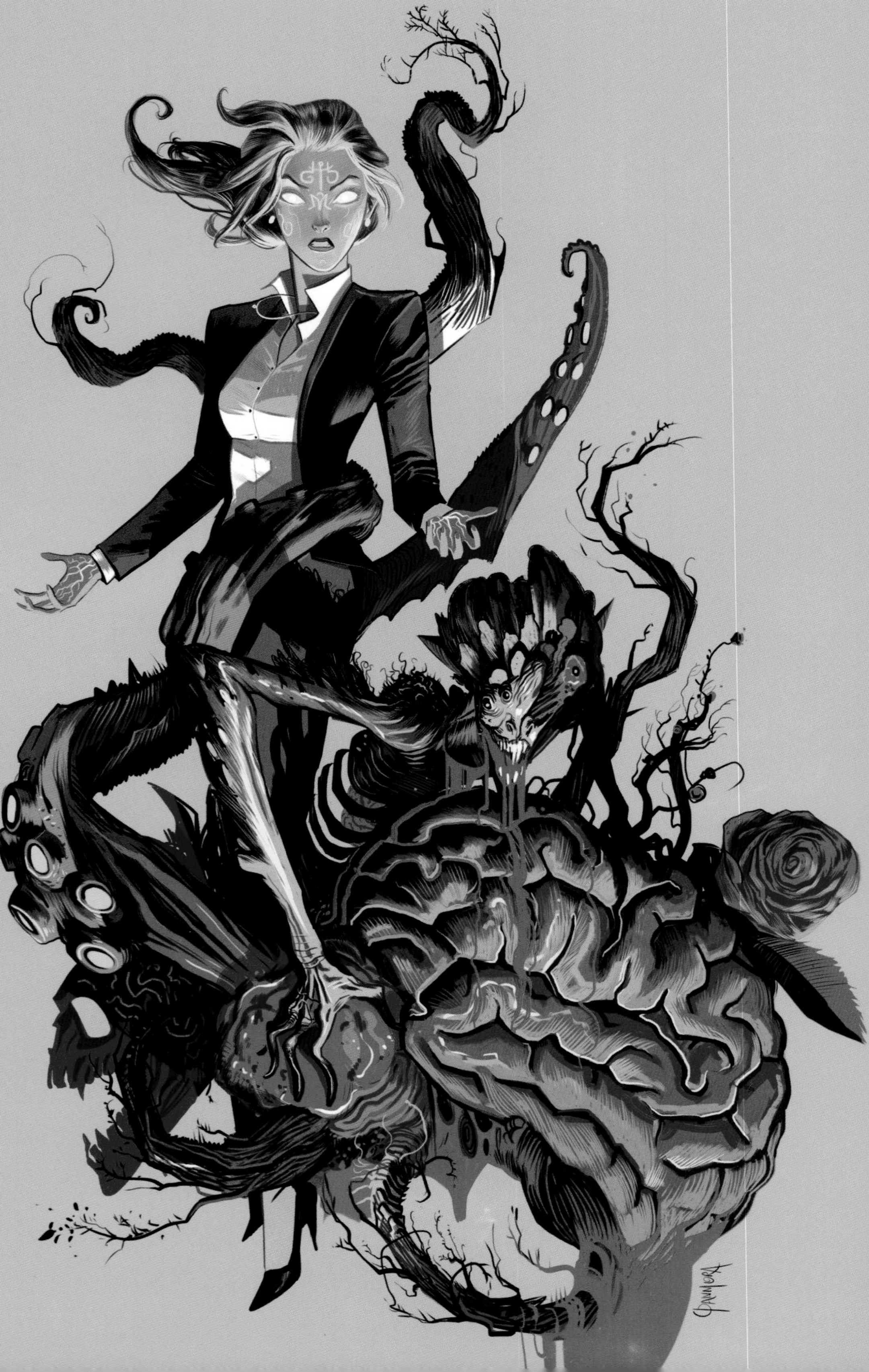

ISSUE SEVEN COVER
DAN MORA

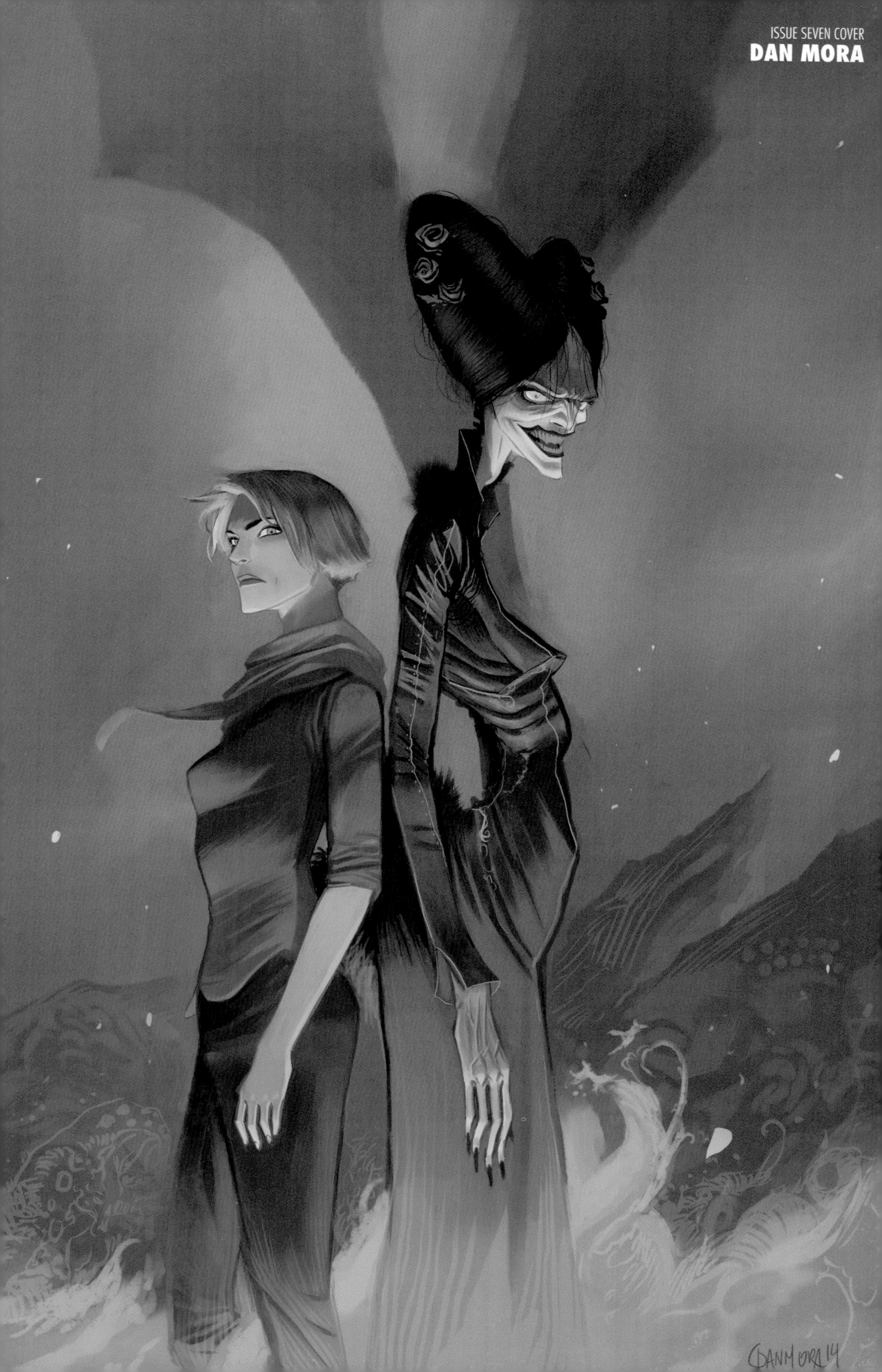

ISSUE EIGHT COVER
DAN MORA

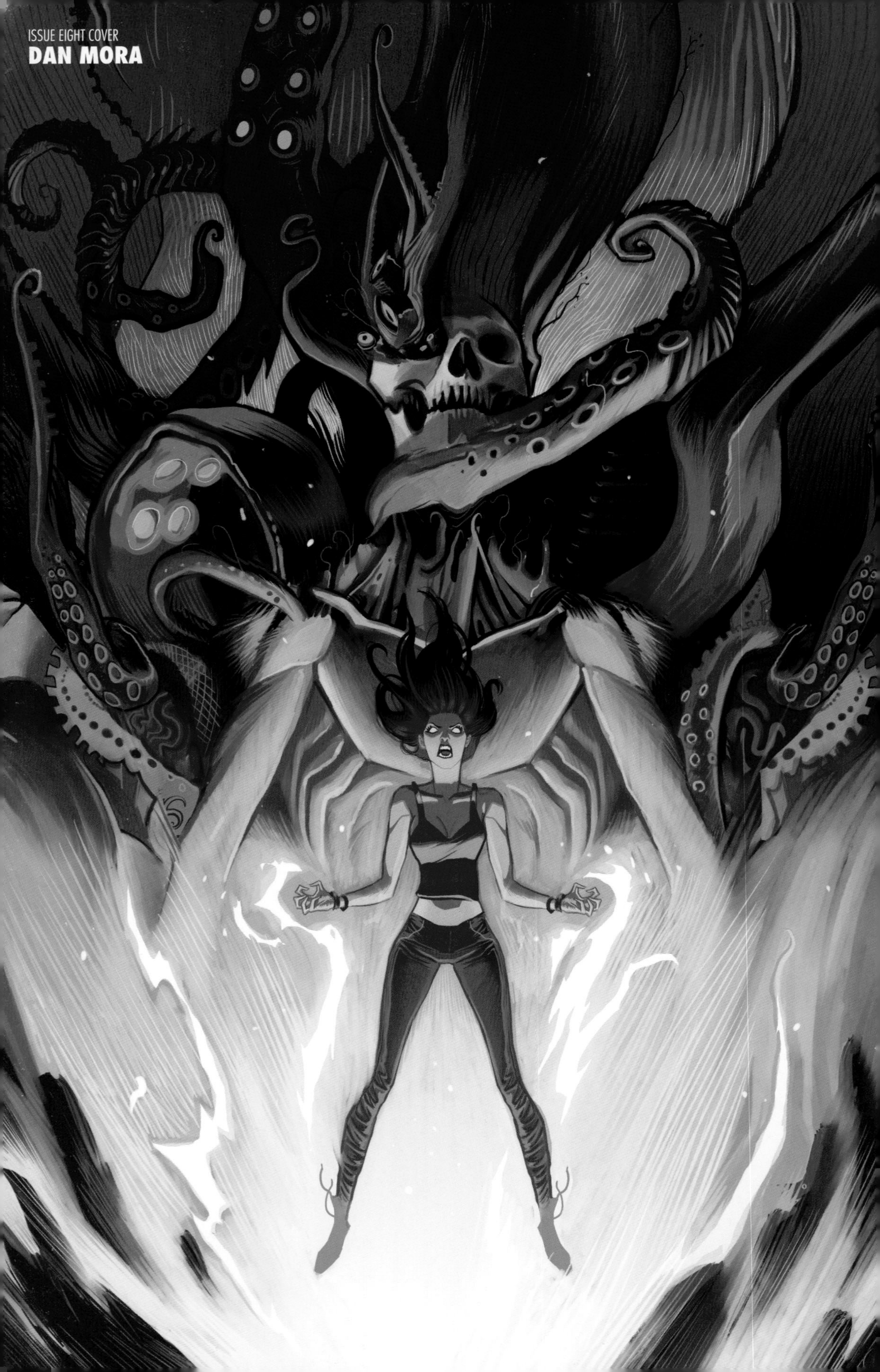

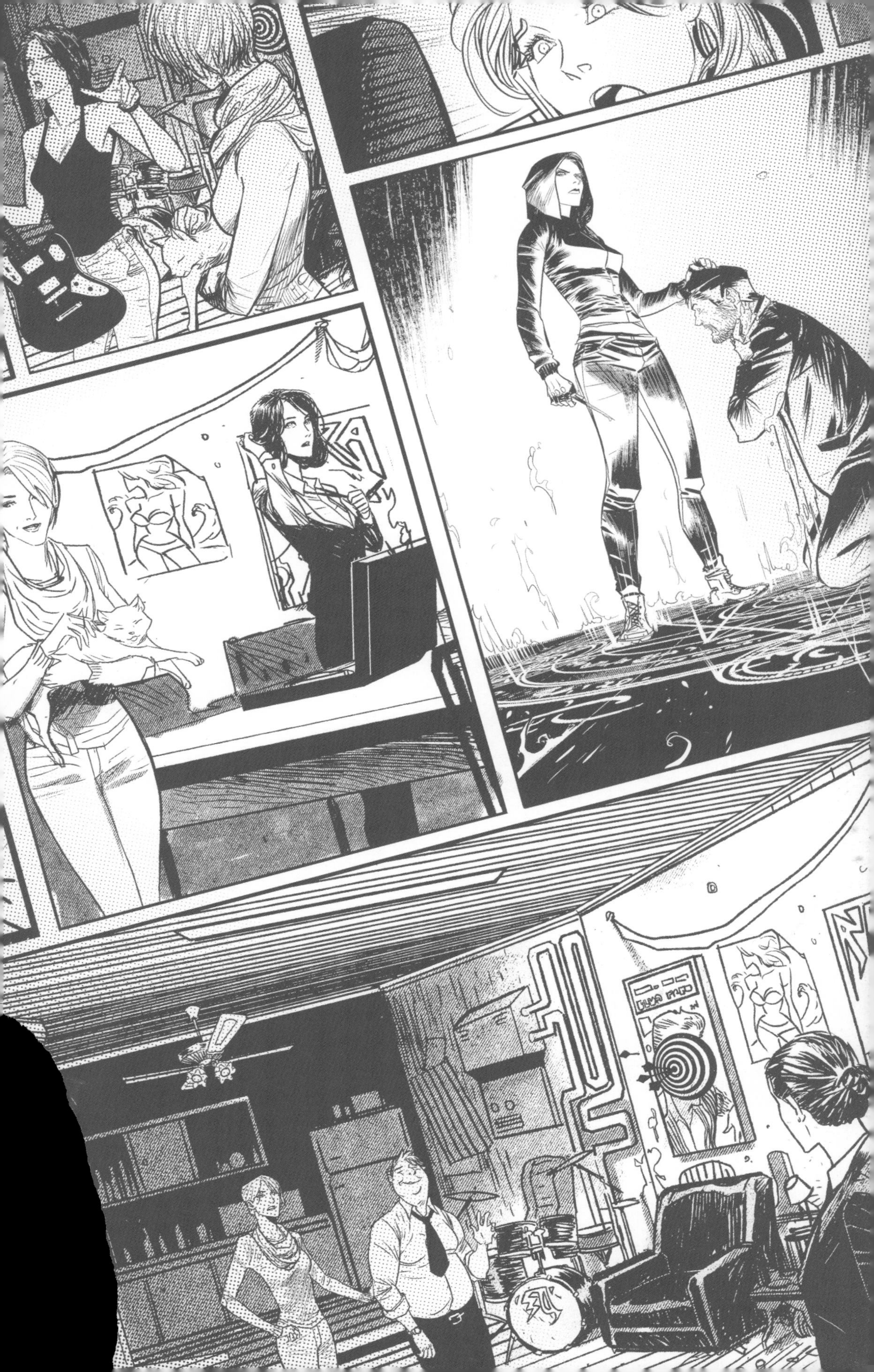

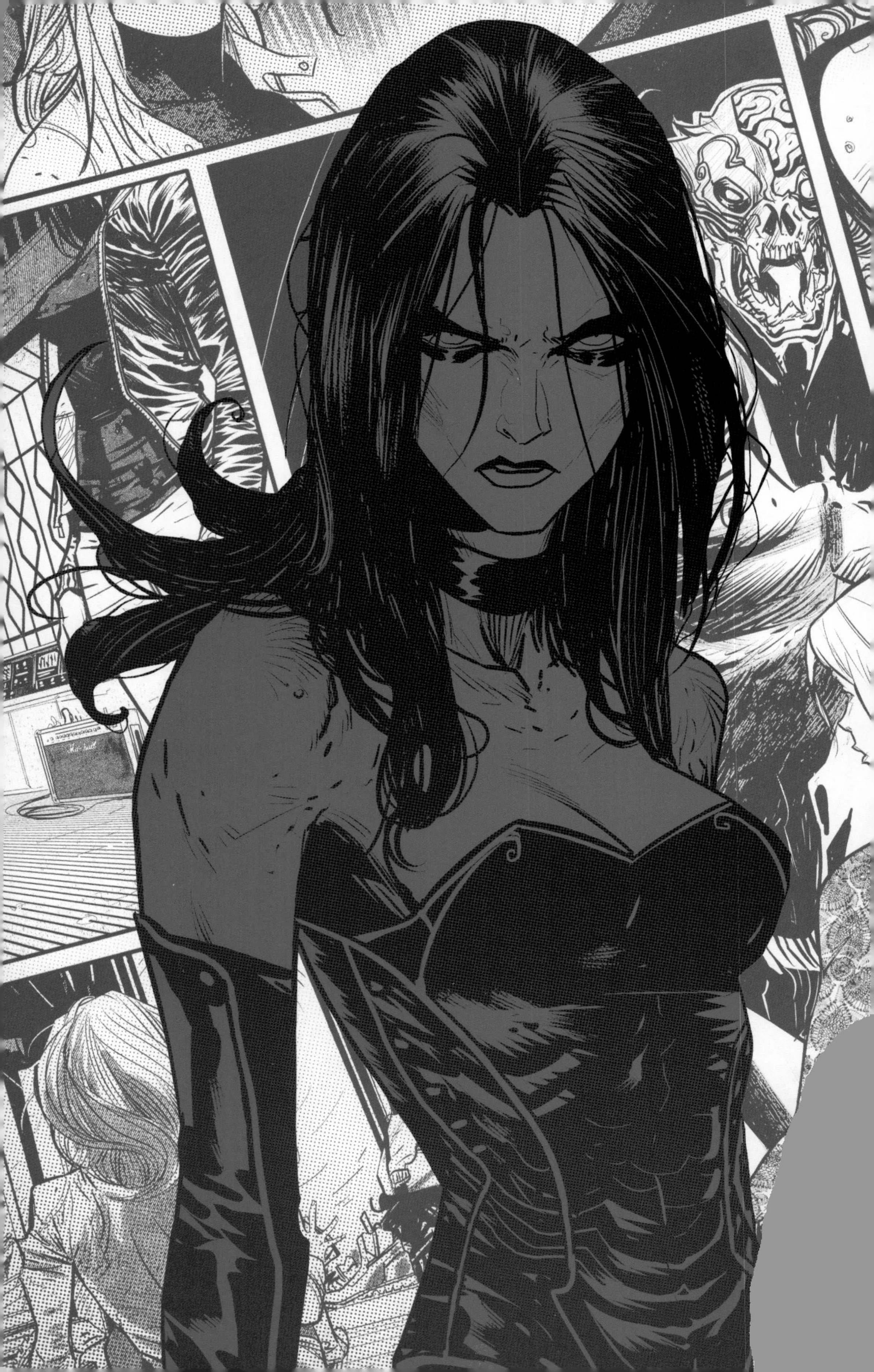

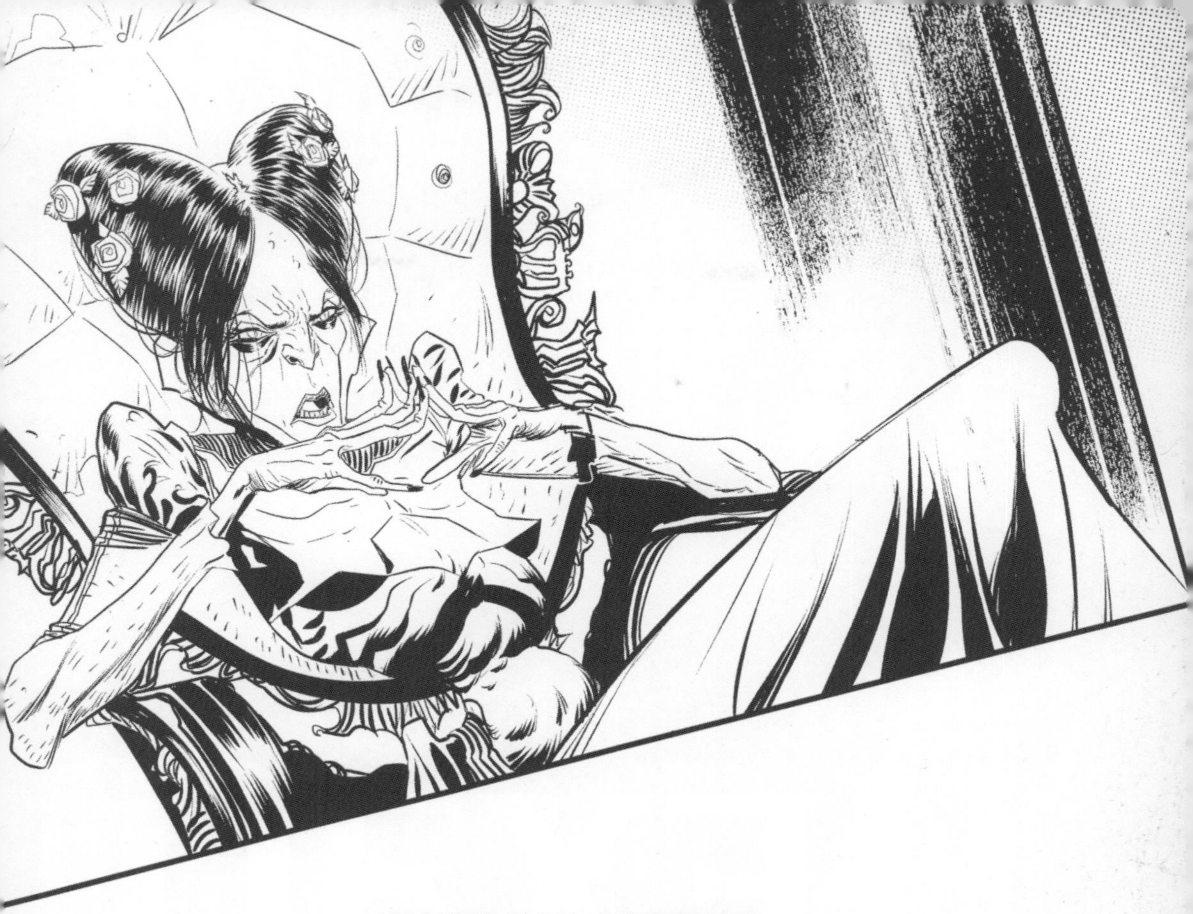

LUCIFER WILL RETURN IN

NELSON • MORA • CASSATA

HEXED™

THE HARLOT & THE THIEF VOLUME THREE

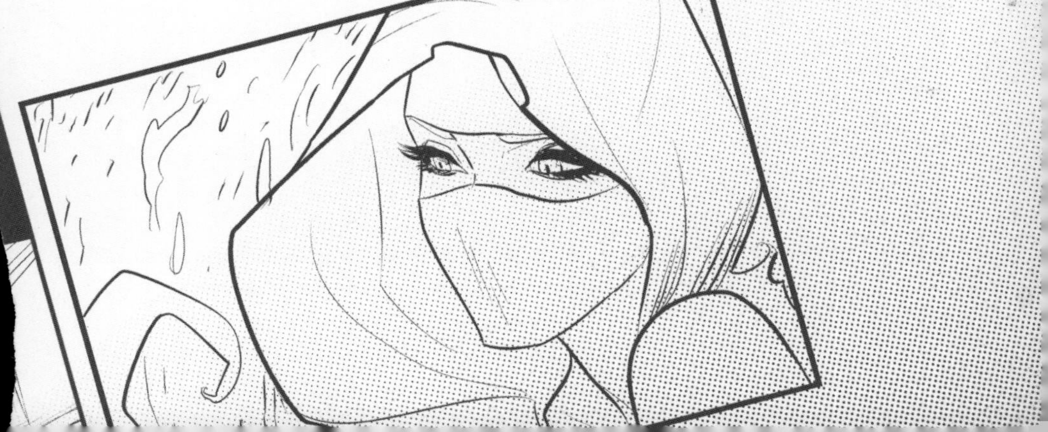

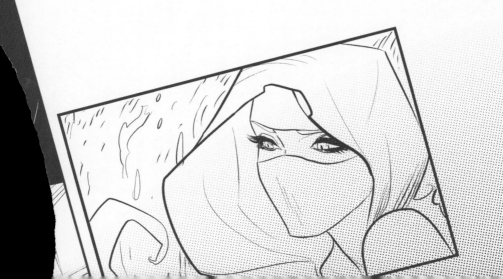